"AN INTRIGUING SNAPSHOT OF THE STOCK CAR RACING WORLD."
—*BookPage*

"*Wide Open* is a flat-out wonderful book. Shaun Assael straps us inside a high-speed narrative that vividly illuminates the world of NASCAR, where moonshine past and megabucks present collide and colorful characters abound."

—JOHN HELYAR
Coauthor of *Barbarians at the Gate*,
Author of *Lords of the Realm:*
The Real History of Baseball

"[A] lavish, detailed, sympathetic, funny, and touching account . . . The drivers he chose to follow . . . are not superstars. But that, in a way, works to Assael's favor. He gets much closer to the bone, achieving far more intimacy with these men than he could have with some of the better-known drivers. . . . NASCAR mechanics talk about a car that is 'just dialed in' when they take it off the transporter and run it around the track and everything is perfect, nothing needs adjustment, and the car is just blowing everyone else's doors off. This book is definitely dialed in."

—*American Way*

"A solid, exciting account of what is one of the most popular and fastest-growing sports in the country."

—*Publishers Weekly*

D0062649

WIDE OPEN

Shaun Assael

BALLANTINE BOOKS • NEW YORK

A Ballantine Book
Published by The Ballantine Publishing Group
Copyright © 1998, 1999 by Shaun Assael

Grateful acknowledgment is made to the following for permission to reprint material: *the insider*: excerpt from "The Top Ten Reasons Richard Petty Was Having Driving Problems" from *the insider*, published by McClatchy New Media, McClatchy Newspapers, Inc., Editor, Seth A. Effron. *John Boy & Billy, Inc.*: parody song about Bobby Hamilton and Dale Earnhardt. Copyright © 1997 by John Boy & Billy, Inc.

www.randomhouse.com/BB/

Library of Congress Catalog Card Number: 98-96469

ISBN 0-345-42677-0

Manufactured in the United States of America

First Hardcover Edition: February 1998
First Mass Market Edition: January 1999

10   9   8   7   6   5   4   3   2   1

ELLIE-L, ALWAYS

CONTENTS

PREFACE

When I showed up to Daytona in February of 1996, I didn't know who the main characters for this book would be, only that I wanted to follow three through a season. The NASCAR books that I'd read were either quickie season-in-reviews written from the pressroom or biographies of individual racers. But more than forty teams show up for each event, and I wanted to feel the breadth of their efforts. By following three racers, I hoped I'd be able to experience Winston Cup racing from very different vantage points.

But whom to choose?

The job of casting wasn't done very scientifically. Brett Bodine was the first person I spoke to. He'd just escaped a fiery wreck, yet he was remarkably open to the idea of having a reporter chronicle his transition from a driver-for-hire to the owner of his own multimillion-dollar team. What followed next were a series of miscues and misfires. Rusty Wallace, I was told by his business agent, didn't make money for anyone who wasn't making money for him. Ditto John Andretti. (No one was paid for interviews for this book.) Ken Schrader thought about it, then backed out. Robert Pressley and Andy Petree, the driver and crew chief of the Skoal team in 1996, agreed but the chemistry wasn't right. Then I stopped by Dave Marcis's trailer. The oldest active driver in Winston Cup listened to what by then had become my intricate sales pitch. (I'd wised up fast after dealing with the multitudes of hangers-on who surround each driver like thick clouds.) Dave wasn't in the least suspicious. He just opened brown eyes wide and guilelessly accepted me, the way he does everyone who wants to hitch a ride on his traveling one-man show. That left the third spot. I'd kept hearing that someone named Bobby Hamilton was a live wire, and, unlike all the other spokesmodel drivers, never failed to say what was on his mind. The accuracy of that description was borne out when I met him after he'd become embroiled in a controversy in Rockingham in late February 1996. He was a racer still looking for his breakout season, but he was feisty as hell.

The businessman racer. The old-time racer. The hungry racer.

I didn't need to look any further.

The season turned out to be a pivotal year in the lives of all three men, and for that I'm fortunate, because it gave me a chance to document some remarkable moments. By the end of my journey, I'd become astounded at what it takes to survive in the fastest soap opera in sport.

Shaun Assael
New York City
October 1997

The 1996 NASCAR Winston Cup Season

NO.	DATE	RACE/LOCATION
1.	Feb. 18	**DAYTONA 500, Daytona Beach, Fla.** 500 miles – 154.308 mph
2.	Feb. 25	**GOODWRENCH 400, Rockingham, N.C.** 400 miles – 109.230 mph
3.	March 3	**PONTIAC EXCITEMENT 400, Richmond, Va.** 300 miles – 102.750 mph
4.	March 10	**PUROLATOR 500, Hampton, Ga.** 500 miles – 161.298 mph
5.	March 24	**TRANSOUTH FINANCIAL 400, Darlington, S.C.** 400 miles – 124.793 mph
6.	March 31	**FOOD CITY 500, Bristol, Tenn.** 266.5 miles – 91.308 mph
7.	April 14	**FIRST UNION 400, North Wilkesboro, N.C.** 250 miles – 96.401 mph
8.	April 21	**GOODY'S HEADACHE POWDERS 500, Martinsville, Va.** 263 miles – 81.396 mph
9.	April 28	**WINSTON SELECT 500, Talladega, Ala.** 500 miles – 149.998 mph
10.	May 5	**SAVE MART SUPERMARKETS 300, Sonoma, Calif.** 186.48 miles – 77.673 mph
11.	May 26	**COCA-COLA 600, Concord, N.C.** 600 miles – 147.581 mph
12.	June 2	**MILLER 500, Dover, Del.** 500 miles – 122.741 mph
13.	June 16	**UAW-GM TEAMWORK 500, Long Pond, Pa.** 500 miles – 139.104 mph
14.	June 23	**MILLER 400, Brooklyn, Mich.** 400 miles – 166.033 mph

15.	July 6	**PEPSI 400, Daytona Beach, Fla.**
		400 miles – 161.602 mph
16.	July 14	**JIFFY LUBE 300, Loudon, N.H.**
		317.4 miles – 98.954 mph
17.	July 21	**MILLER 500, Long Pond, Pa.**
		500 miles – 144.893 mph
18.	July 28	**DIEHARD 500, Talladega, Ala.**
		500 miles – 133.387 mph
19.	Aug. 3	**BRICKYARD 400, Speedway, Ind.**
		400 miles – 139.508 mph
20.	Aug. 11	**THE BUD AT THE GLEN, Watkins Glen, N.Y.**
		220.5 miles – 92.334 mph
21.	Aug. 18	**GM GOODWRENCH DEALER 400, Brooklyn, Mich.**
		400 miles – 139.792 mph
22.	Aug. 24	**GOODY'S HEADACHE POWDERS 500, Bristol, Tenn.**
		266.5 miles – 91.267 mph
23.	Sept. 1	**MOUNTAIN DEW SOUTHERN 500, Darlington, S.C.**
		500 miles – 135.757 mph
24.	Sept. 7	**MILLER 400, Richmond, Va.**
		300 miles – 105.469 mph
25.	Sept. 15	**MBNA 500, Dover, Del.**
		500 miles – 105.646 mph
26.	Sept. 22	**HANES 500, Martinsville, Va.**
		263 miles – 82.223 mph
27.	Sept. 29	**TYSON HOLLY FARMS 400, North Wilkesboro, N.C.**
		250 miles – 96.845 mph
28.	Oct. 6	**UAW-GM QUALITY 500, Concord, N.C.**
		500 miles – 143.143 mph
29.	Oct. 20	**AC-DELCO 400, Rockingham, N.C.**
		400 miles – 122.320 mph
30.	Oct. 27	**DURA-LUBE 500, Phoenix, Ariz.**
		312 miles – 109.709 mph
31.	Nov. 10	**NAPA 500, Hampton, Ga.**
		500 miles – 134.661 mph

Introduction:
"I GOT A FIRE"

Daytona: February 5–17, 1996

The Daytona International Speedway is quiet when the caravan of trailers starts arriving. Without people to bother them, seagulls nest in the infield grass. The air is clean; the overpowering smell of seared rubber hasn't yet settled in. There are no low-hanging clouds, mixing car exhaust with the smoke from a thousand greasy grills.

The arrival of the eighteen-wheelers, in a carnival of color-drenched logos, marks the unofficial start of the season. For the next eleven months they'll be traveling around the country together like a giant medicine revival, selling speed as the salvation for all that ails. Unlike other sports, which put down roots in a place then live there over long seasons, the speed people don't stay in one place for long. Every week they're somewhere else, trying to solve the mystery of how to bleed two-hundredths of a second more out of a car. These are the increments that obsess them. Secrets don't stay secret for long, but they don't have to. Everything changes fast in the speed world.

Because it is a sport of old lineage and trades passed from one generation to the next, sons follow fathers and brothers follow one another. Among the dozens of multi-colored cars spilling onto the speedway for the first Winston Cup practice of the 1996 season, two were piloted by Bodines. For Brett Bodine, the baby-faced, thirty-seven-year-old middle brother of the upstate New York racing clan, it was more than the start of a new season. It was the start of a new life. Over the winter, he'd bought the last pieces of Junior Johnson's faded empire, allowing the white-haired legend to retire to the North Carolina mountains that made him famous. Every penny Brett had was riding on the gamble that he could make it on his own.

Feeling out the track, he veered down from the edge of the front stretch, taking an arc that resembled the flying patterns of the seagulls looping above the grandstands, until he was inside the first turn. It rose over him like an asphalt tidal wave, but to keep from getting lost in it, Brett stayed low, waiting for the mouth of the backstretch to appear so he could go throttle-down. When it's for real, it's called going WFO: *wide fuckin' open*. But this was just practice, so he dove back up and eased into the backstretch, letting it disappear beneath him at a calm 170 mph.

Then, quite suddenly and unexpectedly, Brett felt his legs beginning to bake. His heart tightened when he saw the source: flames snaking out from under the engine. Racers can walk away from catapulting crashes, but if there's one thing that scares them to death, it's fire. It's the one thing they can't outrun. Going into the fourth turn, he leaned hard into the brake, but it did no good because the flames had burned through the lines.

"I got a fire, I got a fire," he radioed, measuring his panic as the flames, being fed by the speed, began eating through the floorboard. He needed time to think, a way to get the car stopped. That's when he reached for the red lever by the driver's seat and sent fire-retardant dust spraying through the cockpit.

Coughing and blinded and still traveling at three times the normal speed limit, Brett threw his Ford into reverse in the hope it might lock the brakes, but nothing happened. That's when he realized he'd have to crash the damn thing to stop it. Bracing for the impact, he rammed the wheel right and scraped the outside wall. The impact threw his head back, but he held on tight, screeching along until he could spin himself into the grassy infield—almost precisely in front of a fire truck.

With flames pouring from beneath the car, he unbuckled his harness and unhooked the black cloth mesh covering his window, staggering out gasping for air and dizzy, but otherwise unharmed. As he was ushered into an ambulance, he looked back on the car that represented every waking hour of his effort for two months and thought, This can't be happening.

By the time he returned to his hauler, Brett's crew was already unloading the backup car that was parked on a lift in the elevated bay of their eighteen-wheeler. It was the car that no one hoped would be needed, the ugly sister. His crew unwrapped it and put it on the track, but its speeds lagged. They tried one engine, then another, and when the clock ticked down on the weekend's practices without improvement, Brett made a desperation visit to a team known for its high-performance motors, and paid $30,000 to lease one of their surplus engines for qualifying day. Even that didn't help. When his time came to go wide open for real, he circled the oval at 185.835 mph, just thirty-sixth fastest of fifty-one cars.

In NASCAR, racers line up in two columns to take the green flag. Given the choice of lining up inside or outside, you want to be inside since the interior car has to travel less distance, and therefore has the advantage in a passing skirmish. The fastest car on qualifying day wins the right to line up in the first position on the inside row, also called the pole position, making that driver the pole-sitter. The second-fastest racer lines up in the first position on the outside row, the third-fastest qualifier gets the second position on the inside row, and so on, until a forty-two-car field is set in twenty-one rows.

The only exception to this system, the only one in a long season, is the Daytona 500. In Daytona the two fastest qualifiers get the first two positions, inside and outside the front row. But NASCAR fills the next fourteen rows by holding a unique pair of qualifying races on the Thursday before the 500. After a week of running practice laps alone, this prerace race gives drivers their first taste of close-contact battle, as well as a feel for how their car works in the often treacherous air currents of heavy traffic. Just as important, fans who've waited a long winter for a new season of racing get a thrilling prologue, and a preliminary look at whether their favorite driver will be strong on Sunday.

After the checkered flags fall on both of Thursday's races, known as the Gatorade Twin 125s because of their distance in miles, the top fourteen finishers in each are awarded spots in the second through fifteenth rows of Sunday's starting grid. With thirty drivers now selected, NASCAR officials populate the sixteenth through nineteenth rows by reexamining the prior week's trial speeds and choosing the fastest eight racers not yet selected.

This leaves four positions. To fill them, NASCAR gives out wild-card berths, known as "provisionals." A provisional is a free pass into the race, but to claim it you must have finished the prior season better than the next racer vying for it. If the four provisionals are doled out, and somehow there is an ex–Winston Cup champion who still hasn't made the cut, a forty-third position is created for him. This freebie is called, not surprisingly, the champion's provisional. If no ex-champion needs it, the slot is not filled, and only forty-two cars start the race.

Looking at his time flash over the computer, 185.835, Brett heaved a long sigh. It wasn't fatal. Though he'd never won a championship, he ended 1995 in twentieth place. The odds were that, of the nineteen racers who finished the '95 season better, four would not need to use a provisional to get into Sunday's race. In other words, Brett's '95 finish was good enough that he'd be at the front of the line, or close to it, when NASCAR started doling them out.

But Brett also understood NASCAR wouldn't let him use an unlimited number of provisionals through the year. In fact, Winston Cup teams get only eight. If Brett could avoid it, he didn't want to waste one on the first race of the season. So he slept fitfully Wednesday night, realizing he had to perform well in the qualifying race. Thursday morning Brett said a small prayer as he slid through the window of the ugly sister, which, because of its poor time-trial speed, was assigned the second-to-last starting spot in his Gatorade 125.

In the early stages of the race, Brett worked the track like a chessboard, weaving his way to eighteenth place, and was about to march up farther when rain clouds burst, prompting race officials, worried about the slickened track, to order the yellow caution flag be waved from the stand above the start/finish line. After the flag drops, everyone must race back to the stripe to ensure their place, but once they pass it, the field is frozen as the pace car pulls in front of the leader. In this case, the top fourteen drivers stayed on the track, protecting their positions, but the rest of the pack turned onto pit road as they came upon the exit lane off the front stretch, grateful for the chance to improve their cars without losing too much position as the leaders circled the track at a crawl.

Brett knew that new tires would make him faster, but this was the maiden pit stop for his newly hired crew. Since the slightest glitch on pit road can kill the painstaking gains a driver makes on the track, Brett hoped for the best when he saw the "11" sign dangling on a pole over the pit wall. It was the mark his team used to tell him where to stop, and as he brought his Ford to a screeching halt, he immediately felt his jack man heave up its left side. At that, the two tire changers went to work, drilling loose the ten lug nuts securing his left-side tires and heaving the old shorn Goodyears off the wheels. The sweating, nervous front changer grabbed a fresh tire, mounted it, and with a move he'd practiced all winter, reached for his air gun to tighten the five lug nuts. Except he forgot to switch the air gun off reverse. Instead of fastening them, it loosened them. In the precious seconds it took to reset the gun, Brett's rivals revved past him. When his crew chief yelled "Go! Go! Go!" Brett had lost so much time that he had nowhere to go but last place again.

But race cars have their own personalities, choosing when they want to kick in, and with ten laps to go, the ugly sister started handling beautifully, hugging the line in the turns, holding the draft in the straights. As Brett came within inches of a black Ford, he heard his crew chief say, "The number seven ahead is the cutoff."

"Ten-four," he radioed back. He knew he had to overtake car number 7 to get one of the fourteen transfer spots into Sunday's race. What he didn't acknowledge to his crew chief was the fact that his older brother Geoff was behind its wheel.

Sweeping inside, Brett took the position away from Geoff. But below him on the track another driver was breathing hard. With the front stretch disappearing under them, Bobby Hillin Jr. ducked out of the draft just long enough to power beneath Brett. But there was so little space between Brett and the car ahead that as Hillin tried wedging back into the draft, he nicked the ugly sister's nose, sending it straight into the wall. Brett's crew raced to their pit-side television in time to see him spinning down the infield and sliding into the Chevy driven by Bobby Labonte. The Chevrolet toppled onto its roof.

Brett finished the race in last place. As a result, he was beside himself as he sweated out the second of the day's races, praying his time-trial speed would still lift him into the race. When the final tally was done, Brett had been beaten out by his brother. The pair, separated by ten years, barely spoke to each other, the result of rifts that had to do with racing and family, but the divide that mattered most to Brett was the six-tenths of a second that Geoff had over him in the time trials. It meant that for his first race as an owner, Brett would need to use a provisional. And all he had left to show for his trouble were two totaled cars.

With four days to go, five bleary-eyed mechanics in Mooresville, North Carolina, were in the midst of a round-the-clock vigil to repair the first wreck. They fixed the front snout, reconstructed the body and repainted it. Then they trucked it to Daytona late Thursday, worked on it in the garage, and when the track closed for the day, stayed up in their hotel parking lot building a fuel cell and exhaust system. Practicing with it on Saturday, February 17, Brett was amazed to find it actually ran faster than before.

Calling his frazzled team together in his trailer that afternoon, he was dizzy from having pulled out the nearly impossible.

"We haven't lost any points," he said. "We're in the same square as Dale Earnhardt and Jeff Gordon. Rusty Wallace is starting behind us. Hey, we're still in this thing."

Hard as it might have seemed to believe, it was true.

The first race of the season hadn't even begun yet.

1

THE OLD MAN AND THE BEACH

Daytona: February 18

From above, the yellow sand looks like the sparkling casing of a turquoise gem. But as the airplane begins its descent and the shoreline starts looking jagged and dirty, something appears that you've never seen on a beach before: traffic. Welcome to Daytona, the birthplace of NASCAR.

Daytona is a spread-out collection of Eisenhower-era hotels and tacky novelty shops, kind of like what Reno would look like if someone booked a surf-punk convention and carburetor show in the same week. Most of the time it does fine by frat boys and bikers, but in the week before the 500, it gussies itself up (which generally means using tablecloths) to host one of the jewels of American sport.

The motels along Route A1A all have signs welcoming the race fans who pay their trebled prices. At topless bars like the Shark Lounge, you can see dancers who've painted the number of their favorite driver on their bouncing breasts. Thirteen hours before the big race, the line to get in the bar backs up two blocks on International Speedway Boulevard, but if you choose not to go, there's another show even more intriguing down the road.

Driving through the main entrance of the Daytona International Speedway, you'll come upon the two most famous tunnels in racing. Shaped like dual exhausts, the cylinders are carved into a huge man-made hill. It's only when you've come out the other side and look behind you and see a nearly vertical mass of concrete that you realize you've just driven under turn four. Welcome to the infield of the Daytona International Speedway, a 180-acre park complete with its own lake, inside the belly of the two-and-a-half-mile oval.

There is a magic to being here, standing atop one of the thousands of Winnebagos, school buses, or pickup trucks that park nose-to-nose, creating a makeshift city of wheeled streets and alleys lit by soft yellow campfires. If you're lucky enough to have arrived early and grabbed a parking place by one of the turns, then you're close enough to press your nose against the fence and feel the cars' awesome power as they speed just a few dozen feet from you at nearly 200 miles an hour. Even in the still of night it's easy to imagine the old legends barreling under the checkered flag, winning races that live on for the NASCAR faithful like the 1955 World Series does for Yankee and Dodger fans.

Of course, the night is rarely still in the days that lead up to the season's inaugural, the race that is referred to as stock car racing's Super Bowl. Even in frigid February, party animals can be found wandering the dark infield, threading between the campers and Confederate flags, draining beers and singing Lynyrd Skynyrd songs off-key. You'd almost think that little has changed since the days when racers drank in local bars, moving easily with their fans. The scene is about community. Family. Continuity.

Except that it's just a set, a backdrop to a show that is as relentlessly choreographed as any Broadway play. The Confederate flags no longer have much resonance for drivers, owners, and crew members who make up NASCAR today. The lowest mechanics on well-heeled race teams make a grand a week, enough to live in nice condos with pools, and at least a third of them come from above the Mason-Dixon line. They report to work in spotless garages that do double duty as tourist stops for hopeful stargazers, decorated with velvet ropes and Plexiglas windows for the fans to stand behind. They're no longer even thought of as simply mechanics, but as athletes, conditioned by personal trainers, energized by dietitians, and pumped up by the same motivational gurus that work with NFL offensive lines. The drivers, meanwhile, rake in staggering amounts of cash from the souvenir trailers whose shelves shudder with product, from pillow covers to $3,000 leather jackets. Dale Earnhardt was a twenty-two-year-old longhair on his second marriage, deep in debt with three kids, when he ran his first Winston Cup race in 1975. Now he sells more T-shirts than the Rolling Stones.

The sheer pace of the explosion caught everyone off guard, not least NASCAR. It used to have a small gift shop in an unassuming single-story office complex that served as its headquarters outside the speedway. But that posed myriad problems, the largest of them being that for a time it was okay to have blue-haired ladies collect a few quarters so fans could see a couple of posters in a cheesy hall of fame, but it became embarrassing when NASCAR suddenly woke up to find itself America's hot new sport. So it erected a 50,000-square-foot interactive museum beside its headquarters, at a cost of $18 million, and dubbed it Daytona USA. With its flickering banks of televisions, an exhibit of a race car that hydraulically lifts to the ceiling in stages, and games that let the fan be both driver and crew chief, the attraction was everything a self-respecting juggernaut needed in the 1990s.

The national press loved the transformation. "NASCAR's growth curve resembles the thirty-one-degree banked turns of the Daytona Speedway," gushed *The Wall Street*

Journal. "If you're looking for trouble, you've come to the wrong place," wrote *TV Guide.*

Grey Robinson, a North Carolina divorce lawyer who represented Flossie Johnson, the ex-wife of Junior Johnson, one of the sport's icons, would read such things and shake his head in amazement. "I've never seen anyplace better at hiding their dirty laundry," he'd say.

The principal reason for this is behind the smoked-glass doors of the headquarters building, and in the corner office of William France Jr.

At sixty-three, he still has his boyish cheeks and chipmunk smile. But even after all these years as the president of NASCAR, few can say they know William France Jr. He has a detached, lawyerly way, which means there are plenty of people who leave his office believing they've gotten what they came for, only later to realize their rivals on the other side think so too. This trait lets him keep two warring car companies, dozens of hypercompetitive race teams, scores of image-conscious sponsors, and the shareholders of International Speedway Corp.—his racetrack company with $336 million in assets—happy while he stifles dissent, ensures that press coverage remains favorable, and keeps the image of his sport squeaky clean.

He can be seen often at the tracks, usually by the fire-red NASCAR trailer, stiff and unsmiling, seeing everything through those cool blue-gray eyes, or at least giving the impression he does. If you look at him long enough, it is easy to understand those who say he never thought about what people could do for him, but what they could do to hurt the sport he's guided since he took its reins from his father in 1972. He's never been as imposing as William France Sr., not as rugged or loud, certainly not as tall or broad. But no one makes the mistake of crossing Bill Jr., or his brother Jim, ISC's president. Their father created NASCAR the same way Jimmy Hoffa created the

Teamsters, using vision, balls, and fear. But unlike Hoffa, the senior France never faced a serious challenge to his leadership. He made fortunes for friends and enemies alike, and passed to his sons the art of keeping both off base.

As a result, NASCAR lives by the credo that if you aren't a France, you're just a nervous guest in their world.

The story that's often told is that after Bill Sr. quit his dead-end gas station job in Washington, D.C., and decided to move his wife and young son south in 1934, he was motoring through Daytona when his car broke down. So he stayed. "Ridiculous," Big Bill would bark when someone asked him about it. "I was a mechanic. If the car had broken down I would have fixed it."

In fact, because an observant hotel owner once discovered that the sand between Ormond and Daytona beaches turned hard when the tides receded, the city became a racing mecca and a good place for a wily mechanic like Bill Sr. to land a job.

France started working for a car dealer and checking out the beach action, which in those days meant Sir Malcolm Campbell pushing his supercharged V-8 "Bluebird" to 276 mph, or straight-line speed-bangs where cars went open-throttle down the beach. But as the speeds got ever higher, cutting-edge drivers like Sir Malcolm decided the winds coming off the ocean played too many tricks, and switched to the flatter, drier Bonneville Flats in Utah. Suddenly without their main attraction, Daytona's fathers changed gears and unveiled something entirely new: a 250-mile race around the road and the shoreline. The first race in 1936 left something to be desired. The wet sands swallowed the heavy stock cars, and by late day the tides washed out the course. The Elks Club took over in 1937, though to scant improvement. Ticket sales were so bleak it could afford only a $43 purse, so for the 1938 race the city set out to find someone who could turn a profit, and asked the opinion of Bill, who by then had opened a Pure Oil gas station that was a hangout for local racers. His first impulse was to call a promoter from a few towns away, but when the man wouldn't take Bill's fifteen-cent collect call, France got a local restaurateur to help pay the cost of printing tickets and posters, and decided to stage the thing himself.

The beach race was suspended during the war, which France spent building submarine chasers at a local boatyard. When he resumed it in 1946, Florida was about to be rebuilt in the suburban vision of Walt Disney, with gleaming neighborhoods stamped out of quarter-acre lots, a new car in every driveway. The smokestacks of Detroit were belching with postwar prosperity, using wartime research to make engines more efficient and powerful. Above Florida, however, there sprawled a Deep South with red clay that didn't lend itself to suburbanization like Florida's dredged swamps. Cotton mill and farm towns turned into the equivalent of the steel towns up north—drab, colorless places where you worked until you were too tired to do much else. Church was the social life. In the 1930s and 1940s, racing helped electrify these towns—like a traveling circus, giving people a reason to leave home on Saturday night. When the moonshiners came down from the hills, racing the supercharged whiskey haulers they'd built to dust the revenuers—mutant cars with three-carburetor engines—a renegade breed of anti-hero was born. The problem was that these early racers—Curtis Turner, Cannonball Baker, and Lee Petty—stood as equal a chance of having their heads split by some farmer's track as by gangsters dressed in a promoter's clothing.

France began listening to the complaints of promoters whose interest in law and order extended no further than their desire to clean up the business so they could make more money.

And so it was that in December 1947, he invited thirty-five of them to the Ebony Bar above Daytona's Streamline Hotel for a four-day summit (stretched out, thanks to the ample drinking). Six-foot-five and as physically intimidating as the men he faced, France helped shape the idea for a single league where rules were uniform, drivers would compete for points, and a single national champion could be crowned. By the end of the four days, those present voted to incorporate the National Association for Stock Car Auto Racing, with France as president. (No one there could have imagined that the secretary's notes of the founding meeting would someday be treated like the Articles of Confederation, and kept preserved in a fireproof safe in the speedway's archives.) It was as if a personality like Jerry Jones had conceived and cornered the NFL. In five years NASCAR was sanctioning 585 races at ninety-one tracks in three different series.* One involved the modified prewar coupes, which were the most popular racing cars of the day. Another was for roadsters. And the third, the Grand National Series, was for these gleaming new wonders coming out of Detroit. The genius of the idea was that since Dad had one just like it in the garage, he could pretend he was the pilot of these supercharged husks. It became the ultimate fantasy for a burgeoning, postwar car culture.

In the fifties, racing moved off the red clay farms (one could bulldoze a circle, fence it in with wood slats, and, presto, have a track in a few hours) and on to more permanent venues. A South Carolina equipment store owner literally paved the way by erecting a quasi-replica of the

---

*As stock car historian Allan Girdler points out, NASCAR "wasn't a southern operation, at least not by intent. There were founding members from New England and the Midwest," and if the West wasn't represented, it was only because the traveling time was so much greater than today.

Indianapolis Motor Speedway beside his home in Darlington. Harold Brasington's neighbors were sure he'd gone insane when they saw him grading his 1.25-mile colossus. But in 1950 nearly 20,000 fans showed up to see the South's longest speedway and its first 500-mile stock car race, held under the NASCAR name. Until then the South had no indigenous sport. Its folks were so used to rooting for someone else's team, they convinced themselves that the Washington Redskins were local. Detroit changed that.

Motown was in its golden era of engine development, and one in particular, the V-8 that Chevy put in its two-door Bel Air, so awed the short-track racers that they called it Mighty Mouse. The motto that shaped NASCAR's future, "Win on Sunday, sell on Monday," was born out of an adman noticing that the Mighty Mouse engine was winning races and causing people to switch to buying Chevrolets. As a result, the car company started financing the winning drivers and building racing parts.

As early as 1949, France saw that the days of his beach race were numbered, that the future was in speedways that could put these new power plants to the test. He began a ten-year campaign to build a dream track—one twice as big as Darlington, where the corners were banked so high that 100,000 fans could watch cars spilling onto the straightaways, door-to-door, at 140 mph. Hot damn, that would be something! On this vision alone he sold $600,000 in shares of stock. It was enough to build another Darlington, but not what he saw in his mind's eye. So he kept plodding, raising money anywhere, including the Brushy Mountains of Wilkes County, North Carolina, where he heard about an old moonshiner with a fortune buried in his yard. The distiller came to their meeting with $25,000 stashed in a paper bag beneath his pickup's front seat, ready to hand it over. But after NASCAR's gawky-looking czar described his plans, the moonshiner drove off, leaving the bag untouched. "I'd never heard tell of such a wild dream in all my life," he was reported to have said. "He's gonna lose his shirt."

Big Bill borrowed $600,000 from an oil tycoon to finance the rest of his vision, and when it first opened in 1959, short-track racers didn't know what to make of the design by Charles Moneypenny, with condorlike grandstands and a forty-four-acre lake in the infield for boat racing. Many years before Humpy Wheeler became the sport's top promoter, he was one of the first visitors there. As he remembers, "It lacked color and finishing because France had run out of money. The consensus was it was just too big. A lot of good short-track drivers insisted they'd never work Daytona."

They were hardly inclined to change their minds when Marshall Teague, a machinist from a local auto parts store, went airborne traveling 160 mph in his Sumar special—a cigar-shaped Indy roadster—and was fatally flung, still belted into his seat, 150 yards down the track.

Daytona ushered in the speedway era. Atlanta and Charlotte opened, then a two-mile track in Michigan, and finally at decade's end, another Big Bill France creation, the Talladega Speedway, a carbon copy of Daytona except that it was in Alabama, within six hours' driving time for twenty million people.

If the old-timers won by driving the bullrings bluntly, Teague's bloody baptism in Daytona taught the new ones they had to be more crafty; they had to seduce the speedways. Richard Petty—whose daddy won the 1959 Daytona race, only to retire when he sailed over its third-turn guardrail in 1961—was the best of this new generation.*

*Ironically, Petty briefly led a union created by drivers who were petrified of Talladega, just as they'd been of Daytona ten years earlier. Some complained of blackouts on its turns, banked two degrees more steeply than Daytona, and boycotted the first race. France went apoplectic, breaking the union

Chrysler poured millions into Petty, turning the quarterback-handsome country boy into stock's first export past the Mason-Dixon line. He became a backwoods version of John Glenn, piloting the most advanced machines that Chrysler's scientists could develop. But Ford, refusing to be outspent, had its own weapons.

Ralph Moody was a gifted, introverted, short-track racer and mechanic from Massachusetts who helped many of his moonshining friends spruce up their whiskey haulers during Prohibition. His partner, John Holman, was a brassy, scheming publicist with an eye for figures. The two couldn't stand each other, yet Holman-Moody became the largest race car builder of its day. At its height, it churned out 400 race cars a year for stars like Bobby Allison and Cale Yarborough, making it so important to Ford that Moody dealt with Henry Ford II himself. But at the close of the sixties, Ford began reconsidering his racing investments. The Environmental Protection Administration was starting to eye safety and emission standards and, says Moody, "raising all sorts of hell." Deciding his money would be better spent on pollution control, Henry Ford ordered a shutdown of his racing programs on November 19, 1970. Moody quit the next year, and though the business continued to bear his name, it never again came close to its 1960s reign.

Ford's seventies hiatus started a bleak period for NASCAR. The Arab oil-producing nations of OPEC began their economic war against the West, jacking up oil prices and causing epidemic scarcity at American gas pumps. Hot-tempered consumers who waited on line for an hour to buy rationed gas at inflated prices didn't look kindly at race cars gorging on opulent supplies of fuel.

---

by fielding all unknowns, and grabbing a car himself. Said the tough old man, "If a sixty-year-old man can drive 176 mph around the track, surely our top drivers can do it safely at twenty miles over that."

Races were shortened. The recession hit. Interest waned. Fans stayed away.

Luckily, the seeds that Junior Johnson planted when he traveled one hour east from his farm to Winston-Salem in 1969 took root during this parched period. He'd lost his sponsor and was coming to ask R.J. Reynolds to step in with a $100,000 check. But looking ahead to January 1972, when it had to end its television advertising under an accord with Congress, RJR decided to go a step further. It would sponsor the entire series. And so it was that Big Bill France renamed his Grand National Series the Winston Cup. (In 1982, Anheuser-Busch offered similar largesse, and he happily renamed his sportsman league the Busch Series.)

RJR did more than throw purse money at NASCAR. It remade the sport of stock car racing in its corporate image. It lured big-time businessmen to the races, cozied up to the major media, and brought its formidable marketing machinery to bear. Perhaps most significant, it pushed France to streamline the schedule to make it more sellable. Promoters had been paying drivers appearance money to entice them to events—a practice NASCAR abetted by sanctioning all the races, even if two were held simultaneously. RJR insisted that drivers compete at the same tracks at the same time, and only then awarded them points in the year-end competition for the Winston Cup.

This makeover coincided with the rise of the corporate sponsor. It used to be that a sponsor was a guy who didn't take your furniture if you were a week late on your payments. That began changing in 1972, when Andy Granatelli gave Richard Petty $25,000 to paint his Plymouth red and blue and drape STP all over it. Soon thereafter, Valvoline, Pennzoil, and a raft of other car care manufacturers followed, insisting their cars be better kept and brightly painted.

The elder France was sixty-three by then, and NASCAR,

like a country under a monarchy, had lived its entire life under him. A generation of southern mechanics were making good livings, and some men like Junior Johnson had retired from driving to become rich, owning race teams. Then, just as NASCAR began to enter its first bust cycle in twenty years, France announced he was handing the reins to his sons, Billy and Jim.

As Bill Jr. became NASCAR's new front man and his brother Jim handled the family's investments, the sport languished from a lack of money and interest. In a recession, racers went begging for sponsorship money. A few racetracks flirted with bankruptcy. As Junior Johnson put it, "That was when the whole deal started gettin' shaky." But then came the 1979 Daytona 500. It all seemed to change overnight.

Until then, television covered NASCAR with truncated, tape-delayed segments on shows like ABC's *Wide World of Sports*. This was the first one to be covered live, flag to flag. Early after the green flag, the two Allisons, Donnie and Bobby, tangled with Cale Yarborough, and all three went spinning into the mud. But Cale, who was put three laps down, was driving Junior Johnson's Oldsmobile, and it was fast as hell. By the last lap he'd motored all the way back into second place, right on Donnie's tail. When two cars run tightly together at Daytona, the lead car is the one doing more work because it's the first to cut a hole in the air. As a result, the rear car has more throttle response, and when it pulls left into the airstream, has the power to slingshot forward. After the white flag fell and Donnie led Cale onto the backstretch—a half a lap ahead of third-place Richard Petty—Cale knew that all he had to do was get by Donnie and he'd slingshot into the lead. Donnie knew the drill, and when Yarborough tried, Donnie veered lower down the track to block him. Speeding into turn three, Cale pulled beside Allison and dropped down a lane. They kept riding one another farther down until finally neither had any room. In a wild melee, they crashed each other a half mile away from the checkered flag, letting a stunned Petty, who was skulking behind, breeze to the win. Enraged, Donnie leapt out of his car and started throwing a flurry of punches at Cale. Then, out of nowhere, brother Bobby joined in "for the hell of it."

"Those cats don't have any class," Petty would deadpan. "When me and David Pearson did it [in 1976], we were by the grandstand where everybody could see us. They did it on the backstretch, out of sight." Maybe out of sight to the fans in the front-stretch seats, but not to a national audience. America was riveted.

Two years later ESPN arrived on the scene, an upstart cable network with no hope of bidding on television rights to the big-time sports. It televised its first stock car race in March 1981. By 1985 it had the rights to thirteen Winston Cup events.

Thanks to a timely visit by an executive of Quaker Oats, some new and distinctly familiar logos were beginning to appear on the cars ESPN's cameras covered. The executive, invited by R.J. Reynolds, was in Daytona when he looked around the grandstands and proclaimed himself astounded at the women. "If you think they're good-looking, you ought to see the ones in the pits," a NASCAR employee tried joking.

"That's not what I'm talking about," the guest interrupted. "I can't believe their numbers." The observation that half of all NASCAR fans were women led to Quaker's involvement, and it was a short skip to Tide, McDonald's, and even the Cartoon Network.

In 1985, 725,000 televisions were tuning in to an average race, and the typical Winston Cup team budget was less than $1 million. In 1989, forty-one million TVs were locked in and the budget figure was $2.5 million. In 1996, when *seventy* million households were watching, the cost of sponsoring a competitive team had doubled to $5 million.

Now, thirty-seven years after Big Bill France opened Daytona International Speedway, its garage was a mass of people who looked more Fifty-seventh Street than Fayetteville. Besides the Winston Cup, which paid an astounding $65 million in purse money, NASCAR also supported ten other divisions—from regional leagues like Winston West, to an ingenious new series that catered to America's fascination with pickups, the Craftsman Truck Series.

For anyone wondering why the season's biggest race was held first, they need only to think of the Daytona 500 as a giant bazaar, stretched out over two weeks so no one would be left without a chance to jump on the gravy train.

Still, through all the years and changes, when all the corporate Kabuki gets stripped away, it is about one thing: what one man can do with a car when the engine isn't quite right and the springs are set up wrong and he refuses to lose.

It is still about what one man can do out there alone.

Race teams are assigned spots in the Daytona garage in order of the points they accumulate in pursuit of the prior year's Winston Cup. A race may pay anywhere from $60,000 to $600,000 to the winner, depending on whether it's held at a small half-mile oval like Martinsville or the Indianapolis Motor Speedway, which is large enough to fit a nine-hole golf course in its center. More crucial than the money, though, are the points that each race adds to a team's cumulative total. A win contributes up to 185 points (depending on whether certain bonuses, such as five points for leading the most laps, get thrown in); a back-thirty finish may be worth less than fifty points.

The spread makes for exciting, down-to-the-wire finishes. In September 1995, with just five races left in the season, for instance, Jeff Gordon held a seemingly insurmountable 275-point lead over Dale Earnhardt. But then bad luck and nerves settled on Gordon, and he averaged 116 points per race while Earnhardt averaged fifty points more. It was nearly enough to propel the veteran past the phenom; Earnhardt, the defending champion, finished the year thirty-four points in arrears.

With Gordon earning an estimated $40 million from his title,* and Earnhardt personally powering a $50-million-a-year souvenir business, the two men accounted for a huge share of NASCAR's profits. As a result, their haulers in the Daytona garage were sealed in a four-deep envelope of fans and prospective business partners, all wanting a piece of their action.

If you walked to the very last of the garage bays, you would find a car that few fans were thinking much about, and few suits were bothering to visit. In fact, the only people in its neck of the woods would probably be fans who'd taken a wrong turn. Dave Marcis finished the previous season with 2,126 points, enough to earn only thirty-fifth place.

For the last twenty-eight seasons he'd shown up to the Daytona Speedway and had never missed the race. People kept expecting him to retire and he kept confounding them. Since he hauled scrap in his father's Wausau, Wisconsin, wrecking yard as a teen, every penny he'd earned came from racing. His best season was in 1975. George Wallace was in his third term as governor of Alabama then. Richard Petty was still building his two-hundred-win record. Four years later Petty would earn the last of his seven titles, and the year after that, in 1980, Dale Earnhardt would win the first of his. Back then, Dave Marcis was still living in the twelve-by-fifty-foot trailer that he'd

*The figure counts souvenir sales, Winston Cup prize and awards money, and increased sponsor activity.

trucked from Wausau to Avery Creek, North Carolina. And he hadn't moved out when Gordon made his NASCAR debut in 1991.

With their easy smiles and porchside midwestern openness, Dave and his wife Helen, a white-haired ex-schoolteacher, were the archetypal mom-and-pop racing family. Every line on their faces suggested a back road, somewhere, where they'd stopped once to make a friend. But at some point—and they'd be hard-pressed to put their finger on when—racing began to cost more than the purses covered. Tire costs alone could eat up what a thirty-fifth place paid. Racing inflation had set in, and it was like living in the same neighborhood for thirty years, only to wake up one morning and see that yours was the only house left. Everyone else had moved to more exclusive territory.

Dave has chestnut brown eyes set far back in a golden face that's framed by wisps of white hair, and an earnest, memorable smile. It's that smile, along with a generous love of company, that kept him going from town to town, state to state, moving seamlessly through living rooms and steak houses and beer barns and tailgate parties. Fans pressed their noses to garage fences, straining for a look at a Winston Cup driver, any driver, and Dave would walk right past them, dressed exactly as he had been thirty years before, in a plaid workshirt with a pocket protector, blue pants, and wing-tip shoes. He'd head into the infield, which most drivers treat as if it's radioactive, looking for an old friend like a miner who'd memorized a map. Then he'd find that friend, someone like Larry Hammond of Wausau, who once sold Dave a race car that he paid for all in single-dollar bills, and Dave would sit down—right there in the middle of everyone—drink a few beers, and warm up his appetite with a steak sandwich. There was no sponsor involved, nobody paying him to do it. As the sun

set over Michigan or Darlington or wherever he happened
to be that weekend, you saw a race car driver who didn't
only live like his fans, but among them.

Which made it easier, but not easy, to get through the
1995 season. Though he'd made the most he'd ever earned
in a single year—$337,853—that said more about what
NASCAR had become than what Dave had. When combined with the $1 million furnished by his sponsor, the
Olive Garden, it still yielded a sum that was a quarter of
the average Winston Cup budget. An engine program
alone costs $1 million for thirty-one races. A tire bill can
exceed $10,000 a weekend. Goodyear cut Dave some
slack because of his intense loyalty. (He once mounted
Goodyears when no one else would, single-handedly allowing the tire maker to boast that it has supplied every
Winston Cup race for twenty-five years.) Richard Childress, an old friend and the owner of Dale Earnhardt's
team, traded engines for technical help. And Helen had the
names of every hotelier from Rockingham to Riverside,
California, who was willing to part with cheap rooms if
there were a few priceless racing stories thrown in.

But as new, big-name sponsors started lavishing money
on teams that had never been so well-funded before, an
unprecedented level of parity was created. The chasm between first and last place on qualifying day became infini-
tesimal. Teams started missing races by just tenths of a
second, a time that very nearly defies understanding. Dave
missed three races in 1995 by a combined total of two-
tenths of a second, including the season's richest, the
Brickyard 400 at the Indianapolis Motor Speedway. His
best finish was fifteenth in the Miller 400 at Michigan in
June, and by September the postrace calls to his sponsor
had become joyless. No one was using the term free fall,
but it was on everyone's mind.

Then the improbable happened. Prodigy, a computer

on-line service, made one of the more curious connections of modern racing, concluding that stock car fans were prime computer users. When they went looking for a driver, they made an even more curious connection. And so it was that Dave Marcis left for Daytona the following February with a neon-green canvas suit and a new logo. He would be spending the year "living digital."

In practice runs for the 500, Dave hardly set the world on fire. His Chevrolet Monte Carlo didn't seem to have the juice of the other cars. The speed he ran during the weekend's two qualifying trials left him vulnerable. If he didn't get a top-fifteen finish in Thursday's preliminary race, he'd get sent home, breaking his record of consecutive appearances.

His crew chief, Terry Shirley, stayed up all night Wednesday trying to figure out where the problem lay. Shirley hadn't risen through the ranks the way the other crew chiefs had, ten years or more to win a job supervising two dozen people. In fact, he hadn't even been in Winston Cup before. The primary thing recommending him was that he was one of the people Dave had met on a back road. It was two o'clock on a freezing, pitch-black December morning, and Dave was driving to Wausau from North Carolina when his pickup broke down outside of Seymour, Indiana. Stranded, he walked until he found a cop who gave him a ride to a local motel beside a service station, which happened to be owned by the pale-blue-eyed Indianan with a gentle manner. Noticing the name on the registration, Terry asked Dave to stop by the Christmas party he was throwing in his little station, and Dave had made a point of coming by every year since. Over time, Terry helped when Dave was shorthanded, and excitedly signed on when Dave called saying he needed a crew chief for the 1996 season.

Now, tossing and turning in his hotel bed, Terry was

thinking about changing the tension of the springs and the shock combinations, moving the lead in the frames around to adjust the body weight, gear, and wedge, and each of the hundreds of things that have to be in perfect alignment. What hadn't he tried?

The next morning, Dave flashed one of the bright smiles that managed to convince those around him to suspend their better judgment. "Relax, Terry," he said, patting him in the small of the back as the cars lined up on the track. "We have a good car."

And he did. As the cars crawled in double file behind the pace car, Dave checked his gauges and jacked the steering wheel back and forth to roughen up the tires so they'd grip better, a process known as scuffing. Then, as the green flag fell and Earnhardt jumped out to an early lead, Dave patiently staked out his turf on the low end of the track, following the STP driver Bobby Hamilton, who was moving up rapidly. "Look at Bobby fly," the CBS announcer Ken Squire said when he noticed Dave. "And that Seventy-one car, Dave Marcis who won back in 'seventy-six, has a brand-new sponsor and a great new outlook. He's making a race out of this."

Indeed, by the tenth time around, he'd passed Hamilton to run thirteenth in a tight, single-file line with the leaders. The eleven others behind him were mixing in pairs of two and three wide, but Dave stayed in the draft, pulled along by the tight winds. Into the turns he had his marks picked—in turn one it was a thick black stripe on the wall—diving down when he reached them, but he missed it in turn four, veered up into the cement tide, and got freight-trained down below, hitting the front stretch in seventeenth place. Damn, he chided himself. After twenty-eight years, he knew better. But there were twenty laps to go, and with plenty of motor left he engineered a new march, with three-wides and S passes, punctuating it with a dip under

Bill Elliott to move into eleventh, then pulling away with the lead pack, leaving Elliott to deal with the boys on the bubble. He needed caution-free racing now, but then Bobby Hillin Jr. swiped Brett Bodine, who sent Bobby Labonte cartwheeling, and the yellow flag that flew brought Elliott back to Dave's tail. The two would jockey side by side through the final laps, mired in a two-column line of cars that neither could break free from, and in a photo finish it was Elliott on the outside with eleventh, Marcis on the inside with twelfth. Still, Dave was ecstatic. His all-time start record was secure.

And so it was that with his gray hair flopping with sweat, he parked his car and began walking back to his trailer when a burly man stopped him with a fresh-faced boy at his arm. "Dave, this here's my brother's boy. He's lookin' for some work. . . ." Dave couldn't help but smile. Six months before they were wondering if he'd even make it through another full season. Now, having made his twenty-ninth consecutive race with a rich new sponsor, he was back on top.

"After all this time, it's finally starting to turn around for us," he said.

Da-da-dum. Da-dum. Da-dum. Da-dum. Da-da-dum. Da-dum. Da-dum. Da-dum. The Gary Glitter theme blared through the megaphones across the oval as the drivers, looking like astronauts in their jumpsuits and helmets, took the long walk from the protective environs of the garage to the tri-oval, a vast grassy plaza that separates the pit road and the front straightaway.

One by one they walked past the fans who were spread out in the city-blocks-long grandstands. Some drivers hate this part of the show, the most public part of a solitary sport. Every week they are paraded out like cattle, and the fans get to howl and boo in what becomes—as the season wears on—a running referendum on their popularity. There are few things more irksome than walking onstage after Earnhardt, when the wild cheers turn to silence for you.

On this day, the other applause magnets were Gordon and the defending 500 champion Sterling Marlin, Terry Labonte, Darrell Waltrip, Dale Jarrett, and Jarrett's team-mate, Ernie Irvan, who was making his comeback after a 1994 wreck that left him near death.

Among the scores who pushed toward the reviewing stand was the normally reserved Helen Marcis. She wasn't there because of her husband, but because of the man about to sing the national anthem. Four days earlier, on Valentine's Day, she got a kiss from her husband but no card. "You know what they're getting for those things?" Dave said. "Three bucks! Forget it." She kind of rolled her eyes at the time and said lovingly, "Well, Dave doesn't really do that kind of thing." Now she was ducking in and out of reporters, craning for the best look at her girlhood crush, Engelbert Humperdinck. "Is that him? It is. [Sigh.] Engelbert!"

Back in the garage, Terry was taking the measure of the NASCAR inspectors going over his car with a fine-tooth comb. It is here, moments before race time, that NASCAR has the final, gut-wrenching say over what a team puts on the track. The three makes of cars that race in Winston Cup events—the Ford Thunderbird*, Chevy Monte Carlo, and Pontiac Grand Prix—all must use preapproved parts. The prior year, Junior Johnson was caught with an illegal engine part and fined $45,000. No one wanted to explain to an image-conscious sponsor that they lost because they cheated.

The inspectors did their job with all the warmth of a Georgia state trooper on a hundred-degree day. Terry no-

*Ford switched to its Taurus model for the 1998 season.

ticed the other crew chiefs joking with them, explaining things, trying to steal what edge they could. Some were rebuked for having quarter panels too close to the wheels, something that could create an aerodynamic advantage, or rear spoilers that weren't lined up at precisely forty degrees. The lump in Terry's throat grew. He didn't know what these men wanted, how to joke with them, how to sidestep their thornier questions. He couldn't remember the last time he felt this scared.

As it turned out, he had little to worry about. The Prodigy Monte Carlo went through fine. Terry and his crew wheeled it to the track in the twelfth row.

If there was one thing every driver was thinking about, it was finding a place in line and getting out of traffic early. Unlike IndyCar racing, NASCAR tries to keep speeds *down* in Daytona and its sister track, Talladega. It does this with a special part called a restrictor plate. When installed between the carburetor and intake manifold, it reduces the mixture of air and fuel to the engine, leaving it with 450 horsepower, a third less than what Winston Cup cars run elsewhere. The flip side of the safety coin is that since no one has superior muscle, everyone races in tight packs, unable to break out. Earlier in the week, practice had to be stopped several times because racers were taking turns four wide, unable to pull away from one another.

And so, when the green flag finally fell on the season's two-hundred-lap inaugural race, each of the forty-two cars struggled to find a safe patch of track to run on. Gordon became the first casualty, trying to squeeze too tightly into a space he had no place being. He went into the wall hard.

With Gordon out of the hunt, Irvan had one less worry. He'd leapt to an early lead and then settled in the top three, creating the possibility of a storybook comeback. Then Earnhardt, whom he was trailing, developed ignition trouble and slowed. Ernie checked up, causing a chain reaction in which he got rammed from behind and went spinning out of the race. Earnhardt switched on his backup ignition box and drove off untouched.

All this time, Sterling Marlin had been watching his rivals struggle through the second turn. He, however, had no such problems with handling. Radioing his crew chief, Marlin said, "We have 'em where we want 'em" as he stole the lead. But upon forging into the open track, his Kodak car started smoking and losing power with a broken piston. He, too, was out.

(Racers are superstitious, but none more so than Marlin. Before the race, it seemed everything was revolving around the number four. When he picked up his rental car, it had four miles on it; when he stopped at a convenience store later, the bill came to $4.44. And he was driving the same number 4 car that won Daytona the year before. But after examining the broken piston and discovering it was the fourth one, the team decided to get a new superstition. "We got over that four thing pretty quick," his engine builder, Sheldon "Runt" Pittman, said, sighing.)

Brett Bodine, meanwhile, was thinking his luck might just be holding out. His car—the one his crew had so slavishly worked on to get ready after the devastating fire of the prior week—was handling, if not superbly, then well enough to keep him in twenty-fourth, and therefore in the middling hunt. When John Andretti had problems—a lug nut during a tire change wasn't fastened, causing the tire to come loose and the car to crash—Brett decided to stay on the track as all the other drivers pitted, taking the lead for one lap. But it was illusory. A lap and a half later Mike Wallace's black Ford fishtailed as it barreled into the back straight, T-boning nose first into the wall and collecting Bobby Labonte's Chevy. As Wallace was repelled backward, his nose facing speeding traffic, he formed the perfect target for Brett, who dug into his brake but in a cloud of burning rubber had nowhere to go but head-on into Wallace.

The carnage thinned the field for what now increasingly seemed like Earnhardt's day. As the race wore on, he dueled with Dale Jarrett, who denied him a win in 1993 by passing him on the last lap. This time Jarrett took the lead earlier—with eighty miles to go. But Earnhardt was in no hurry. He wanted Jarrett to stare at him for a while in his rearview mirror.

Earnhardt's race-ending assault came as the final lap unfurled before a fist-waving, standing crowd. In the infield, beer-soaked fans stood on top of their RVs, screaming their throats raw as Earnhardt swung himself on either side of Jarrett, looking as if he had the power to pass. But running the damn thing as hard as it would go, he couldn't bridge the distance to Jarrett in front of him. He realized his only hope was to do a deal at 190 mph.

Two cars together can go faster at Daytona than either can alone. The reason is that when tucked tightly together, they split the air resistance, slicing a sleeker path through the wind; the technique is called drafting. As he scanned his rearview mirror, Earnhardt saw his closest potential partner was Ken Schrader, the likable Budweiser driver who'd toughed his way to third. Together they could draft past Jarrett. But with one lap left, it was now or never.

As Jarrett disappeared into turn two still leading, his crew chief, Todd Parrott, put his head against the pit wall, closed his eyes, and said a small prayer. This was the first race he'd worked with Jarrett, the maiden voyage for their rookie Ford team. When he heard the screaming fans, he just assumed Schrader had done the expected and hooked up with Earnhardt, two Chevrolet teams drafting past a Ford one. But looking up, he was stunned to find it wasn't so. Their Ford was still in front. Then he heard Jarrett's easy southern drawl crackle through the radio. "We've got this one baby! We've got it!"

A blink later Jarrett took the checkered flag twelve-tenths of a second ahead of Earnhardt, filling the garage with talk of Schrader's stubborn and apparently self-defeating calculation. "My job isn't to help Dale Earnhardt win," Schrader sourly told reporters as a seething Earnhardt ducked behind a chain-link fence to escape the cameras, sniping, "Finished second, no problem."

Lost in all the hullabaloo was the fact that Dave Marcis had run a remarkably trouble-free race and finished fifteenth. Returning to his trailer, he was ebullient. Helen kissed him sweetly as he passed into the back to change from his neon-green jumpsuit into the more Marcislike plaid workshirt and blue slacks.

Perhaps he didn't notice, perhaps he didn't care. But Dave had stripped butt naked as a crowd of fans and admirers began collecting in front of his open trailer bay. Someone shouted something, and he was about to turn around when Helen leapt up to spread her arms in front of him. Oblivious, he gathered up his effects and walked off to get ready for the next week's race in Rockingham.

The last sight that the Marcis well-wishers had was Dave walking into the sunset, arm in arm with Helen, devouring a huge ham sandwich.

The season had officially begun.

2

THE BREAKOUT

Rockingham & Richmond: February 23 to March 3

Bobby Hamilton said a silent prayer to his father under the maple trees of the Nashville cemetery, wishing him peace in death after a lifetime of restlessness.

Bobby and his father had recently come to a reconciliation—the kind that families reach when their sadness becomes unbearable. Bud Hamilton had lung cancer. When his longtime girlfriend had died a few years before, he had doubled the amount of Canadian whiskey he drank, hoping to cloud the pain of her death and what he was sure was his own imminent demise. Bobby had never tried to get close to his father. His parents divorced when he was just one year old. But seeing Bud walk away from radiation treatments with legs so spindly that he couldn't go far without losing his breath, Bobby had to do something. It didn't take a genius to see that Bud was taking *his* father's route out.

Bobby's grandfather, who went by the name Preacher, was one of the best engine builders in Nashville. His wife Annie was a stern, stout woman who minded his money and morals. Together they ran one of the busiest service stations in town. It took care of the public by day, but at night it filled with racers. Bobby would play around it when he was young, calling himself Baba until all the racers did too. The one who seemed to like him the most was Marty Robbins, the country music singer who raced at the Nashville Speedway. On many late nights, Robbins sang his mournful melodies as Preacher worked on engines.

When Bobby was just eleven, doctors diagnosed his grandmother as having pulmonary fibrosis and confined her to bed. The boy did his homework by her bedside, and usually awoke three times a night to change her oxygen tanks. The house looked like a hospital on October 16, 1968, the day she died, with her husband holding her hand.

Preacher didn't drink before that day—as Bobby says, "He woulda thrown you out of his shop sooner than see you take a drop"—but the next year he was rarely sober. Bobby wasn't old enough to legally drive, yet Preacher made him drive to Annie's grave every evening, leave him with a bottle of whiskey, and pick him up before Bobby went to school the next morning.

Preacher died seven months later. Bobby watched them ease the casket into the plot where he'd dropped his grandfather off so many nights. He resolved to live his life differently. He was fifteen.

Now, as Bobby's wife Debbie watched the next two generations of Hamiltons, she marveled that he hadn't even mentioned having a living father until the third year of their marriage.

At first blush, the two men didn't even look as if they were related. Try as she might, Debbie just couldn't find Bobby's square, smooth face in Bud's gaunt profile. But the longer she observed them, the more she noticed that they moved to the same rhythms—whether it was the way they tapped their fingers at the dinner table or held their beer as they watched television. Bud was one of the wiliest mechanics in racing, and charming when sober. After she helped nurse him back to health, bringing bounce to his legs and a ruddy hue to his cheeks, he talked endlessly about how proud he was of his son.

But then he used his newfound health to start drinking

again, and it became plain to Debbie that Bud simply didn't care to be alive. The only thing she thought he was hanging on to see was Bobby win one for the King.

To a race fan of Bud's generation, the only King worth mentioning was Richard Petty. He was Joe DiMaggio, Elvis, and Lee Petty in one wrapping. Lee was the iconoclastic farmer who ditched his plow for a Plymouth, stole the number 42 off the first two digits of his license plate, and became a working-man's hero in countless southern mill towns where stock car racing was becoming the local sport.

Lee didn't so much encourage Richard to drive as not stand in his way. As Richard got older, his dreamy good looks and tufts of thick black hair began setting him apart from the other broken and soiled men, many of whom would not make it through the 1960s, an era when the craving for speed surpassed any desire for safety regulation. Most of these racing men were poor, many illiterate. When Bud and his friends went to the tracks, they were good for little more in the way of autographs than a gnarled, angry scrawl, maybe just an X. But Richard gave his fans a beautiful incongruity—a flowery, curling signature that looked as if it belonged to royalty. And so it was that the King, that wonderful creation, that alter ego, that smiling, relentlessly polite autograph signer, was born.

He was fortunate in that his arrival dovetailed with the birth of the speedways. Since there weren't any drivers who knew how to tame them, he became the first. Richard drove closer to the wall than anyone, which is like leaning into a Mike Tyson punch, except that the wall hits harder. But Richard got along well with the wall. It seemed to know that he was the last guy out there who'd do anything rash. He was economical, deliberative, patient. When he saw that your tires were getting bald after all your foolish banging, he'd come down off the high groove like the devil himself, and you'd be passed, son.

He took his fans—who by the mid-sixties included a young Bobby Hamilton—on a miraculous ride that lasted all the way up to his 200th win on Independence Day 1984, when Ronald Reagan helped him celebrate the national milestone with fireworks. But it was as if on that magical moment the racing deity froze him and said, "No more."

"Ya know, when I was born, God said you've got twenty-five years of good luck," Petty liked to say. "I just tried to stretch it to thirty-five."

Never to win again, Richard became something of an eccentric, hiring engineers with far-fetched ideas about re-designing the most basic elements of the race car. His crew of aspiring young hopefuls watched helplessly as one idea after another failed, as the once-fearsome car number 43 became a sideshow act for nostalgia buffs, run-ning in the back thirty. With half his stomach eaten away from ulcers, the King's famed toughness turned into frailty. His face twisted with pain, he'd stumble from his car to an oxygen mask after races. Those years didn't do his image proud, and by the early nineties Richard was making less from his race winnings than he had twenty years earlier.

Then a small group of friends started tinkering with an idea they privately called the Richard Petty 401-K tour. It began at the 1992 Daytona 500, when they minted 25,000 die-cast cars and sprinkled them through dozens of sou-venir booths. The lot sold out in days and by the morning of the race were fetching scalper's prices. It was the first indication that Richard's good-bye season, dubbed "The Fan Appreciation Tour," would become the single largest marketing bonanza ever in NASCAR. It was as if every hand Richard shook over thirty-five years was a deposit in the bank and it was suddenly time to make a withdrawal. With an Olympics-style strategy of sponsors paying up to a half-million dollars for official logos, Petty lent his name to everything from Magnum revolvers to chicken-on-a-stick.

The yearlong farewell made evident how narrowly NASCAR was managing itself. It had no central branding arm, no version of NFL Properties. Richard, who helped invent NASCAR with his driving, helped *re*invent it with his retirement. If the Petty name could bring out stock's silent majority with their wallets wide open—often WFO— imagine what the NASCAR name could do. It wasn't a long trip from that question to NASCAR batteries and NASCAR Thunder stores.

But Richard Petty was foremost a racer, and when he ran his last fiery lap in Atlanta, when he suddenly couldn't do the very thing he'd done for thirty-five years, all his new millions couldn't paper over the gnawing fact that Petty Enterprises hadn't won since 1984. Richard briefly hired John Andretti, the nephew of Mario Andretti, as his driver, but the marriage of two great racing names ended when Richard refused to pay Indy-size wages to the jockey-size upstart. Then Richard's son Kyle suggested he take a look at this Hamilton guy, who'd spent the season with him at Felix Sabates's Sabco shop. He said Bobby Hamilton was a hell of a driver, and just about to hit his prime.

After his father's funeral in Nashville that Thursday, Bobby caught a flight into Daytona that arrived early Friday for the first practice of the season.

Strapping himself into the car, he took the first few laps in a brand-new Grand Prix that was being introduced by Pontiac. Working deep into the banking of turn one, he found his mind clear, almost serene.

Nearly a year later he'd say, "When I got in that car a day after I buried my father, I didn't think about him at all. That night, I went home and I asked Debbie, 'Does that make me mean or sick?' I don't know. All I can tell you is I'd never felt focused like I did on those first few laps in Daytona. I don't know how it happened. It just did."

His first Daytona was five years before. He'd shot out of Nashville after his big break came driving the Tom Cruise car in the movie *Days of Thunder*. The exposure turned into a full-time job driving Winston Cup, and he became its 1991 Rookie of the Year.

But racing is a mystical thing. A car that wins once can finish last under nearly the exact same conditions the next time out. Some have compared it to alchemy, and more than one crew chief has shrugged his shoulders while standing over a winning car, wondering what the hell he did right. The same is true of losing. A top-ten car can get a virus halfway through a race and start doing maddening things. When it happens a few weekends in a row, teams get superstitious and begin referring to themselves as snakebit.

Bobby's sophomore season was snakebit. By his third year the owners of his team were doubting his resolve in a whisper campaign that preceded his firing. By late 1993 he was showing up to the tracks alone, watching old friends and rivals in blurs of motion as he searched for someone to help pick up the pieces. Jeff Hammond, a veteran crew chief who was scouting a new team for the millionaire Felix Sabates, listened to Bobby explain his failures, waiting, as he always does, to see whom a driver blames. Hammond made a note that although the garage was rife with gossip about Bobby being a problem case, moody and laconic, the racer didn't engage the subject. Instead, he looked at Hammond purposefully and said, "I know I can drive that race car." Hammond hired him, but just as Bobby's life seemed on the verge of a major turnaround, a silent investor in the operation with modest racing credentials stopped being silent. He second-guessed the gentle way Hammond was setting about rebuilding Bobby's confidence, and ultimately axed the Nashville racer. It was the kind of denouement Bobby came to expect: a messy end to a messy year.

And so it was that Kyle Petty introduced Bobby to his father. And from the moment he walked into the old white plank barn on a winding road in Level Cross, Bobby would find the people he'd waited a career for.

In the silver-haired Dale Inman, the man behind most of Richard's two hundred wins, Bobby found the old pro he'd always wanted. In Robbie Loomis, the self-critical crew chief who'd never orchestrated his own race win, he found a hungry thirty-year-old eager to make a name for himself. In the crew who worked for them, he found a clean-cut group that rarely partied.

In other words, he found men very much like himself. All of which combined for a season of surprising good fortune. Bobby posted a personal-best four top-five finishes, and finished 1995 in fourteenth place.

The 1996 season looked to be even more promising, particularly since Pontiac was bringing out a new aerodynamically advanced Grand Prix. But after the Daytona 500 it was clear the car had been released from the lab too early. Air went under its new nose instead of over it, causing the front end to lift, making it harder to turn through the corners. Racers call this a "push." Battling a savage push all day, the Forty-three team ended the race in twentieth.

When the crew got together for their regular Tuesday-morning meeting, Robbie Loomis tried not to lose enthusiasm. There are thirty races left, he said, and twenty-three

of them are on ovals of a mile and a half or less, where all
the GM data suggested the Grand Prix excelled.

Bobby slid his hand along the Pontiac's rounded nose
Sunday morning like a father taking his child's forehead
temperature. Word around the garage was that Terry
Labonte had the car to beat at this week's Goodwrench
400. But Earnhardt, who'd spent his days after Daytona
chain-sawing and chopping old poplar trees on his farm,
figured to have something to say about that. Upon being
told that Earnhardt looked surprisingly rested and relaxed,
his crew chief rolled his eyes. "He's been set on kill the
whole weekend," David Smith said.

Through the first half of the race, the predictions about
Labonte looked true. He was so dominating, he'd passed
half the field by the eightieth lap. The only thing making
the race mildly interesting was Jimmy Spencer, a back-
twenty driver best known for his crashes, who was having
a career day trying to wrest the lead away from the Texan.
Earnhardt and Labonte obligingly let Spencer wear down
the tread on his tires, then dusted him as they raced for the
$10,000 halfway leader bonus, their sleek noses rocking
in rhythm side by side.

Robbie Loomis chewed his lip watching Bobby run behind the three Winston Cup cars. Seven laps earlier his men
kicked ass with a picture-perfect stop, moving Bobby up
four spots to fourth. Now, as Labonte and Earnhardt
stalked each other for the lead, Bobby shadowed the third-
place Spencer through the corners, finally showing what he
had under the hood with a power pass to Spencer's outside.

That was all the convincing Robbie needed to know that
they had a car capable of winning. Now what they needed
was green-flag racing. But a caution flag soon thereafter
let Spencer rearm with fresh rubber, and in the ten laps that
followed, the lead changed every corner. First it was Jar-

rett, then Labonte, then Labonte's engine went up in smoke, sidelining him, and it was Ricky Rudd, Earnhardt, Spencer, and Hamilton in dizzying succession. Bobby was hot now, his heart was pounding. Those GM people were right. He could put the Grand Prix anywhere. Speeding into the sun hovering over the first turn, he closed on Rudd, forcing himself inside, retaking second. He'd never led a lap here, but when Spencer blew an engine cylinder, Bobby glided into a lead filled on all sides with daylight. Spencer wasn't done, not yet. He tangled for a few more laps, then spilled oil, drawing a caution that reshaped the race. Thirty seconds after Earnhardt followed Bobby onto the pit road, they pulled off in reverse order.

The next few minutes and the headlines they produced would haunt both men over the coming year. Earnhardt throttled hard off the restart but a few laps later pushed as he came off the backstretch, getting lost up in turn three's asphalt tide. That let Bobby plow into the open track beneath him. He held the lead for one lap. In the same place on the next lap, Earnhardt dove in lower, pulling close enough to Bobby to disrupt the path of the air over his Pontiac's spoiler. With no downforce to hold its back end down, it drifted up, clearing the way for Earnhardt to dive under it and again take the lead. Having picked their patch of track for battle, Bobby took the wind off Earnhardt's spoiler in the same place on the next pass, changing the lead for the third time in as many laps.

Debbie was watching on the STP hauler's television, thinking about Bobby's father and wishing he'd hung on just this much longer. Robbie Loomis was running between the pit road TV and the track. "Hang in there," he said to himself as his driver entered new territory. They'd spent a year waiting for their chance to break into the elite. Now it was suddenly, wonderfully, here. All they needed was another couple of laps.

But Dale Earnhardt had a champion's faith in his ability to handle his car. As they took each other around the track for the fourth time, the spoiler trick wasn't working. Earnhardt was right on Bobby's tail into turn three, doing all he could to disrupt the air, but Bobby's knuckles were white on the wheel and he was holding his course. In the middle of the turn Earnhardt tried again, but Bobby wasn't giving up the low line, not this time. The STP crew was glued to their television as Earnhardt came closer, closer. Then, right by the turn-four exit, right when it seemed Bobby was about to break away, Earnhardt made contact.

Dale Inman, who was spotting from the observation tower above the track, couldn't believe his eyes. The faint touch redirected Bobby's car, the wind sending it sideways into the wall, as if sliding on a smooth sheet of ice. Bobby frantically countersteered, trying to keep from smacking on the right side, managing to contain the hit to a small corner of his right rear. The impact sent him nosediving back down the track.

Inman had been pained as much as anyone by the team's winless drought, and all race had tried to keep Bobby in the hunt, playing Earnhardt even up, making Bobby believe he was every bit as good. They'd just about had the damn thing won and now Earnhardt stole it. Oh, there'd be hell to pay down the road. He'd make sure of that. But for now he had to keep Bobby, who'd straightened the car to stay in sixth, from going berserk.

"Let's get our act together, now, bud," he said into the radio, stifling his own outrage. "We can still get a good finish." But Bobby was beyond reach—pissed off and convinced he was fast enough to retake the lead.

"Good finish?" he said over the radio incredulously. "Hell, we're gonna win this bitch."

By saying this, he committed the cardinal sin: trying to win a race with a car that had only a tenth-place finish left in it. On the 345th lap he spun out and crashed in the fourth turn, further blackening the stripe he'd left earlier. It guaranteed he'd go home in twenty-fourth place with a check for $27,300.

In the days to come, Pontiac would calculate what "the bump" actually cost. The list, which was distributed to the press, read:

$240,000:	Winner's Circle program
$60,000:	Pontiac contingency money
$50,000:	STP contingency money
$62,000:	Additional purse money
$18,000:	Starting Spot Winston Select (minimum)
$30,000:	Cost to fix car

$460,000: Total*

Earnhardt received $83,840 for the win. But more important, he won 180 points toward his quest for a record-setting eighth championship.

Weeks later a sheepish Earnhardt came up to Inman and asked, "How long you gonna be mad at me?"

Inman looked him squarely in the eyes and replied, "How long you gonna be alive?"

As clouds moved in over Richmond on Friday, the March 1 edition of the *Richmond Times Dispatch* carried stories about a congressional vote to end crop subsidies, a pair of bootlegging brothers who'd been arrested, and a mini-scandal about a driver for the state's lieutenant governor

---

*The Winner's Circle program is a licensing vehicle that pays drivers who win races to appear in Winner's Circle promotions. Pontiac and STP both pay extra for wins. The Winston is an invitation-only all-star race held in April at the Charlotte Motor Speedway. No points are awarded, but the purse is rich and drivers who've won a race in the prior year are guaranteed admission.

who somehow avoided paying a speeding ticket while trafficking hizzonor.

But as traffic started filling downtown, John Boy and Billy, the syndicated disc jockeys from Charlotte's Fox 99.7 FM, were filling the airwaves with news of the bumping incident six days before. All across Richmond that morning, listeners heard them singing this song, recorded to a quick, tinny riff:

There's a man in black his name is Dale/ He's fast as lightning and mean as hell/ He's not afraid to bump and grind/ If it means he can leave your butt behind.

It's February in Rockingham/ And that Goodwrench crew is ready to jam/ As the number 'three moves through the field/ Big Bobby Hamilton refuses to yield.

Coming out of turn four, what a sight to see/ It was blue and red and Forty-three/ But Earnhardt gave that Chevy the gas, and the 'three tried to pass/ Petty said, "Hold on man." And Earnhardt said, "Watch this y'all."/ Next thing ya know, the Forty-three tagged the wall . . .

The man in black he flipped along/ And drove as if he could do no wrong/ Took the flag and pumped his fists/ Petty's fans were really pissed.

The press caught Dale in Vict'ry Lane/ And asked if he could please explain/ Well, Dale said, I was racin' hard/ I don't know what else to tell you, pard'.

All the crew at STP, was mad as mad could be/ And lots of folks seemed surprised/ That 'three car didn't get penalized/ But NASCAR says it's just hard racing/ And that's the kind of stuff you're facing.

I guess some guys have all the luck/ And sometimes life just seems to suck.

On race day in Richmond, Bobby found himself besieged by reporters. He hated the attention, and it showed in his curt, crisp answers. After a while he retreated into his transporter and locked the door. When asked how Bobby was doing, Doug Murph, the team's chief chassis man, took a knife from the counter and sliced the air with it.

Earnhardt had tried to engage Hamilton in a rapprochement that Bobby rebuffed with a cold shoulder. It was the perfect response for the weather, which had turned freezing and wet. Snow fell through the morning, and the temperature hadn't peaked over 45 degrees.

The STP pit was located by the entrance of the first turn, which the whipping winds made feel like an open prairie. Being a typically superstitious crew chief, Loomis had to smile when someone pointed out that the wind was blowing at precisely 43 mph.

As ESPN went to air, a national television audience of three and a half million—the largest for a NASCAR event up to that time—got yet another dose of the feud. The pretaped segment had Earnhardt saying, "I didn't wreck him. [Dale] Jarrett got into me [from behind], and I saved my car . . . Guys wrecked each other all day . . . I hate that it happened, but it's over and done with." Asked whether that cleared the air, Bobby decided not to let things die down entirely. "No, not really," he said, deadpan. "I seen him. He talked. I listened for about two minutes and walked off. He was still talking."

If anyone thought they were going to see fireworks early, though, it wasn't to be. Starting in third, six places ahead of Earnhardt, Bobby picked up right where he'd left off the week before.

Jumping off the green flag, Bobby quickly dispatched second-place starter Jeff Gordon, then hung on pole-sitter Terry Labonte's bumper until Labonte decided it was way too early to start gunslinging. He eased high, giving Bobby just enough open road to sneak out front. ESPN analyst Benny Parsons was impressed. "Boy, he went into that turn hard," he said.

Loomis also noticed. Wintry weather had forced the cancellation of many of the track's January practices, and the paltry few hours they'd been given in the last two days wasn't nearly enough to make him feel good about how the car would handle over four hundred laps of hard charging. As Bobby drove by pit road, the crew pumped its fists in the air, but Robbie said into his headset, "Easy does it, easy does it. Don't abuse the car."

"I'm not," crackled back the confident voice. "I just wanted to lead a few laps and get comfortable. I'm really not punching."

For a brief stretch Bobby ran a torrid pace. But unlike the week before, when he ran better on old tires, this time it was the reverse. He could march through the field at will on new ones, yet started losing traction on old ones. He was hardly unique. The shorter track with its constant turning was hell on tires. Geoff Bodine tempted fate by driving fifty-four laps on the same set, and was rewarded by skidding into the wall after he spun, cutting a sharp arc through turn three.

Still, Bobby was able to get in and out of the pits quickly enough to dominate the first two hundred laps, picking up $10,000 in bonus prize money.

But two-thirds of the way through, Robbie's fears began to be realized. After the Pontiac had drifted out of the top ten and pitted near the 300th lap, Petty examined the tires like an archaeologist and shook his head. Except for the occasional lumpy patches that the road hadn't yet sheared, they were worn down to grainy pebbles of rubber. "Too fast," he muttered. He'd already done the mental calculations everyone else was doing, and it didn't bode well. At this rate Bobby would have to stop three more times. And because of the bitter cold, his crew wasn't at their best. Twice already they'd lost a place or three on the track with their delays getting the car off pit road.

It would be one of the day's ironies that Earnhardt would be the one to help Hamilton out of his jam.

Despite the cool temperatures, Richmond was a flat-out brake killer. Many street cars use brake calipers—the device that squeezes the brake pads against the rotor—with one or two pistons. (The pistons get pushed by brake fluid into the brake pad, slowing the car.) By contrast, Winston Cup cars have twice that because of the pressure it takes to slow down 3,400 pounds of speeding car an average of once every ten seconds. By late in a race, the brake rotor begins glowing burnt orange.

Earnhardt had trouble with his calipers forty-three laps from the end of the four-hundred-lap race. A leak in his front right one sent bubbling brake fluid squirting onto the caliper, causing smoke to pour from under the car. This called for an unscheduled pit, and as cars whizzed past him, he grew irksome. "What the hell are these people doin'?" he barked.

"They're putting brake fluid in, Dale," his owner, Richard Childress, replied.

"The hell they are. They ain't doin' nothing!"

Finally, the crew sent him back out with only left front and rear brakes. It would prove inadequate. On the 372nd lap a car skidded and spun before Earnhardt, causing his spotter high above the racetrack to warn him to slow down. "You're not payin' attention," Earnhardt shouted back. "I can't stop this fuckin' race car." He then forced himself into the wall so he could spin out and stop himself by sliding to the bottom wall.

This drew a caution, which is exactly what Bobby, who was driving on old tires, needed. He was in fourteenth place, and the last car on the lead lap. No car was better on the field with new tires, and now it would be a thirty-lap duel that he'd be fully armed to fight.

"Okay, driver," Robbie said as he sent Bobby out of the pits. "You know what to do." And Bobby did. For a whole week his name had been the one on everyone's lips. He'd been through years of people questioning his grit. Now there was no question. He'd had his coming-out party in Rockingham. It was time to mature before the cameras here in Richmond.

Marching hard up the field, he was relentless. If the knock on him before was that he was listless, he was going to show his critics just what he'd learned from Earnhardt.

John Andretti found that out the hard way. With fourteen to go and Bobby blowing past Ward Burton to take ninth, the two cars were neck and neck. Unable to pass in traffic, Bobby bumped Andretti, nearly causing him to lose control. Somehow, he managed to hold on, and when a four-car pileup occurred later that lap, a caution flag flew, freezing the field until it could be cleared for a final five-lap mad dash.

On the restart, Andretti was fighting off Terry Labonte on his outside when Bobby booted him again, this time nearly sending him sideways into the Kellogg's car. Again Andretti managed to correct, but he had to veer high to do it, giving Bobby the middle of the track to speed past him. He was in eighth place. Now it was time for sheer power. With two laps to go, he passed Labonte. As the white flag fell, Bobby spilled onto the front straight with Rusty Wallace. Both wanted to go into the first turn as low as they could, but Bobby held on to the lane, forcing Rusty outside enough that Bobby was able to swipe sixth, and stay there when the checkered flag fell.

"Way to go, driver," Robbie said into his radio. Bobby was about to answer when he felt a bump from behind. It was Andretti. He kept driving on, thinking it was an accident. But Andretti did it again, this time harder. Bobby locked his brakes and Andretti pushed him into the infield wall, tearing apart the rear of a car Hamilton had managed to drive four hundred laps without damaging.

In racing, this is as clear a declaration of war as one can make. You aren't just throwing a punch at a driver. You're wrecking a $100,000 race car that a half dozen over-worked crewmen with families are going to have to stay after hours to fix. As Bobby drove it to the garage, the Petty people were already trading angry words with the Andretti crew.

Along with being a singular presence in the garage, Petty was something of an oracle on matters of protocol. Noticing Andretti's veteran chief, Tim Brewer, he walked over and slid his arm around Brewer's shoulder. Knowing what was coming, Brewer said, "I didn't see anything, King." So Petty asked where Andretti was, and Brewer pointed into the hauler.

Petty walked in and stayed for a few minutes. Then he returned to his car with a perfectly serene look on his face. "What didya say?" Loomis asked him from the side of his mouth.

"I told him I was gonna whip his ass if he ever took it out on my car again. He wants to beat on my driver? Fine. But don't take it out on my race car."

3

JUNIOR AND FLOSSIE

On Friday afternoon, April 12, the school bells rang early, as they always did in North Wilkesboro when racing came to town. By the afternoon, the cars would be heard all the way back from the small brick city hall on Main Street to the apple orchards up in the mountains. It had been like that for fifty years. So it would do no good to try to keep the kids behind their desks, especially since their fathers had probably called into work sick and their moms had put everything on the back burner.

Qualifying day in North Wilkesboro was a local holiday.

The town recently produced a commemorative book. It's a thick, impressive hardcover with a seal on the front— a train steaming across Cherry Street. Between entries for the chartering of a YMCA in March 1944, and the reorganization of the Junior Women's Club in June 1947, is a photo of the North Wilkesboro Speedway, along with this caption:

According to Junior Johnson, racer and car builder, the first race (unofficial) was by haulers of locally made illicit whiskey, who had honed their driving skills outrunning law officers. The first official race was run on May 18, 1947.

North Wilkesboro is Yadkin River country, where Daniel Boone lived, where deed books still contain language preventing the sale of some land to blacks. Stock car racing may have started on Daytona's beaches, but it found its soul here. Looking down from the Brushy Mountains, over the orchards and cornfields, across to the Blue Ridges that look like part of a painted museum exhibit, it's easy to imagine the way this lazy county was on that May day when a bunch of red-eyed moonshiners came out of the hills to kick up its dirt.

The hills act as an inoculant, preserving its past like fossil stone. But its greatest fossil wasn't getting anywhere near the racetrack this day. Having retired at the end of the previous season, Junior Johnson sat in his new Georgian mansion telling all comers that NASCAR was losing its soul.

"There is not any loyalty in racing anymore," he said. "They used to kind of go for the throat. Now they go for the jugular vein, to put it kinda mildly."

The visiting reporters lapped this up, for Junior was racing royalty. But around the track, there were people just as glad he was staying away. These were friends of his ex-wife Flossie, people who'd never forgiven him for the way he dumped her after forty years to have children with a woman less than half his age.

Junior and Flossie were teenage sweethearts, and already living together (they didn't legally marry until 1975) when Tom Wolfe heard about Junior's exploits under Wilkes County's moonlit hills, and how the revenuers who hunted his kind were making him an outlaw legend. Wolfe introduced Junior, and by extension stock car racing, to the New York literati with his seminal article in *Esquire*, "The Last Great American Hero Is Junior Johnson, Yes." He described Junior as their Dillinger, from a part of the country that bred Purple Heart winners

in astounding numbers. Robert Glen Johnson Sr.'s 1935
bust with hundreds of cases of illegal whiskey was the
largest inland seizure ever, and years after his son Junior
came out of the hills to become a stock car star, the boy
kept close to the family tree. Early one morning when Junior had come back from a race wanting nothing but to
sleep and his brother was sick and couldn't fire the still,
Junior, then age twenty-two, went for him. Four revenuers
who'd discovered it hidden deep in brush were lying in
wait. They were stunned when their ambush produced
only the pearly-toothed tomcat, and pissed off when he
tried to run. He ran straight into barbed wire and federal
time: eleven months and three days of it.

But that wasn't the largest case in Wilkes County history. That came a year later, when the feds stung his entire
family. In the gripping 1959 trial, Junior was acquitted, but
his mother wasn't so lucky. She got fined $7,500 for selling
two pints to an undercover. One brother got two years, another six months more. Long after Junior became big
enough to entertain the presidents of Ford and Chrysler at
his house on Highway 421, he remained at odds with police. To show he was never far from their thoughts, they
subpoenaed him on the eve of the 1974 Firecracker 400 in
Daytona, claiming he hadn't paid an eighteen-year-old
fine. He fought the nuisance rather than pay. He hated the
bastards that much.

Junior put his garages where he could always see them,
a few dozen yards down the sloping hill where he built the
shingled A-frame home that came to be synonymous with
its town, Ingle Hollow. Junior would amble out the door of
his home in white T-shirt and slacks that matched his
snowy hair and disappear into the garages until noon,
when work stopped for supper from Flossie's kitchen.

The role of the doting southern bride came naturally to
Flossie, even if she wasn't Junior's first wife (he was

briefly married as a teen in 1949), or even his wife at all for
the first twenty years they lived together. Plump, with
a trim, delicate mouth and round eyes made for soul-
searching, Flossie turned Ingle Hollow into more than a
race shop. She made it NASCAR's White House, where
everyone from the Edsel Ford to actors portraying them in
movies could sit at a long wood table looking over the
garage bays, and taste her sausage pinwheels or pretzel
salad. Flossie kept the values country, kept cussing to a
minimum, and wasn't shy about sharing her front-porch
pearls of common sense when she spotted a marriage in
need of saving, or an ego in need of checking—even if that
ego belonged to her husband. They were NASCAR's First
Couple, and because their mail was sorted by the post office in Ronda, North Carolina, hundreds of mechanics
would say they got their education at the small but presti-
gious University of Ronda.

In the 1970s the Johnsons won three championships
with Cale Yarborough as their driver. In the 1980s there
were three more with Darrell Waltrip. In 1985, Junior had
his federal conviction lifted by Ronald Reagan's presidential pardon. In 1992 the Johnsons nearly won a seventh
title with Bill Elliott.

All in all, it was a good life for Flossie. Until one day
the phone rang in the kitchen. A woman on the other end of
the line said, "You need to know. Junior's going to leave
you."

"Who is this?" Flossie demanded.

"That's not important," she said. "Call me the other
woman. All you need to know is he's leaving me too."

Flossie knew about the women from the past, but she
thought that part of his life was over. She also assumed the
issues surrounding their inability to have children were
long since retired.

"Is there anything to it, Junior?" she asked when she hung up.

"Might be," he said.

For nearly three years rumors had circulated around the NASCAR garage that Junior was having an affair with a twenty-eight-year-old strawberry blonde who was raised in a home so close to Flossie that she could look out of her kitchen window and see it up the hill.

"Oh, Junior," Flossie sighed, dumbstruck that they appeared now to be more than rumors. "What a tangled web we weave."

"Ain't it so," said Junior. He would always deny having sexual relations with his Lisa Day while he lived in Ingle Hollow. But he left that night, and since North Carolina is a no-fault divorce state, was granted a divorce after living apart from Flossie for a year.

With his life in tumult, it was hardly surprising that Junior's fabled feel for his race cars began to slip. During the summer of 1992, Bill Elliott was tearing up the Winston Cup circuit. As Tim Brewer, Junior's crew chief for over twenty years, remembered, "We were in Dover and we had Alan Kulwicki 342 points behind us. Comes to where it's the end of the race and I want to put on two tires because we're racing Davey Allison for the title and Ricky Rudd for the win. I called for two left-sides and fuel, and about the time the car got to pit road Junior said, 'No, put on four.' Out of respect, because he owned the team, I did. Well, Ricky won the race, we came in second, and at the end of the year we'd lose the championship by the number of points that cost us. After the race someone yells, 'Brewer, you was robbed.' One of my guys whispered under his breath, 'Yeah, it was an inside job.'"

When the increasingly bitter divorce was settled in the fall of 1993, Flossie got the house and Junior kept the business behind it. He drove to work every morning, but they never spoke. By then he and Lisa Day, a plain country girl prone to mothering her man in public, were married and living ten minutes away, in a mansion with columns, a circular drive, and a brass plaque outside that announced *they* were the Johnsons.

While Lisa was becoming the lady of the manor, and the maid minded their three-year-old son and newborn daughter, Flossie was in Junior's old house, filled with baby dolls—some in lace gowns, others in Sunday hats and antique pajamas, and one in a white wicker bassinet in the living room, sucking its thumb.

No one knows better than Flossie what it is to be a racing wife. She admits that she was willfully blind to many things, yet in the next breath says she never expected to be sixty and alone.

The wood-paneled downstairs is filled with photos of young Junior smiling from behind the wheel of his old Ford, a collage of headlines, a mural of his life. But the kitchen is the heart of the home, and it's where she chose to speak. Staring into the skillet, she started by saying, "Well, I suppose you've heard about me and Junior.

"I guess I've known him all my life. When we were twelve and thirteen years old, we used to go to the movies together. Skating. To the drive-ins. We always were friends. Later we became sweethearts. I guess you can say we were still sweethearts when Junior left."

Lifting her blue eyes, she went on, "We had a lot of struggles puttin' a racin' team together, and it took both of us. I always thought we had the best combination in racing. At least until the last few years. Then things weren't the way they used to be. You know, you have a guy that's on top for a long time, and then he slides away. Well, it hurts. It hurts that guy. It hurts racing. And I guess that's what we seen here. We had a really good life

together. We were best friends. I don't know what happened. It just happened."

Flossie doesn't talk about this easily, so she put down
the pan, scraping the eggs onto a china plate, and pulled
out a chair for herself at the table.

"Junior loves this house," she said, looking around.
"We built it together. We struggled to do it. I drove a truck
to git the lumber. We dug the bricks for the fireplace out of
an old furniture factory. We raised chickens in those days,
and Junior had a bulldozer he leased to the state. Every
time we had any extra money, we put it in."

A smile started across her wide, soft face, brought on by
those memories. "On Saturdays we got ready and went to
the races, and most of the time Junior would win. Then
we'd go out to eat. We'd talk about it, and then go to
church the next day. 'Course, you had to shampoo your
head the next day, it being full of red mud. There was
times it was a struggle for both of us, but I guess I can
compare myself to Cinderella at the ball. We always got
along so well. And I think I can say that I'm still Junior's
best friend. I don't know that he would say I still am. But I
feel like I was the best friend he had. He's told me that lots
of times."

Flossie's voice turned small as she said this, and then disappeared altogether. She walked out into the sunroom for a
moment, pretending to have left something there. "And
when things weren't like that," she continued on her return,
"when he stopped being on top in the last few years . . . I
could see the hurt in Junior. And it hurt me for him.

"See, to everyone who ever worked here, we was like
their mom and dad. When Junior left, they all said they
didn't think they could have been hurt any more than if it
had been their own parents. They were like our kids. I
helped them with their lives, with their marriages."

She paused, steeling herself. "I guess mine is the only

one that really failed in these walls. But it just happened. If Junior didn't want to be here anymore, I didn't want him to be."

Junior's leaving made the NASCAR world understand that a rule had changed. Yes, drivers fucked famously on the road, but in exchange for that liberty, they became family men on Sundays. How else could NASCAR sell itself as the one sport above all others that prized family values? Now its most public family was breaking apart.

"I used to say you have to be blind when you're a racing wife," Flossie said, understanding this was what the conversation would come down to. "You see a lot of things you don't want to see. You hear a lot of things you don't want to hear. You put up with a lot of stuff you don't want to put up with.

"If you've got a strong marriage, you're lucky. I always thought I did. That was the last thing in the world I ever would have thought woulda happened to us. When things happened to other people's marriages, he'd say, 'Floss, that'll never happen to us.' And then it did. There was never a day he told me he didn't love me. He said it as he was walkin' out that door. You coulda taken a butcher knife to my heart and it wouldn'ta hurt me as bad."

She kneaded her knuckles until they turned ruddy red. "What hurt me the worst of anything was the disappointment I had in somebody I loved so much. For a long time I couldn't even comprehend Junior not being here. Us not being together. Even after he was gone, I cared. I wanted to tell him a lot of times what I thought was going wrong with the race team. But he never talked to me after he left."

Not at all?

"No. His new house is ten minutes away from here. I've never been there. Never been by, or anything. I've seen a little bit about it in the paper. You know Junior was raised up in the country, an old country boy. If he'd just built him an old country house, big fireplace where his dogs coulda come in and laid down, that's Junior. Nothing about that new house is Junior."

Here, Flossie put a period on her marriage. She did it for herself and for the many people who write to ask how she's faring.

"After he left me, I did a lot of praying. I can't say I haven't missed Junior. But I can truthfully say that I can go to bed and sleep. I dream about him once in a while, I probably always will. He was such a part of me for such a long time.

"I don't know if he'd say the same thing or not, but it wouldn't matter to me if he did. I've never wished him no bad luck. I've never done anything to hurt Junior. He knows that. And everyone else does too."

Conceding nothing to age, Junior had gone into the 1990s with as great a pool of talent as anyone in NASCAR, and all of the biggest sponsors. But it was becoming plain that he couldn't keep his mini-empire together, or simply no longer had the desire to try. Most of his contemporaries had sons to take over. Richard Petty had Kyle. Bobby Allison still had Davey and Clifford. But Junior had no one to pour a remarkable life's work into.

That's why he clung so tightly to Brent Kauthen, the almond-eyed child who began spending summers at Ingle Hollow at the young age of seven. Brent's mother, divorced and struggling to raise two kids in Detroit, met the Johnsons through her job with Chevrolet and gladly let them bring the boy to the country to have the kinds of summers that any kid would envy. He became a fixture around the tracks and, more important as the years passed, the son Flossie and Junior never had. When he turned eighteen, they paid his way through North Carolina State. Junior began talking about the day when he could take it easy and watch from their sunporch as Brent took over running things. On the rainy night of April 27, 1990, that dream died when Brent, then twenty-five, died in a car crash on a back Wilkes County road.

By the spring of 1993 the divorce and the pressure of running his teams had left Junior in declining health. Never a particularly healthy eater, his eyes took on a yellow tint. In March after the Rockingham race, he left Ingle Hollow and didn't come back. A few crewmen convinced themselves he was dead until they heard that his new wife, a cardiological nurse, admitted him into the hospital for a triple bypass.

Returning the next month, he found his Bill Elliott Budweiser team, which finished 1992 in second place, struggling in twenty-fifth. Worse, McDonald's, the highest-profile sponsor in the sport, was growing edgy over the performance of Hut Stricklin, a Birmingham native whom Junior had installed in the high-profile ride despite a tepid track record. Though Elliott rebounded to finish 1993 in eighth place, Stricklin's twenty-fourth-place showing that year prompted McDonald's to open a back channel to Elliott after the 1994 Daytona 500, and ultimately led it to abandon Junior in favor of a new race team Elliott started in 1995.

In the midst of all this, Flossie's attorneys were hiring accountants to pore through Junior's books, so sure were they that he was undervaluing his teams to cheat her out of millions. In fact, Junior had allowed Ingle Hollow to fall behind in technology and get tapped out of talent. It would have taken a full-scale turnaround, not a tired Junior with two young children and a twenty-something wife, to breathe life into its old husk. Rather than try, Junior settled the divorce by selling two of his three teams. But he wasn't ready to get out entirely. Not that way. So he kept a fragment of a team, the Eleven car, and went to work every day to the garage a hundred yards from Flossie's kitchen. She pretended not to notice he was there.

Going into 1995, Junior had neither a driver for his Eleven car (Elliott had left to form his own team) nor a sponsor (Budweiser bolted too). So it was fortuitous that the Lowe's home-improvement chain had decided to sponsor a Winston Cup car as a way of building awareness for itself in the Midwest, where it was expanding. As Lowe's and Junior were staples of the same small town, Lowe's sponsorship of his Eleven team couldn't have been more natural. Junior assured everyone concerned that they would do well with a new driver he'd selected— Brett Bodine.

The image-conscious company was shaken, then, when Junior arrived at Daytona in 1995 with a secret helper: an illegal manifold that allowed in more air, increasing the car's horsepower. In years past it might have slid by, but Bill France had hired an inventive crew chief named Gary Nelson to be his Winston Cup series director, and Nelson was taking his job deadly seriously. Believing fines were an empty threat in the era of the $5 million race budget, Nelson reasoned that only a chagrined sponsor could help him get tough. And so he cannily decided to start publicizing infractions that once were dealt with quietly. Who better to start with than the pearly-toothed tomcat himself? The $45,000 fine that he levied became national news and, as Nelson predicted, mortified Lowe's executives, who were anticipating a decidedly classier debut.

It didn't get better from there. Four races into the season, crew chief Mike Beam left, ripping a gaping hole in a ship that was rapidly taking on water. As a stopgap, Junior hired the son of an old friend who hadn't even been to most of the Winston Cup tracks. The team finished that year in twentieth place, the worst finish ever for a Junior Johnson car. He'd had enough. He was getting out.

Now, for the first time in North Wilkesboro's history, Junior Johnson wouldn't be at one of its races. Instead he would be sitting in his new home, receiving reporters as a kind of grumpy oracle. As he spoke, his three-year-old son rode a go-cart past the sliding glass doors that open onto a farm where he tends six hundred head of cattle.

His cheeks hung off their mounts like weights, and when his mouth moved, it was slowly, with carefully chosen words. "I didn't want to pack a bag on Thursday, be gone till Sunday night, and be off to the shop Monday morning. I just made up my mind that it weren't the way I was going to bring up my family," he started.

"Some things have their priorities. Now I'm just doing things that I like to do. Like being with my family and children. The old dedication to racing is pretty much gone."

Like Flossie, he'd chosen the kitchen to talk. Dirty from having been bulldozing a private drive from his mansion to the road, wearing clay-crusted overalls and sod on his work boots, he carefully maneuvered himself behind a white linoleum table. Explaining his decision to retire from racing, he said, simply, "There's not any loyalty anymore.

"I've had people leave me over twenty-five dollars after I taught them everything. I've had [rivals] steal 'em, keep 'em for two weeks, and then fire 'em just to tear me up. It takes ten people to run on race day, and they'd try to get me by leavin' me nine."

His voice was barely above a whisper, but he seemed to be shouting. Then he threw up his hands, big meaty hands, and let them hit the table with a thud. "There's just so much money in it now. It's taken a lot away from the way it was really brought up. Anything that happens on the racetrack is put on TV. Everybody sees it. If you got a big sponsor, they're gonna lower the blame on you for somethin'. It makes the drivers today into . . ." The next word came out sounding vile. ". . . sissies."

He spoke for a while about the past, saying, "Moonshine was a way of life here, cultivated by our grandfathers and great-grandfathers. It wasn't like we thought it was against the law. We didn't see any harm in it. The government made whiskey and we wasn't doing anything different. We just wasn't paying taxes. The way we saw it, we was as legit as our country.

"We used to have 'forty Fords with supercharged Cadillac motors, awesome vehicles way, way ahead of Detroit in the technology of speed. And being in the moonshine business, it was natural for us to test our skills against each other. That's how I got going. People started payin' me to run races in 'fifty-five, but I didn't take it real seriously until about 1960. I'd got caught runnin' a still for my father and went off to prison for two years. But I made parole in eleven months and three days. When I came out, I went back to driving race cars. I had a contract with Ford Motor company and I coulda made good money, 'bout $50,000 a year. Then, in 1965, I won thirteen races of the twenty-nine they ran. It was my best year, and I just walked away to make even better money as a race team owner."

It's mentioned that he created the modern era by having sponsors that financed his teams. "Yeah, all that stuff I started. But without it, we wouldn't have survived. See, you couldn't race with just the winnings the tracks were payin'. At least I couldn't, not if I wanted to keep my edge. We were innovating. If anybody had an idea how to win, I'd say go on and spend the money."

Here Junior leaned forward, wanting to set something straight. He was talking about the seventies, the era when "it all started gettin' shaky." Ford dropped out of racing. The gas crisis hit. Bill France Sr., who built the sport, handed the reins to his untested son. "Everyone gives the Frances all the credit, but it was us, the owners and drivers, who saved NASCAR. We couldn't afford for it to go broke, 'cause if it did, we was outta business. And, whether Billy likes it—or whether he wants to admit it or not—that's the truth."

This is the Junior that Flossie talked about, the man who invented the science of stock. Yet his new house is decorated with few suggestions of who he was. There's an old black-and-white photo of Junior, the movie poster of the film about his life, *The Last Great American Hero,* a trophy or two. They're hung as if they were bought by a designer. Most everything else is back in Flossie's basement. It's her past now, not his.

The more he spoke, the clearer it became how much distance Junior was putting between himself and the world he'd walked away from. "It's not even all the money that gets me," he said, rolling the eyes one writer described as flashing gun turrets. "It's how they spend it. Today, the drivers and the mechanics get all the money. Not the people that own the teams. In a business, the man that owns the thing should make something out of it. Not every damn body around him. So let them run it. I'll do something else."

Junior exhaled deeply, in a sign that he was getting itchy to go back to his bulldozer.

But there was one last question.

What did he think of the person who bought his Eleven team, Brett Bodine?

"He'll have a lot of trouble," Junior said. "I don't wanna go to the racetrack and be around Brett and his guys, because someone will ask me what I think, and I'm the type of person, I don't care who it is, I'm not gonna go off and tell a lie. I just don't think they're knowledgeable enough to know what they're gettin' themselves into."

4

GROWING PAINS

Rockingham to North Wilkesboro: February 25 to April 14

Brett Bodine is a sunny person. At five-seven with curly, thin brown hair, the thirty-seven-year-old racer wouldn't look out of place as the owner of an airy L.A. wine bar or as a golf pro, which he once flirted with becoming. His smile is so natural, you believe that he wakes up every day happy, and it takes an enormous amount of effort to change that. But only a couple of weeks into the 1996 season, he was already running on fumes.

After the Daytona 500, Brett and his fifteen exhausted employees stayed up early each morning trying to reshape the mangled wreckage of their Ford for the next race, two hours southeast in Rockingham. They arrived in town at one o'clock Friday morning and were at the track five hours after that. There was a brief flurry of excitement when Brett ran the fastest practice lap, but by Sunday the crew was glassy-eyed. The driver too. Early in the race he veered up into Rusty Wallace coming out of the fourth turn, pinching him into the wall and mashing his own Ford's right rear. He got back on the track, but it was ugly. The day ended with a twenty-eighth-place finish.

In his hauler, Bodine threaded his fingers through his wet hair, trying to remember when he'd first noticed the men in suits traipsing through Ingle Hollow. Was it only nine months ago? Junior never said a word to him, but Brett didn't need his engineering degree to figure out that after unloading two teams, Junior was starting to shop around his Eleven team.

When he signed on for the 1995 season, Brett did so with eyes wide open. Junior gave him his first Winston Cup break, tapping him to drive in relief of Terry Labonte for two races in 1986.* He'd driven the wheels off the cars, finishing eighth and ninth, and it earned him a full-time ride the next season. Now he was coming back to Junior, hoping to rediscover a bit of that fire. He knew Junior would retire soon, maybe even at the end of the year, but one good season was all he needed. Unfortunately, he didn't get even one good race. In their first week in Daytona, the illegal manifold scandal flared, and after ten races crew chief Mike Beam defected with all but two of his pit crew, ripping a hole in the operation's hull.

As the season that was supposed to answer the skeptics turned into the longest of his career, Brett looked at all the other drivers, wondering when the bottom was going to fall out of their rides. They were the back twenty, the ones who would retire into car dealerships after frustrating careers filling out the field, who would have one good day followed by fifteen bad ones, whose lines were the same: "The *fill-in-the-sponsor* Ford/Chevy/Pontiac was running real good today. We could have had a top ten if not for *fill-in-the-problem*. But we'll have a real good car ready for *fill-in-the-next-race*."

His eight-year Winston Cup career had been a struggle to keep off their carousel. He spent the 1988 and '89 seasons with Bud Moore, finishing twentieth and nineteenth. Then he moved to a new team started by drag-racing titan

---

*Brett's substitutions are a little-remembered footnote to the record of most consecutive starts that Labonte would set on April 21. The rules at the time were that a driver merely had to drive the car off pit road to be awarded credit for a start. Soon thereafter, the rules would be changed to read that a driver had to take the green flag to get credit.

Kenny Bernstein, and in five years there finished twelfth, nineteenth, fifteenth, twentieth, and nineteenth again. Junior's team was only the third he'd worked for, and amid the chaos he eked out a twentieth-place year there.

Only a handful of NASCAR racers can sell the licensing rights to their name for $30 million, as Dale Earnhardt had. But Brett came along just when the purses were starting to explode. His brother Geoff won $3.8 million for notching fifty-four top-five finishes in his first eight years on the circuit, 1982–89. In Brett's first eight years, 1988–1995, he had sixteen top fives and won $4.3 million. With a contract allowing him to keep a quarter of the purse, in addition to an annual salary that averaged about $400,000, Brett had few financial worries.

He may not have had the best record, but the omnipresence of ESPN, TNN, and countless local affiliate stations meant television had an insatiable appetite for drivers, and being smart, telegenic, and smooth, Brett was one of the easiest and best interviews. That, combined with his ability to bring his race cars home in one piece, meant there'd always be an owner preferring his steadiness to the uncertainty of a young gun who'd run through a million dollars' worth of cars before he learned to drive. Yeah, Brett could always get a ride. But he wanted more.

"Some people in this garage walk right into great rides. But we all can't be Jeff Gordon," Brett would say, his blue eyes wide and clear, his voice even and convincing on the point that his best years weren't behind him. "The rest of us have to make it happen for ourselves."

So while he was still in the middle of his 1995 season with Junior, he rang the old man up at the mansion. "Junior," he said, "if you're going to sell this team, then sell it to me."

*   *   *

The Bodines did just about everything in Chemung, New York, from hatching chickens to running a dairy barn on Main Street—a map speck that fit only one grocery store, a gas station, a springwater company, the town garage, and a post office. When Eli Bodine built a five-eighths-mile dirt track in 1951 and began running races on summer Saturday nights, Chemung's population grew twelvefold. The kids did everything from sweeping to scoring, and it wasn't hard for them to become mini-celebrities before they were old enough to drive. The Bodine farm always had a dinner table filled with noisy kids, because that's the way Eli's wife Carol liked it. When her daughter Denise and son Geoff were well into elementary school, Carol said to her husband, "It's so quiet. We really need another baby."

Ask Brett and Geoff about their upbringing, and they'll invariably say, "It wasn't your normal childhood," by which they mean that their ten-year age difference kept them apart. But it was more complex than just that. Carol remembers her two oldest boys this way: "Geoff was always more quiet and self-conscious. When he was little, he was very timid. If someone came in the house, he'd stand behind me. Brett was outgoing. From the day he was born he smiled."

It's been said of the brothers that Geoff is the best engineer, Brett the best businessman, Todd the best driver. Todd, who keeps two of Geoff's horses on a farm he's building near Brett—an apt metaphor for his role in the family—weighs in with the observation that "Geoff was so focused on his racing, people thought he was ill. He just didn't want to talk. Brett grew up seeing that and became the opposite. Very outgoing. Very giving."

Engaging any of them on a discourse about the other is nearly impossible; more tight-lipped brothers can't be found. When it comes to Brett and Geoff, maybe the fairest thing to say is that despite the ten years' distance, they've shadowed each other across their careers, sometimes to their betterment, often not.

Both had equal obsessions for racing from a very young age. Geoff laughs about once dressing in drag to compete in a Powder Puff derby without his parents' consent, pulling off the track before he'd get caught. On his high school graduation day his uncle qualified his car so he could race it that night, unconcerned about the school parties. By the mid-seventies he'd become the Northeast's most prolific modified racer, setting a single-season win mark (fifty-five out of seventy-four) that still stands in the *Guinness Book of World Records*. When the Chemung Speedrome's fortunes faded and the town refused to let Eli build a larger track, Geoff moved his family to Massachusetts.

Brett chose to stay behind, living with an aunt as he finished high school. He worked on a college degree while he raced on the side—or maybe it was the other way around—paying his own way rustproofing cars, coming home past midnight with the fumes still in his nose. By 1980 he'd worked his way up to the larger tracks, like Pocono, where he one day caught a glimpse of a twenty-one-year-old race fan named Diane Dallaire. Afraid he wouldn't see her again, he followed her all the way out of the track and to a gas station, where he hung on the window talking to her until her twin sister threatened to pull away with Brett half inside. On their first date, they drove to Ohio to drop off a motor. They were married four months later.

With infant daughter Heidi in tow, the couple moved into a cramped trailer in the Pocono Mountains, then a small Connecticut apartment. "If you'da seen Brett, he was a rolling caravan with nothing," Clyde McLoud, his crew chief in those days, remembers. "In 'eighty and 'eighty-one we won a couple of races, but in 'eighty-two he went crazy. All over the Northeast we were a threat to win. By 'eighty-four we were at the top of the heap."

Geoff had already made the move south, winning the 1982 Winston Cup Rookie of the Year Award and three races in 1984 on Rick Hendrick's fledgling All-Star Racing Team. His natural aloofness was taken as Yankee superiority, and, perhaps inevitably, he found himself feuding with Dale Earnhardt. "I've thought about inviting him to go deer hunting," Earnhardt was quoted as saying in Frank Vehorn's book, *The Intimidator*. "But I can't ask with a sincere look on my face. I'd make him wear antlers. After all, hunting accidents do happen."

Brett, meanwhile, exhausted his stay in the Northeast and rejoined the family in North Carolina with a job fabricating sheet metal for race car chassis at Hendrick's race shop. But lightning would strike quickly, and literally, for the younger brother. Storms canceled two races in the summer of 1985 and both were rescheduled for the same day, leaving Hendrick in a lurch since Geoff was his driver for each. Brett was called upon to sub for Geoff at the Dogwood 500 in Martinsville, a Busch Series race, and in storybook fashion, he won it, leading to a short-term Hendrick contract that yielded two more Busch wins and *eight* poles in thirteen races. *Stock Car Racing* magazine called it an "amazing rise to stardom," and the next season Brett exploded with top fives everywhere, finishing as the runner-up to Larry Pearson, a scant twenty points away from the Busch Series title.

And so it was that five years after his brother was anointed Rookie of the Year, Brett would join him in Winston Cup, a twenty-eight-year-old on a tear.

What happened next? Brett sees the question coming and he exhales. You can see him preparing the brief for an uneven career. There's a word for this. Brett sees it and grabs it before it lands on him. "I know there are people who think I'm a *recycled* driver, but they're wrong. It's been a combination of things. Not being in the right place when certain rides opened up. Not being able to affect track performance as much as I wanted. This sport puts a target on the driver when things go bad."

In January of 1993, Brett made the first move to remove that target by buying a race shop in the sparse outskirts of Mooresville. Geoff waved off his younger brother, insisting he was crazy for wasting his money, only to later find that a plane crash in the mountains of northern Tennessee would make him wish he'd have heeded his own words.

One of the passengers in that 1993 crash was Alan Kulwicki, the defending Winston Cup champion who was en route to a race in Bristol. Kulwicki's personality was typified by a photo taken during a snowfall in Atlanta three weeks before his death. Everyone else had abandoned the garage, but the photo shows Kulwicki standing alone, knee-deep in snow with his helmet on. It captured the insular, workaholic man. Though few in the garage ever got to know him well, his crewmen were devastated by his death and determined to stay together. Gerry Kulwicki, Alan's father, studied several offers, in the end winnowing the list to two: PGA golfer Payne Stewart and Geoff. Two years later Geoff would lean forward with a hollow look and say, "I've tried to tell Todd this, because he's still young and has time. Think hard before you buy a race team, because your life changes more dramatically than you could ever imagine. I ended up going through so much."

Here's what he means.

Six weeks after his son's funeral, Gerry Kulwicki signed the team over to Geoff, but, still under contract with Bud Moore, Geoff couldn't get in its driver's seat. He wound up burning the candle at both ends, fulfilling his own driver duties while trying to land a full-time sponsor for his new team in 1994. He'd hoped Pat Robertson's Family Channel would deepen its involvement past a few one-shot deals, but the team was doing poorly with fill-in drivers, and the channel's Christian executives chafed at his coarse-tongued wife, Kathy. In September, they told him they were going with Jack Roush.

At about this time, a soft-spoken Indianapolis tire maker named Bob Newton was making a comeback in NASCAR. The ex-racer had a factory on an eighty-acre farm in Lakeville that made racing tires. He made eight hundred different types, one for every short track he served.* Though this was all he'd made since 1962, an invitation from Bill France caused Newton to try to create a speedways tire in 1988. Goodyear had narrowly averted a takeover by the English corporate raider Sir James Goldsmith, who'd loudly insisted he'd cut its racing program if he won, and France was starting to worry that he was relying too much on only one manufacturer. By inviting Newton to supply a rival product, France instigated what came to be known as the Great Tire War. Newton's Hoosier brand finished fourth in the 1988 Daytona 500, and went on to win eleven races through the summer of 1989. But in a sport built on generational loyalties, Newton was shunned as an outsider, and when Goodyear poured its resources into developing a radial that Newton couldn't match, he was forced to withdraw.

Newton retreated to the Busch Series to develop his own radial. At the same time, Continental of Germany was licensing the Hoosier name for a performance brand of retail tire. Though sales of this brand proved sluggish, Montgomery Ward decided to stock it late in 1993. The

---

*Most short tracks have their own rules, requiring that specific tire types be used. It is a difficult way to do business, but Hoosier has made a name for itself with its customized service.

timing was ideal, because Newton, having perfected his radial in the Busch Series, was preparing to challenge Goodyear again in Winston Cup. It was plain to the executives at Montgomery Ward that if Newton could find a high-profile driver to run his rubber, they'd get free publicity.

"I might get in trouble for saying this," Geoff allows, "but it was a well-known fact, if not publicized, that Goodyear played favorites" by giving better compounds and more attention to its star drivers. "The fan doesn't know it, so you look like a schmuck. I just got tired of looking like a schmuck." (Goodyear denies giving preferential treatment to stars.) By agreeing to become one of the controversial few to buck the establishment and run Hoosiers, Geoff also got help filling the hole left by the Family Channel's exit. Montgomery Ward used its clout to prod executives at the Exide battery company into Geoff's corner. By 1994 he was arriving to the Daytona 500 with Hoosiers under the car and Exide, his new sponsor, draped over it.

Then unprecedented tragedy hit. In the first half hour of practice, the veteran driver Neil Bonnett died in a savage wreck when he hit the fourth-turn wall. Three days later the rookie Rodney Orr hit the second-turn wall and had the roof of his car sheared off. He was pronounced dead at the scene. The only common thread was that both drivers were running Hoosiers. Though an investigative series in the *Orlando Sentinel* would later establish that the tires had nothing to do with the deaths, the heat of the moment singed the Exide team, and Newton started the year by ignominiously withdrawing the tires he'd spent years developing.

Geoff finished Daytona in twentieth place, and by August had only crept up to eighteenth place in the standings when the inaugural Brickyard 400 in Indianapolis rolled around. On the best tire Newton had made yet, Geoff qualified fourth and leapt out early when the race began, taking the lead on the ninetieth lap. A handful of passes later a yellow flag let him rearm with fresh Hoosiers, but his own brother beat him off pit road, shuffling him back to second. Racing hard after the green flag, Geoff tapped Brett to loosen him so he could get past in turn three, and though the next moment would be debated in the family for years, a replay shows Brett booted back harder in turn four, spinning Geoff into the wall.

While Brett continued on into the lead, a shell-shocked Geoff was telling ABC's national audience, "We've had some personal problems, and he took it out on the racetrack. I never expected he'd do it." Geoff started to leave, but ABC's Gary Gerould had a follow-up: When would the brothers talk? "He won't talk to me," Geoff replied, "so maybe never."

What went on between them? No two brothers have worked harder to keep a secret buried. Cal Lawson, Geoff's ex–team manager, downplays it, saying, "The whole thing was overblown. Geoff had a souvenir business that his brothers got involved with. When Brett got bigger, he took away his rights. He wanted to be independent, that's all."

Maybe. But the fallout from the feud kept Geoff from focusing on the troubles brewing under his own roof. Friends could see that his wife Kathy wanted out of the racing life, but Geoff didn't have any idea until he returned home from the Goody's 500 in Bristol to find her about to move out. "We were the least likely couple to have that happen," Geoff says now. "I was destroyed. I was ready to end it." Lawson, who was by Geoff's side, remembers him "barely being there in 1994, though our record didn't show it. In Darlington he was crying before he got in the car, got in, won the pole, and kept crying when he got out. We were seriously thinking about getting him psychiatric help. He was a mess."

With the help of his children, doctors, and close friends, Geoff got through the depression and the divorce. Then, in December, one of those close friends, Bob Newton, announced he was withdrawing from Winston Cup. Newton had been dragged through the mud after the deaths in Daytona, and unfairly tarred inside the garage. With so few teams willing to switch to his side, the Great Tire War II bled $6 million from his family coffers,* threatening his bread-and-butter short-track business. He'd had enough.

"Want to know about my first year of owning a car?" Geoff says now. "I almost won the Brickyard, then got spun out by my brother. Then my kid's mom leaves me. Then Hoosier leaves racing."

He thinks about what he's said and shakes his head.

"Unbelievable."

Brett thought he could do better.

He got the chance to find out how much in the summer of 1995. Executives at the image-conscious Lowe's home-improvement company had become uneasy about Junior's fine in Daytona, the defection of his crew, and their twentieth-place standing. Certainly, they expected more for their $100,000 per race. So in late July the company's top marketing man walked into a Lone Star restaurant near Charlotte for an off-the-record lunch with Brett. As the conversation seesawed, it became clear that Lowe's wanted out of its deal with Junior as much as Brett wanted to fill his garage in Mooresville with a new team. And though it would be hard to remember who said what first, the two men got up having hatched a plan to move Lowe's spon-

---

*Newton insists he could have been successful if not for a NASCAR rule requiring a tire maker to supply enough tires for the entire field at every race, even if only one driver uses them. Though this causes immense waste, the rule was designed to prevent manufacturers from supplying only a few stars at a few high-profile events.

sorship to a new Brett team, thereby setting the stage for Junior's retirement.

With Lowe's on board, Brett could sign over to Junior the entire $4.2 million that Lowe's was scheduled to pay in 1996—amounting to a sale price that many considered wildly inflated. Then, with no need for Junior's shop at Ingle Hollow, Brett would auction off everything except the cars, netting roughly $2 million, and move the whole operation to Mooresville. That would finance him well into the summer, and a line of credit and their winnings would do the rest. When it was all done, Brett and Diane would be buying a race team for next to nothing.

Sounds easy, right? Not so fast.

After his Busch success, Brett moved his family into a ranch-style starter home on a three-quarter-acre lot in Harrisburg, North Carolina, with a pool and enough room in back for Diane to keep her 175-pound pet Vietnamese pig, Felicia. But in the summer of 1995 the Bodines visited a golf course development outside Mooresville and found their dream house. Its design suggests a French countryside manor. The roof has five peaks, and the facade is made of Victorian stone, with brick trimming around the windows. Inside, the feel is more West Virginia, with huge ceilings that give the living room an airy feel, and a columned balcony around it that feeds into two well-appointed loft rooms. It is a successful man's home, and Brett unfolds his frame on a plush living room couch as sunlight streams through French doors, overlooking the golf course's first hole. About taking over from Junior Johnson, he says:

"I'd never been so scared in my life. We'd just moved here, into our dream house. I had to use it as collateral. I had to sign over everything that we'd saved. And then the deal just took forever. There were lawyers talking to lawyers, environmental people had to look at the gas tanks Junior had stored down there. And the press was all over me."

By October he was in a full-scale panic. The season was ending in less than a month. He needed to move the entire operation out of Ingle Hollow, hold the auctions, and get the cars ready for racing. The Lowe's contract was good only through 1996. If the deal didn't happen now, it wasn't going to.

It was a once-in-a-lifetime chance, and in Rockingham, in the speedway's parking lot with October rain pelting the windshield of his van, Brett felt it coming apart. "It was all closing in on me. I said, 'It's not happening. We're not gonna make it. Diane, I need to find a ride for next year or I'm gonna be out of work.' " But Diane Bodine had every bit as much ambition as her husband. She walked from the van to the yellow transporter and into the back lounge, where she took a seat on the leather sofa and relentlessly negotiated the final details.

The new team would be called BDR Motorsports—initials that covered Brett, Diane, Diane's twin sister Donna, and Donna's husband, Donnie Richeson. Donnie, a poker-faced thirty-six-year-old, was reprising the role of crew chief that he had had with Brett in the years both men worked for Kenny Bernstein.

Sunday, April 1, was the first of the springlike days of 1996, sunny and about 70 degrees. Outside the entrance to the North Wilkesboro racetrack, which was built fifty years ago in remote woods, a Christian quartet was singing Bible songs in a tin livestock barn.

"Come all ye to the river, rest near the evergreen trees. I carry my cross through the midnight. Come all ye there's glory for ye.

"Sometimes I despise and reject it. And question O Father how long. Then I take one look back at the calvary. And it gives me the strength to go on."

The lyrics filtered across the pasture that spread before the speedway. A biker poked his head into the barn and then decided to stay, pulling up a bridge chair beside a leathery old man. The old man stopped tapping his leg long enough to tip the edge of his Goodyear hat. The biker nodded back and let himself get lost in the music. It was early, just eleven o'clock. The race wouldn't be starting for a couple more hours. There was still plenty of time to drain a few beers and browse the souvenir trailers before going inside.

Through the gates and across the track in the garage area, Brett was making his way to the roof of the media center, which faces the grandstands, an ideal place to hold the driver introductions.

After the late-February debacle in Rockingham, he'd taken a car to Richmond that was hard to steer into the corners. The crew tried fixing it in the pits, but before they knew it they were three laps down, and finished in twenty-fifth place. The next week in Atlanta, Brett took the checkered flag fourteen laps down. He had an in-car camera for that race, and all it showed were cars passing him left and right. In Darlington a piston went bad and Brett had to retire with just a dozen laps to go for moving too slowly. It was a perfect metaphor for his first five races as an owner.

But there was something special about the Bodine name here. For one thing, it was the site of Brett's one and only Winston Cup win. It was also the place where he had his best qualifying run of 1995. If Jeff Gordon hadn't run .88 seconds faster, Brett would have sat on the pole. Add to that it was home turf for Junior Johnson and Lowe's, and the grandstands were packed with fans who wanted Brett to kick some ass. Passing before them, he drank in the loud applause.

At about the same time, Donnie Richeson was holding a prerace meeting in their hauler.

"There's more green-flag pits here than any race all year," he was saying. "So be ready. Expect pits from fifty to seventy laps. Somebody will run till they can't take it anymore, and then it will start a chain reaction. If you see a car make that decision, then get ready and hang tough."

They chanted, "Let's have a win."

When the green flag fell in the First Union 400 and the two columns of neatly ordered cars turned into scattered puzzle pieces, pole-sitter Terry Labonte sped out to an early lead. Nineteen spots behind him, Brett dove in and out of the congestion, holding his own. He may not have been a threat to the front-runner, but neither was he fading early. After he took on four new tires in a seventy-fifth-lap pit stop, he was nearly where he started. Then, eight laps later, he ran over a stone, cut down his left front tire, and had to return to pit road, a devastating setback on such a short track, and one that shot him back to two places off last place. As he cursed his luck, it got worse: The unmistakable odor that brought him back to Daytona started wafting into his cockpit.

"We got smoke," he radioed into his pit.

Donnie measured his anxiety and kept his voice steady. He needed to know where. "I think it's under me," Brett said. As Brett dropped into the box, Donnie frantically doused the cockpit. His crew looked everywhere for signs of a fire. The damned thing was, they couldn't find one. Brett would drive the next three hundred laps soaking wet and nauseous from the fumes, and he still managed to climb out of the cellar, finishing the day in twenty-third place. After he'd stormed off in a mean spirit, his brother-in-law blamed a block of wood in the frame of the chassis, inserted to keep lead balance weights from sliding. The 300-degree header pipes bolted to the frame had caused the wood blocks to start smoldering.

Looking at the soot-stained cockpit that smelled oddly like hickory, Donnie forced his frustration down deep, because doing otherwise would mean going insane.

"Don't that beat all," he'd say, as if he had just found a new weed in his garden.

Robin Pemberton was in a decidedly better mood. Rusty Wallace's crew chief had watched his driver slowly work up the field. At about the time Brett was fighting the hickory fumes, Rusty was diving under Earnhardt in the fourth turn to take over second place. An early pit stop near the half gave him four new tires, and enough grip to get to the front with a three-second advantage.

After hanging on his tail for sixty laps, Labonte made a decisive move to the inside, allowing him to pass cleanly into first. But Rusty reclaimed it by beating Labonte off pit road in lap 320. If Pemberton was thinking about anything twenty minutes later—when Rusty was just twenty-five laps away from winning—it was tire wear, and the four fresher tires on Labonte's car.

He certainly wasn't thinking about the bump-fest that Geoff and John Andretti had had in Darlington two weeks earlier, causing both to crash out. But their déjà vu was about to become his nightmare.

Geoff was in twentieth place, three laps down, when he saw Andretti in front of him. At that point Andretti was in twenty-third and one lap behind. Geoff tried to cut under him, and Andretti dipped down to stave him off. So Bodine went high. Andretti stopped him up there too. Going into turn three, Geoff again tried to pass low. Depending

on whom you believe, either Andretti turned left to cut
him off or Geoff lost control of his car.

The pair connected, and Andretti went crashing sideways into the wall. The impact ricocheted him into traffic,
nose down, when another car clipped his rear, sending him
spinning with no steering control into the three huge water
canisters by the entrance to pit road. They exploded into a
waterfall.

To Pemberton's horror, all of this was playing out right
in front of the speeding Wallace. "Go high! Go high!" his
spotter screamed, but Rusty was low, and everyone was
clogging the outside lane to escape. With nowhere to go,
Wallace bashed right into Andretti, causing a fireball to
pierce the smoke.

In the garage, Pemberton led the rescue effort to get the
wreckage back out onto the track. Wallace sat on the edge
of his transporter and let out a tiny strain of stunned
laughter. "Don't this just beat all," he said. "I don't think
I've ever had luck like this my whole life."

Just then Andretti's Ford rolled by on the hanging tooth
of a tow truck. Sprayed with fire retardant and still smoking heavily, it looked like an angry ghost. Comparing the
doused car to Wallace's face, it was hard to tell which was
whiter.

Months later, when Rusty was 399 points out of first
place and Pemberton was asked about the race, he'd say,
"You mean the one where I was in total disbelief as the
cars careened in front of me? Those guys weren't even in
the race. They were acting like boneheads. My guys had to
work 'round the clock for three days to fix the suspension
and the front end. Then we go to Martinsville, and the
same two guys are at it again. I was shaking my fist at the
[Andretti] bunch. I couldn't believe it."

The thing about racing is that on any given day there
will always be someone with more money and a higher

profile who'll do worse than you. It's not consolation and it's nothing to feel happy about. It's just a small bit of therapeutic schadenfreude.

Rusty Wallace finished the race in thirty-third place. Brett finished in twenty-third.

5

SURVIVING ON THE SHORT TRACKS

Martinsville, Bristol, & North Wilkesboro: March 31 to April 21

In his Prodigy office in White Plains, New York, Brian Simons looked at the phone ringing and wondered whether he really wanted to pick it up. It was three o'clock on Saturday, April 13, which meant that second-round qualifying was just about ending in North Wilkesboro. He'd had a knot in his stomach about Dave Marcis all week. Somehow, he couldn't convince himself that the news would be good.

Reaching for the phone, Simons heard the voice he was expecting. "Brian. I'm in my car." It was Dave's business manager, Dwayne Leik. "I've got a gun to my head."

"What happened?" Brian asked dryly.

Dwayne grew uncomfortable behind the wheel of his black Jeep Cherokee. Brian was more understanding than most. After all, he and Dwayne had become friends. Brian was a thirty-year-old divorcé, Dwayne a thirty-two-year-old bachelor. They went out to bars, skied together, and shared a stake in Dave's success. Dwayne knew that the cofounders of Prodigy, Sears and IBM, were desperately trying to make their billion-dollar baby pay off. That's why he pitched them on Dave, arguing that by sponsoring him, Prodigy would tap a gold mine of new NASCAR subscribers. They agreed, but now it was six months later. Sears and IBM were selling the service to austere new owners. How could Brian hide a $1.5 million budget item? Worse, how could he explain Dave Marcis?

If you headed north out of Wausau on Highway W in the 1950s—the Wausau that is township of Texas in the county of Marathon in the state of Wisconsin—you'd pass Tony Marcis's P&M Auto Service station. Tony dabbled in IndyCar racing in the 1930s, but by the time David, the first of his three children, was born in 1941, he'd settled down to selling Cities Service Gas and doing the best overhauls in town. Dave and his brother Donald were fixtures at the P&M, and when the weather turned warm they also biked over the fairgrounds to watch the jalopy races, sitting in the tops of trees so as not to pay admission. Like most boys their age, they fantasized about piloting the huge hulks, and by their teens they were scouring the skeletal heaps of their dad's wrecking yard, looking for parts to create their own.

In the fall of 1956, Dave was working on an old Chevy and spilled gas on his leg, and that one spill changed his life. After it dried, Dave lifted a piece of metal to the flame of an acetylene torch. A sliver dropped on his boot, igniting the dried gas, and the flames covered him from head to toe. The resulting six-month stay in a hospital caused the young Dave to miss his first year of high school, and though he was an A and B student, he never went back. Figuring life was too short, he became a stock car driver.

By his twenties, Dave was running a bar he'd bought near the P&M and racing on weekends, finding every possible method of wrecking his car, including flipping upside down into a pond at the Tomahawk Race Track, the place where in 1965 he met a pretty high school business teacher named Helen Rennhak. They went fishing on their first date and were married a year later. She loved his spontaneity, but even Helen was unnerved when he gathered her up and drove to Daytona in 1967 to join the undercard for the Daytona 500, and then again a year later to get into The Show. Dave finished that race in twentieth place, and since it paid five times anything he'd made up to that moment, he decided to keep going. After seven years of cobbled financing, he got his big break in 1974, when Harry Hyde, the inspiration for the crew chief in *Days of Thunder*, hired the balding midwesterner with bronzed skin, a crooked smile, and the biggest appetite Hyde had ever seen.

At the season's inaugural, then held in Riverside, California, Dave took the checkered flag in fourth place, and by midseason was finishing every other race in the top five. Yet the old guard was slow to take him seriously, pointing out that while Bobby Isaac and Bobby Allison managed to win in Hyde's K&K car, Dave had not. Wrote one columnist, "The red Number Seventy-one hasn't been too impressive this year, and the rap is on the man driving it." But almost as soon as those words saw print, Dave won in Martinsville, and six races later he was finishing the year as runner-up to Richard Petty. It was the apex of a career, and the *Los Angeles Times* gave it the headline "Damn Yankee Breaks NASCAR Southern Elite."

In 1976, his last with Hyde, Dave finished sixth. In 1978, after the K&K outfit dissolved, he notched a fifth-place season driving for a California construction magnate. But then came one of those principled moments that get looked back on with, if not quite regret, then at least forensic curiosity. It was the last race of the season in Atlanta, and a member of Dave's Wausau mafia found himself pink-slipped as crew chief. Marcis was determined to save the man's job or get an explanation, and when he got neither, he stormed into the pressroom to announce he was quitting. It was the worst hubris. A young Dale Earnhardt got his job. Dave got to go out on his own.

The Zen of racing is in the remembering. If you can remember how a certain gear with a certain spoiler angle worked five years ago on an overcast day on a certain track, then you're a step ahead of the new guy with his flashy tool truck. Over the next twenty years Dave's encyclopedic memory kept his ragtag team in contention on many a day when they should have gone home empty. In the early 1980s he stayed in the top fifteen, in the late eighties the top twenty. But his last, best edge was taken away in the early nineties, when high-speed computers began to reshape racing.

Walk around a well-financed race shop today. You'll see a suspension specialist using a Windows '98 program to generate overlapping bell curve charts, magnetic imaging machines scanning for minute imperfections in parts, dynamometers measuring the horsepower of engines nakedly suspended in midair, or computer-controlled welding machines that ensure the weld on each chassis is precisely the same. Every year Dave pushed a little harder to keep up. And every year he lost a little more ground to the machines. In 1990 he finished twenty-first, in 1991 and 1992 twenty-ninth, in 1993 thirty-third.

Dwayne Leik, a stockbroker from Naples, Florida, didn't see that clearly on his first visit to Dave's garage in the summer of 1993. He was supposed to be in Chicago, where a seat on the Commodities Exchange was waiting for him, but he'd detoured to Charlotte to cool his heels for a while, not at all sure that was what he wanted to do. In his heart he wanted to be a racer, and having heard that the penny-pinching legend Dave Marcis worked around there, made an appointment to drop by. On the afternoon he arrived, he found Dave sitting in a wood-paneled office that looked as if it hadn't been touched since the mid-seventies, wondering how he was going to make it to the next race.

The two men talked for hours about how the racing

world had changed beneath Dave's feet, and before Leik knew it, he was grabbing a yellow pages, calling car dealers and supermarkets in the town where Dave was next headed to race, drumming up business, entirely forgetting he'd come to talk about himself. Dave asked if he'd be interested in coming back the next day, and the day after that, and before Leik knew it, he'd traded Comex for Marcis.

The Prodigy sponsorship was the culmination of three years of his work, a fresh start for an old lion. The company's money let Dave trim the age of his car fleet from six years to a year and a half, buy better parts, and even splurge on a few nifty gadgets. It let him finish fifteenth in Daytona, and a less exciting but respectable twenty-first in Rockingham.

But then came three suggestions that things might not be turning around as quickly as first hoped: a thirty-fifth-place finish in Richmond; a twenty-ninth-place finish in Atlanta; and a twenty-third-place finish in Darlington.

Heading to Bristol, Tennessee, on March 29, Brian Simons didn't need to tell Dwayne that they needed a good finish. Dwayne Leik didn't have to tell Dave Marcis.

There's a saying about a race season—that it's really three races. There's the yearlong race for the points championship, the race to be first when the checkered flag drops every week, and a third race that gets little notice: the race to get into the race.

Upon arriving at a track on Friday mornings to practice, teams rarely get more than ninety minutes. If you're lucky enough to have set up your car perfectly at the shop, then you don't need to worry. In the slang of the garage, you've "rolled off the truck fast."

But if problems arise, then you're madly fighting the clock, watching it tick down as you flail, looking for elusive answers. Dave was upbeat when he pulled into the Bristol Motor Speedway on Friday morning. But from the moment the car hit the track he knew he was in trouble. It swam all over the thirty-six-degree turns like liquid in a blender.

"What do you think, Terry?"

This was usually a rhetorical question. Dave sought opinions to get his crew to agree with things he'd already decided. But this time he was genuinely stumped. They tried adjusting springs to change the car's balance. They tried placing tape over the air ducts on the front grille so the air flowed over the hood rather than through it. Usually that helped the front end stick to the asphalt better. Not this time. With just minutes left to practice, Terry screamed, "I got it!" He might have found the answer to a murder, the way everyone gathered around.

Dave shook his head so fast he nearly lost his cap. "You gotta be shittin' me," he said when he saw it.

Shock absorbers come with what's called a "rebound adjuster." It's a switch that lets mechanics change the pressure. When Terry tried changing the rear left adjuster, it didn't respond. That told him the internal housing was shot. It was a brand-new shock, the last place they would think to look. And by the time they had it replaced, the clock had ticked down on their practice. There they sat, with their original setup untested.

It killed them in qualifying. The fastest car was Mark Martin's Ford. He tore around the bowl in 15.527 seconds. Michael Waltrip would run the track in a half blink less, .243 seconds off Martin's speed. As tiny a chasm as that was, it was wide enough for twenty-three other cars to fit between them. Dave's time was nearly eight-hundredths off Waltrip's pace, leaving him in thirty-third place.

Only the fastest twenty-five qualifying cars get guaranteed starting spots. Everyone else can try again on Saturday

for the remaining spots. (Usually there's room for seventeen more cars, but the short tracks get so crowded, Bristol
only had room for another twelve.) While this second
round of qualifying is usually done quickly and away from
the camera's eye, it holds its own unique drama.

It begins with a simple choice: Do you try to run a faster
lap, or stand on your time of the day before? Dave took
some more practice laps Saturday morning to help him decide, but they were inconclusive. The car was handling
better, but still not well. Then Dave noticed the sun poking
through the clouds.

Requalifying would be at noon. That meant it would be
a few degrees hotter than it was yesterday at three o'clock.
More heat would loosen the grease on the track. Dave ran
the numbers through his head and calculated he'd lose
three more hundredths sliding around. Why would he
want to try again if it meant he had to be three-hundredths
faster just to *match* Friday's speed?

Because there was another consideration: Dave qualified thirty-fifth. Bristol had room for thirty-seven cars.
That meant that if he stayed put, and only two cars bested
his Friday speed, he'd make the race, right?

Wrong. NASCAR holds the last five spots of the starting
lineup for provisionals. Think of them as tables at a
crowded restaurant that the maître d' keeps for friends. The
first four tables go to whoever is highest in the point standings at the moment. The fifth is saved for ex-champions.*

Dave was now twenty-fourth in the standings, and looking down the list of drivers also trying to get into the

---

*The champion's provisional, like many rules in NASCAR, has become
something of an anachronism. It was originally instituted in 1989, after
Richard Petty missed the race in Richmond, to keep him from the embarrassment of having it happen again. Now it exists to protect Darrell Waltrip, Dale
Earnhardt, Bill Elliott, Rusty Wallace, Jeff Gordon, and Terry Labonte.

race, he could see many had more points than he. They'd surely gobble up the reserved spots, making his spot absolutely worthless. He had to go back out with a car that didn't want to dance, and hope he could bleed out every last ounce of speed.

As the seven-hundred-horsepower engine in his Chevrolet roared to life, he reminded himself how the track liked to be driven, low and fast out of the turns. Then he cleared his mind, and when the signal came, let her rip. Terry clicked his stopwatch as Dave sailed off pit road and flew into turn one. Exactly 15.877 seconds later—three-hundredths of a second slower than Friday's pace—he clicked it again.

Damn, he thought, staring at the speed. It left him behind the thirty-second-spot cutoff. He'd be spending Sunday on his couch at home drinking a beer.

Looking at the speed flash across the laptop he kept in the trailer, Dwayne Leik went pale.

Dave was even less prepared for North Wilkesboro than he'd been for Bristol. He was just now finishing building a new car for the race, and there was no guarantee how it would act. And bringing an untested car to North Wilkesboro was like bringing a horse whose hooves had never dug into dirt to the Kentucky Derby.

Needing as much practice time as they could get, Terry bit his lip as he stood behind a long trail of cars waiting to get checked out in the NASCAR inspection bay. If he'd learned one thing about this Friday-morning ritual—the very first thing that teams do before they get on the track—it was that the inspectors are painfully thorough about enforcing the rule book. Every engine spec and chassis measurement counts. Teams go in order of their standings in the points, which means that such thoroughness can cost those at the bottom a half hour or more of valuable practice time. By the time an inspector got to Marcis, there was scarcely time to run two dozen laps.

Those laps were enough for them to realize that they were in trouble. When the time came for qualifying, Dave's stomach was tied in knots. He was sweating. His mind was racing with numbers. Hired drivers are paid handsomely to have clear heads in moments like these. But Dave, the one-man computer, the air traffic controller and pilot, didn't. So exactly 19.646 seconds after he took the checkered flag, NASCAR's computers recorded another Marcis miss.

As he pulled back into the garage and climbed out of the window of his car, Dave knelt there silently for a moment, as if in prayer. His face was sunburned, and for the first time all season it seemed as if he couldn't get up.

"How'd we do?" he asked, not really wanting to know.

"Thirty-third."

He balled up his fist and slammed it toward the car. Then he pulled up at the last second, before he could make a dent. "Son of a bitch."

"You want to hear the times?"

"Nah, it won't do any good."

Dave knew he was toast. In the past two weeks he'd dropped from twenty-fourth to thirty-seventh in the standings. And like the week before, only thirty-two cars would get into this race based on qualifying. If Dave stood on his time, he'd get displaced by someone higher in the standings entitled to one of the five provisionals.

He stared at the tires as if he expected them to answer him. "We'll change the shocks and springs tomorrow," he announced halfheartedly. "See what we can do."

But Saturday, with the sun hotter and the track greasier, everyone ran slower. Dave's time wasn't the worst—Hut Stricklin lost three-tenths of a second—but it was bad enough: 19.841.

"I don't understand it," Dave said as he walked around the garage, now out of his Prodigy suit and in his trademark plaid shirt, navy blue slacks, and black wing-tips. He prided himself on being able to get out of holes like these at the last minute. Sometimes it was hard to watch, but near misses produced a high-wire adrenaline rush. It usually lasted until Sunday, just in time for a new race-day rush to take over. But this time it wasn't working. The last good rush he had had was three Saturdays before.

He stopped by Earnhardt's trailer for moral support. He asked Jeff Gordon's crew chief, Ray Evernham, for advice. Hours after he climbed out of his Chevy, he was still looking for answers, sitting in a little brick house by the Unocal gas pumps.

By then Dwayne was in his car heading home. Halfway there he picked up the phone and dialed Brian Simons at the Prodigy office in New York. "Brian. I'm in my car," he began. "I've got a gun to my head."

"What happened?" Brian asked dryly.

"We missed the show again, that's what happened."

Brian breathed deeply. "What are you gonna do now?"

"I'm going to the golf course," Dwayne said, "and I'm going to write the number of every car that's racing Sunday on the balls. Then I'm gonna whack the hell out of them."

"Helen, *hey Helen,* we need more sauce . . . and mushrooms! Can you believe that woman? Huh, what'd'ya say? *No, mushrooms!* Lord. How can you make a good sauce without mushrooms?"

Exactly eight days later, everything changed. After puttering around his front lawn on Sunday, Dave went back into the shop Monday ready to act upon the lessons he'd learned about "Sonofabitch"—the nickname he'd given the frustrating new car. He and Terry recalibrated the suspension and shifted lead weights from front to back. He trucked it to Martinsville at the end of the week, trying not to think what a third straight miss would do to his season, his career.

But then the oddest thing happened: Sonofabitch rolled onto the claustrophobic little half-mile oval Friday morning as if it had found home. It hugged the track so beautifully, Dave couldn't think of a thing he wanted to change. When his turn came to qualify, he was able to run the track in 20.431 seconds. That was faster than Jeff Gordon, Dale Jarrett, Ernie Irvan, and Bobby Hamilton.

It meant Dave would be starting on the inside of the sixth row, safely out of the way of all the drivers who'd no doubt start wrecking when they tried to pass. It meant, for the first time in nearly a month, he could relax and enjoy being a racer again.

So now on Saturday night, he was leading a convoy down Route 220, out of Virginia and into North Carolina, past the Miller brewery and into Eden, where, if you turn left at the only stoplight, you see the cherry-red awning of Homer Wood's Railroad Cafe.

For twenty years Dave has been going there, making his special spaghetti for half the town as they show up to dance in the space that Homer clears away in the front of the kitchenette, by the country-western jukebox. On this Saturday night, while some very drunk Edenites were stomping their feet, Dave was submerged in a cloud of steam in the kitchen, shouting, "Hey, Helen, where are those mushrooms?"

"Right in front of you," she yelled back. Dave lowered his bifocals, spotted them, and grabbed handfuls that he sent sailing into bubbling vats.

Homer, a stocky man with a long speckled gray beard, watched the out-of-towners approvingly from his lunch counter, his hands firmly inside his overalls. "When did I first meet Dave?" he mused. "Musta been either the late sixties or the early seventies. It was him and John Sears. You know John Sears? He's a race car driver from Ellerbe, North Carolina, peach country. They wound up eatin', man, and I mean eatin.' Dave been comin' back twice a year ever since."

"Show the man the museum, Homer," someone shouted from the crowd. Homer looked out toward the kitchen, convinced himself the Marcises couldn't do any more damage, and led a small group to a house beside his restaurant. The inside was just a storage room with a desk and some tin shelves, but Homer invested it with an air of privilege. He opened up two mason jars, one filled with strawberry moonshine, the other with straight corn whiskey, and gave a hearty laugh as it burned down his visitors' throats. Amid the coughing and mopping of eyes, Homer said, "All right, then, where to begin?"

He began by carefully unwrapping a prized portrait of Richard Petty staring godlike into a powder-blue sky, proceeded through scores of Marcis mementos, and ended with what all agreed had to be one of the most unusual collectibles in racing—a poster of the twenty men who competed in the 1987 Winston. There is a version of the poster that is still widely sold, but it's a touched-up, second-generation iteration. This was the original, the one that was pulled from circulation when a fan noticed an odd shadow by Tim Richmond, who was positioned in the back row, behind a kneeling Neil Bonnett. A close study suggests that the shadow was Richmond's exposed penis. Tim Richmond was a womanizer who came within a hair of winning the championship over Dale Earnhardt that year. He would die of AIDS on August 7, 1989. The photo captures his reckless, sexually insouciant spirit to perfection.

With the tour of his museum complete, Homer led his now unsteady visitors back to the restaurant, where Dave was dishing out ample heaps of meat sauce onto bending paper plates. As the evening wore on, and the eating gave way to drinking and storytelling, it was easy to imagine it was twenty years before, easy to see the way big-time racing used to be in small-town America.

On Sunday morning the big story had to do with longevity, though not Dave's. Reporters were following Terry Labonte, who was about to break Richard Petty's record of 513 starts. Someone decided it would be terrific to pair him with Cal Ripken Jr., so Labonte had spent the prior week throwing out a ball at Camden Yards, and posing for photos with the great shortstop. Both athletes blithely smiled their way through the session, even though it was evident that until the national press decided they had to become fast friends, neither had given the other much consideration.

(Actually, Labonte almost didn't make it. The Tuesday before, he was stepping out of his truck shop when he noticed a woman sunbathing across the way. He thought she was topless, and not looking where he was going, tripped over a step and twisted his ankle. As it turned out, the woman was clothed, but the trip made his heart stop for a brief second.)

Dave Marcis had warm wishes for Labonte. He liked him. He thought he was a survivor who knew what it was to work with small budgets as well as large. But Dave had more immediate things on his mind, namely a twenty-nine-year-old from nearby Lynchburg whose transporter was a few parking places away.

Stacy Compton, who'd roped off the area around his trailer in a showy demand for privacy, was a late-model champion—one of those Winston Cup wanna-bes who tended to be good on just one track. He hadn't made it into any other Winston Cup events in the year, yet his familiarity with Martinsville led to a qualifying lap that won him ninth place on the starting grid. Marcis knew that Compton's heart would be pumping, and that he was in over his head. So he told him, "I just want to let you know that you don't have to worry about me. If you get high, I'll give you a break. I won't be pokin' my nose under ya."

Compton thanked him and walked off, leaving Dave to find Jeff Gordon, who was starting behind Dave in thirteenth. "Be patient with me, Jeff," he said, "because I'm cuttin' the kid some slack." Gordon agreed that if he saw the Prodigy Monte Carlo staying high, he'd try not to cut underneath and spook Compton.

As the green flag fell, the double-wide line broke into single file, snaking around the oval. Compton delighted his hometown fans by racing side by side with Gordon. But soon the champion tired of that and began his march ahead, leaving Compton to settle in behind Marcis. The two developed a rhythm: diving low into the turns, then braking hard, steering sharply to get into position for the exit and throttling hard out, dropping from the crest of the turn to the low white line. After ninety-two laps of this, Dave's spotter thought little of telling him it was okay to drop down as he throttled out turn four.

"Okay, Dave. He's inside you. You're clear. Come on down."

Obeying the direction, Dave dropped to the inside. It turned out to be a disastrous move.

Terry Shirley's stomach sank as the next thing he saw was Dave spinning. Compton had bumped him from behind, sending him into the grass that was wet from an earlier rain. On a track that small, the accident sent Marcis from eighteenth to thirty-fifth. His day ruined by a single bonehead move, Dave was livid.

"What about that son of a bitch?" he shouted. "I work with him and he fucking does that."

It got worse as the race turned into a graveyard for

brakes and gears. The first out was John Andretti, whose rear gear was so hot, minutes after it was removed it sat smoldering on the asphalt, smelling like something dead and infectious. But Dave was soon to follow him into the garage. "I don't have enough brakes to race around anyone," he exclaimed when Rusty Wallace put him a second lap down at the 120-lap mark. A few minutes later he pulled off the track and to his trailer, getting a new transmission that would keep him out until sixty-three laps from the end.

Compton, who'd gotten his wish and finished the race, came up to Dave afterward to apologize. "Sorry, Dave," he'd say. "I didn't mean it. It was a rookie mistake."

"What was I gonna say?" Dave said later, sighing. *"Rookies."*

6

CAR WARS

Throw the chair, Gary Claudio thought. Let 'em know you're serious. *Throw the damned chair.*

It was early May in Charlotte, and Claudio, the chief of Pontiac's racing program,* was studying the faces of the men who flew his company's flag. Collectively, they'd garnered just thirty points in the manufacturers' championship, placing them a distant third behind Ford and their wealthier GM relation, Chevrolet, which was in the lead by twelve points.

The manufacturers' championship is a show within the show. The rules are simple: The first make across the finish line gets nine points, the second six, and the third four.

It's hard to imagine getting Sunday-afternoon rah-rah about the fortunes of one multinational over another. (Imagine reading *The Wall Street Journal* and saying, "Yes! John Deere got the exclusive Akron contract. That'll show Caterpillar. Ten points for us.") But fans do care. Sit in a traffic jam near someone with an "I'd rather push a Ford than drive a Chevy" bumper sticker. Listen to the horn-honking it causes. Or walk through an infield and look at all the Chevy bow ties, plastered on everything from fenders to foreheads.

Ever since Bill France Sr. brainstormed the idea of

*He has since been elevated to manager of Chevrolet's racing program.

using new stock cars that looked like Dad's five-seater, Detroit has lived by the credo "Win on Sunday, sell on Monday."

So it was odd, considering this decades-long love affair, that GM had an internal policy against using racing to advertise its products until 1989. As one executive put it, the fear was some kid would "start believing all this Smokey and the Bandit shit, get hurt in one of our cars, and start hunting for a deep pocket."

Once it got over that fear, however, GM poured massive resources into linking its cars with racing. When the new Monte Carlo debuted in February 1995, GM plastered Daytona with billboards of Dale Earnhardt, Jeff Gordon, Darrell Waltrip, and others. Three hundred dealers were flown to Florida at GM expense. In the grandstands, fans were given peanuts stamped with *M.C.* A plane flew loops above, pulling the banner "Monte Carlo Is Back." When Sterling Marlin won the race, GM rushed Victory Lane photos to *Sports Illustrated* and *Time*—both of which were holding their presses for the advertiser. Ten months later the Monte Carlo had won twenty-one of thirty-one races and was well on its way to becoming the best-selling midsize model in America.

Now the new Grand Prix was debuting on the heels of that success. GM spent $2 billion developing it (along with the Intrigue and Century), and Claudio knew what his bosses wanted to see: a strong finish. Maybe even a repeat of what the Monte Carlo did a year earlier.

Yet over forty-eight attempts in ten races, his teams had come up with only five top-ten finishes. The average finish was twenty-first.

He had a $2 billion car that was rolling into showrooms this very week. *Twenty-first?!* Unacceptable!

It was time for a Come to Jesus meeting. It was time for

the five men who owned his teams to understand the stakes.

So Claudio gathered them in this Holiday Inn in Mooresville and stood before them in a near-empty conference room. He knew he had to be careful. If he came down too hard, they could decide to jump off the unsteady ship. He had to be both good cop and bad cop.

The artfulness with which he approached that task was aided by the fact that Claudio is an ex–New York police officer. A native of Long Island, he worked for Pontiac in his twenties, but "I always liked fast cars and cops and robbers." So in the early 1980s he applied and was accepted to the Suffolk County Police Department. For four years he worked street crime, stalking the shadowy doorways where deals go down.

"I remember we rolled up to this school; it's dark and four mopes were clearing it out of computers around back. They see us and scurry like roaches. Two guys bailed on foot, two in this Econoline van. We go after the van, and I'll tell you, this one guy drove like goddamned Mario Andretti. We're chasing him the wrong way down one-way streets, into alleys. Now I'm pissed. I got my gun out. Finally, we get alongside the son of a bitch. I swear I was gonna shoot him. I mean, I *hate* to lose. But my partner drives into him and we get the guys.

"So we do the paperwork, then I go to the hospital 'cause my arm's all banged up. I got two bruised ribs. I get home the next morning. My wife sees me. She says, 'Look at what you do. This is the third time you've been in the hospital this month. You walk around with two guns and a switchblade. And you want to shoot a guy through a van. What kind of life is that?'

"I looked at her and I said, 'Shit, you're right.' "

Which is how he ended up back at Pontiac. Over eight years, he went from Charlotte to Cincinnati. Then, in 1994, the carmaker moved him to its headquarters in Pontiac, Michigan, and promoted him to Motorsports Manager.

It is a title that requires a man to be equal parts spy, seducer, and salesman. Claudio wears the suspicious, furtive look of a man perfectly suited to it. And he was wearing just that look as he took in the Holiday Inn conference room.

In the corner was Felix Sabates. Sabates was raised in great wealth in Cuba in the 1950s, but after Fidel Castro came to power and nationalized his family's far-flung business interests, he joined the underground, burning buildings and distributing propaganda. At his father's insistence, he came to America when he was seventeen, and went from making eighty-five cents an hour as a furniture stripper in Lexington, Kentucky, to becoming one of the country's top electronics importers. He'd been in NASCAR since 1983, and was paying Kyle Petty handsomely to drive the Coors Lite car. But his riches-to-rags-to-riches history, not to mention his Cuban temperament, made him impulsive and meddlesome with personnel. His team just wasn't meshing this year.

In the row ahead was Bill Davis, the Arkansas trucking czar who'd forever be known as the man who discovered Jeff Gordon, only to be burned when the upstart defected to Hendrick Motorsports. Now Davis had the considerably lower-profile Ward Burton and a season mired in thirty-sixth place. Burton needed more attention than most drivers, and Claudio worried that Davis wasn't communicative enough for the task.

To Davis's right was Richard Jackson, the gentlemanly engine builder whose new driver, Rick Mast, was incensed at what he saw as Pontiac's underfunded, scattershot program. Would they defect?

He felt better about Chuck Rider, owner of the Bahari team, who also had a new driver in rookie Johnny Benson. Great things were expected of Benson—certainly more than Mike Waltrip, who left Rider after earning the igno-minious distinction of being the most senior driver in Win-ston Cup without a win. But it would take time for him to adjust. Claudio had to be patient.

Then his eyes locked on Richard Petty, who was wear-ing his cowboy hat and sunglasses inside.

Petty and Pontiac go back to 1982, when the car com-pany was adrift. It had no image back then, no soul. Perilously close to the cutting block, its executives decided to associate it with the richest period in its history—its postwar racing years. Looking for a big name to push the image, Pontiac bought into Petty. He was at his height then, but even through the fallow years he gave them the kind of PR that companies dream about. When the Grand Prix de-buted in February at the 1996 auto show in Chicago, the King was there to smile for the cameras.

But now it was April, and Claudio needed the King to do more than smile. He needed him to start winning. Sensing the number 43 car was the ticket to saving his year—maybe his job—Claudio tried to give team manager Dale Inman and crew chief Robbie Loomis what they needed. But his biggest concern was with Bobby Hamilton. Clau-dio wondered if the Nashville native had the psychological stamina to handle the pressure. Based on what he'd heard around the garage, he wasn't sure.

After going from a near win to twenty-fourth in Rock-ingham, the month of March told the story of a team that had its confidence badly shaken. Just look at the finishes: sixteenth in Atlanta; the same in Darlington; thirty-second in Bristol. Fortunately, the Petty team's eighth-place finish in North Wilkesboro, sixth in Martinsville, and eleventh in Talladega suggested they were coming back. They were now up to ninth in the standings.

That's why Claudio was on the phone to Inman after Sonoma. A possum had darted in front of Bobby's car, sending it spinning into the dirt and into a seventeenth-place finish.

"How's his confidence?" Claudio asked.

It was okay, Inman said. "His body ain't great, though. All bruised." A thermos full of Gatorade came loose in the cockpit and kept careening into Bobby's helmet like a missile. "He was pretty pissed."

Claudio liked Inman. He thought he was a straight shooter. He also understood that Inman was better than anyone in the garage at getting inside a driver's head. That's why he wanted to keep him happy too.

But Inman wasn't happy. If he was a psychologist, that just came from years hanging around racers. Foremost, Inman was a builder. He'd built a car every year since 1959. He'd seen every model. He'd seen every advance. In the garage, he was a teacher of revered rank.

You couldn't put much past him. And as far as Inman was concerned, GM's engineers were lying through their damned teeth about the new Grand Prix. They insisted it was the aerodynamic equal of the Chevrolet Monte Carlo. But Inman didn't believe that for a second. He'd been around long enough to know that as far as GM is concerned, Chevy is the mother ship. GM wasn't going to do anything to upset the division's Monte Carlo, including letting Pontiac's rival Grand Prix outperform it.

Claudio tried to assure him it wasn't so. But in his heart he wasn't so sure Inman was wrong. Which is why, after a fashion, he asked the GM representatives who were also in the Holiday Inn conference room to leave. He was going to address those internecine concerns head-on.

There is very, very little love lost between Pontiac and Chevrolet. As Inman's suspicions showed, Pontiac people live with an inferiority complex. The new Grand Prix was supposed to change that. But instead, its debut became a bungled enterprise. With plenty of blame to go around, its introduction offers a window into how a race is shaped long before the green flag ever flies.

Its story really begins in the mid-1980s, when General Motors went through one of the darkest periods of its history—the GM-10 program. Between 1987 and 1988 nine recalls were issued—for everything from wheels coming off to cruise controls randomly engaging. Overbuilding was eating up profits (four plants were turning out cars whose sales justified the services of just two), as was a ridiculous level of custom ordering (by some estimates, 100,000 build combinations existed). In their book, *Comeback,* authors Paul Ingrassia and Joseph White figured that GM was losing $1,800 on every GM-10 car sold. At the end of the decade, GM's share of the midsize market shriveled from 51 to 35 percent.

One of the cars that carried GM through these dark years was the Monte Carlo. Chevrolet was going to retire it in 1984, but at the last minute unveiled a sporty NASCAR-inspired coupe that became a sensation. It had a nose that always looked pissed off, and a build that reminded boomers of the muscle cars they drove in their youth. The SS coupe would account for roughly half of all Monte Carlo sales through the mid to late 1980s.

When Chevy finally retired the nameplate in 1989, it was to make room for its 1990s gamble: the Lumina. It was a bizarre, ill-fated move. Chevy was taking the spiritual descendant of the revered muscle cars and replacing it with the automotive equivalent of a toaster. Says one GM racing veteran, "It was an appliance designed to do a job. If not for the rental car companies and computer salesmen, they wouldn't have sold any." Another GMer quipped incredulously, "A *Lumina*? What's that? They fed a computer a bunch of letters and that's what it spit out."

Sensing that it was in trouble, GM fast-tracked its new-generation Monte Carlo. As early as 1989, designers decided that the mid- to late-1990s look would be rounded, and the Monte Carlo's corners were made saucerlike. Its convex rear window—called the greenhouse—looks like a falling wave drenching the rear end.

At about this time, some fairly novel notions of aerodynamic architecture were circulating around the NASCAR garage as well. As Ford owner Robert Yates told writer Bob Zeller in *Car & Driver*, "Back then we thought the needle-nosed front end was the greatest thing in the world. But once in a while we'd end up wrecking the car, patching it up, and taking our not-so-aerodynamic car back out. And it would actually run faster.

"The most aerodynamic shape that everybody can relate to is a teardrop. You want to get the air displaced and then let it return and let the same little molecule buddies get back together without any turbulence. So it takes the teardrop shape. We were running our teardrops backward. If we had studied the drops of water dripping off the truck sometime while we were sitting around in the rain, we probably would have realized that. But we didn't."

If not for the king's ransom that Richard Childress spent debugging the Lumina in the early 1990s, Ford would no doubt have run away with the manufacturers' championships. At least half of Chevy's points came from Earnhardt in those years. As the GMer put it, "Childress was the one who made chicken salad out of chicken shit."

The 1996 Monte Carlo, by contrast, was a car GM's racers could like, maybe even love, out of the gate. There was just one problem. In keeping with NASCAR's dictates that the racing version of a car look exactly like the showroom version, the Monte Carlo had a fifty-one-inch-wide rear end. The problem was NASCAR's rule mandating that every car use the same fifty-seven-inch-wide spoiler. The Monte Carlo was six inches too short!

It wasn't as if this went unnoticed in Chevrolet's laboratories. In fact, GM's designers had put a fifty-seven-inch spoiler on the car, allowing a few inches to hang off either side. The results were disastrous. It totally ruined the aerodynamics of an otherwise masterful design.

NASCAR's Winston Cup director, Gary Nelson, knew there would be trouble. But by forging ahead on the design, GM's engineers had backed him into a corner. They didn't volunteer a solution. Instead they waited for him to offer one. In late 1994, with the Chevy teams waiting for the final designs so they could start building their 1995 race cars, Nelson made the most controversial decision of the decade to that point.

Just make the back end six inches wider so it can fit the spoiler, he offered.

Ford executives went apoplectic when they heard the news. If NASCAR had one central orthodoxy, one building block that had remained unchanged since its beginnings, it was that the body of a race car had to be a carbon copy of its showroom twin. This was the National Association of *Stock* Car Auto Racing. Though the machinery beneath the body was as advanced as anything in racing, the body itself had to be strictly stock. Now Nelson was allowing two different Monte Carlos to exist: a street model with a fifty-one-inch rear end, and a racing version with one six inches wider.

"You have to remember," says Ford publicist Kevin Kennedy, "they went through an unprecedented two years of testing. GM knew that little bit of widening in the rear would make all the difference. When the wind travels over the car and hits the back, it has more surface to sweep across. That helps the car stick to the track, which is everything when you're going through a high-banked corner at 170 mph.

"But Chevrolet went on a total misinformation campaign. Look at the quotes from back then. All you read about was what a pig the car was. They knew what they had, and they knew we'd complain. So they planted the seed in the fans' minds that we were whiners. I remember Darrell Waltrip stepping in front of the TV cameras and grabbing a template," an aluminum silhouette NASCAR inspectors use during inspection to ensure that all bodies have been built to the dimensions prescribed by the rule book. "Darrell put it on the Monte Carlo's deck lid and said, 'I don't know what they're talking about. It fits.' Well, of course it did! It was the fifty-one-inch *production* model that the race template didn't fit. That was the point! It was a classic little evasion.

"At the end of the day, you couldn't get around the fact that the Thunderbird had to fit fourteen of fourteen templates, and the Monte Carlo fit twelve of fourteen. NASCAR had never given a concession like that. And this was before their car even hit the track. We didn't appreciate that."

What came to be known inside Ford as "the Gift" changed the rules of engagement. Whereas before an unofficial group of crew chiefs and owners would agree upon rules and submit them to NASCAR, "the Gift" raised the stakes to a much higher level.

The Monte Carlo won twenty-one of thirty-one races in 1995. This would be war.

The new battles were fought in the wind tunnels, not in the pits. After a race, Ford would besiege Bill France with charts of aerodynamic data that supposedly proved it was an underdog, only to have Chevy counterpunch with numbers that it said proved parity. (Ford went so far as to build its own Monte Carlo and wind-test it both in the United States and Europe.)

"Even before this, France felt like the manufacturers all lied to him," said a source with a bird's-eye view of the action. "When everyone tried selling him these aero numbers he didn't understand, he *really* felt like they were screwing him."

The solution? NASCAR would get into the aero business itself.

For the first time in its history, NASCAR started seizing cars as they finished races and bringing them to wind tunnels for its own downforce tests. By May of 1995, NASCAR decided to repay Ford with a series of small concessions, but this made Chevrolet scream. Soon Nelson and NASCAR's vice president for competition, Mike Helton, were changing the rules for nearly every race.

Just a few years earlier, stock cars were the aerodynamic equivalent of fat Aunt Ethel. Now, even lowly mechanics were talking like Princeton engineering students as they chomped on beef jerkies. A well-intentioned suggestion had changed more than the way the car companies were acting. It changed the very language of the garage.

As the well-heeled Hendrick and Childress teams began testing their new weapon in summer 1994, their Pontiac cousins—already prone to feelings of neglect—were growing restless.

Rusty Wallace had just deserted their ranks, leaving them without owner Roger Penske's deep pockets. Worse, the car wasn't winning. After nearly snaring the manufacturers' championship thanks to Wallace in 1993, it didn't win a single race in 1994. That August, Claudio called his teams to GM's design center in Warren, Michigan, to let them know, as he put it, "that we had our own silver bullet."

Other than the security guard at the entrance, there's little about this unremarkable collection of sixties-era glass-and-steel buildings that suggests anything vaguely intriguing, let alone top-secret. It has the feel of a vocational college, not the research hub of a multibillion-dollar company. But as Kyle Petty remembers:

"We were led into this long hall, and it's like the beginning of *Get Smart*, with all these doors opening and closing. And all along the hall there were full-size clay models covered up with tarps, like they'd have to kill us if we saw it. They brought us to this cul-de-sac, with lots of rooms jutting off it, and there in the center, on a platform with a canvas cover, was the car. They pulled the cover off, throw on the lights, and, da-dum, it's the 1997 Pontiac Grand Prix. Except for one thing. It was a four-door. They didn't even have a two-door version yet!"

Claudio desperately wanted his teams to feel encouraged, but the fact was that the project already had a stink of setback. This prototype was two years delayed, and needed work. "It had a lot of potential," Kyle recalls. "For one thing, it had nice lines. But it had a lot of bad stuff too. Like the deck lid. It was too short for a race car and dropped off."

Predictably, the metamorphosis from street car to race car would be a troubled one.

To start, engineers had to turn a V-6 front-wheel-drive car into a V-8 rear-wheel-drive. To fit the V-8 engine, they had to move the car back on the chassis, as well as raising and lengthening the hood. Then they had to flatten the doors, because NASCAR wanted them to look identical to those used by Ford and Chevy. And finally, because the trunk on the production car was too low to make the car stick to a racetrack at high speed, it needed lengthening.

In the fall of 1994, Felix Sabates was given the blueprint

and asked to build a prototype. Time was of the essence, since the car would be racing in seventeen months. But fall turned to winter, and winter to spring, and nothing got done. Internal strife at Sabco—crew chief Robin Pemberton defected to Rusty Wallace's new team—paralyzed the operation. Frustrated, Claudio moved the development operation to Chuck Rider's Bahari team.

Within months a dull-black Bahari car had been molded and brought to Atlanta for closed, top-secret testing. The work was painstaking. They moved the chassis up and down, back and forth, trying to get just the right balance, trying in vain to match the Monte Carlo's incomparable aero numbers. If Sabates delivered on time, they'd have had more than a year to do this. As it was, November 1995 was upon them far too quickly. The Daytona 500 was three months off. NASCAR needed to approve the car. Claudio's clients needed to get started building their fleets.

The Grand Prix was nowhere near competitive. But the clock had simply run out.

On November 3 a covered trailer pulled up to an unassuming warehouse on the outskirts of Charlotte. If anyone was watching, they wouldn't have thought twice about the midday delivery to Richardson Racing Products, which is just the way Claudio wanted it. As Richardson's employees closed the garage bay behind the truck, securing it from prying eyes, Gary Nelson stepped out to see what the new GM entry would look like. It had a sloped rear and a broad semicircular hood that melted like wet candle wax into the rounded nose.

Though the Bahari team was the development leader, this particular car had been built by Richard Jackson's Hooters outfit. In principle, it shouldn't have made a difference. After all, the specs were the same. But as soon as the car was wheeled into the center of the room, a young engineer named Jeff Kettman saw that it wasn't right. No, not at all.

Nelson had been upset over a rash of episodes where racers were poking their cars' noses under the bumpers of the cars in front of them. This would force the lead car to lift and crash. So to avoid repeats, he decreed that all noses be seventeen inches off the ground. It wasn't an unreasonable request, but it required that special instructions be followed in building the assembly. Somehow, Jackson's fabricator had misread those directions. Instead of lifting the whole front end in unison seventeen inches high, he merely tilted the nose up so it reached that height.

Standing there in the warehouse, Kettman didn't know how big a problem it would be. Only that it was a problem.

"You know, Gary," he said as Nelson began measuring the nose. "This isn't really the one we prefer." But Nelson had come to get this deal done, and wasn't about to work piecemeal. They could do it all now, he said, or they could come back and do it all later.

Claudio looked at Kettman, who shrugged his shoulders. "I guess we'll do it all now," he replied.

"Something happened, and we were damned if we knew what it was," says Kevin Hamlin, then the crew chief for Jackson's car. "We really had something good going in October. Then in February it's a different car. We kept asking ourselves, 'What got lost?' "

The Pontiac engineers became an easy target for the increasingly frustrated racers, but the fact was that no one could be sure who or what was at fault. Was it the engineers, who let the misshapen nose slip through their fingers? Or was it the race teams, who might not have been up to the R&D challenge of debugging a brand-new car under the gun of a season-in-progress?

Either way, all sides knew that if they were going to ask NASCAR for help, they'd better figure out what they were asking for.

France was taking so much heat from Ford, he wasn't about to step into another political headache. Jack Roush, the leading Ford attack dog, had been all over the airwaves, complaining about the Monte Carlo leading the most laps in Rockingham and Richmond. But the greater problem was with the two races coming up. The turns in Atlanta and Darlington are steep and wide—precisely the traits that require a car to have a good downforce coefficient. In other words, these were the tracks that the Monte Carlo, with its abnormally wide rear end, excelled at. Ford scientists had already done their own wind tunnel comparisons and declared Ford in need of relief. France's message pads were filling up with their calls.

With Pontiac crying for a new nose, and Ford crying foul, France decided he was going to prove to himself who was lying.

On March 11 a Thunderbird, Monte Carlo, and Grand Prix were wheeled into a wind tunnel in Marietta, Georgia, under trailer cover. The results of the tests that followed frustrated Ford's engineers. It found the wind hit the back of all three cars about the same, contradicting Ford's in-house tests, which purported to show its cars were at a disadvantage.

But there was another finding that caused more mixed emotions for the Pontiac brigade. The NASCAR tunnel test showed the wind came down more lightly on the front of a Pontiac than a Ford or Chevy.

On one hand, this was good news for Claudio. Now he could go to Nelson with hard proof that Pontiac was at a disadvantage and ask that Pontiac's teams be allowed to build a new nose. But there was also an ominous side to

the discovery: It was now clear the Grand Prix was infe-
rior to the Monte Carlo.

If Claudio wanted to look at this generously, he might
conclude that GM's engineers were simply wrong when
they said the two cars were equal. But what if GM's engineers were as good as everyone thought they were?
Claudio didn't like thinking about that alternative. If they
really were that good, then it meant that Inman was right,
that they'd been lying to him. Either way, he wondered
how he could trust them.

Standing on the stage in the Holiday Inn conference
room, he looked over the room. In addition to the owners,
two high-ranking members of GM racing were in atten-
dance. The first was aerodynamicist Terry Laise. The
second was Don Taylor, who ostensibly oversaw tech support for Pontiac and Chevy, but mainly worked with the
Chevy teams.

"Excuse me, Terry, Don," Claudio said. "Could you
leave us alone for a second?"

There was a strained silence as they left the room.
Claudio sensed the mistrust in the air. Inman had nearly
come to blows with Laise, threatening to punch him as he
reached his own conclusion about what the results of
NASCAR's wind tunnel test meant.

"I'm sick of you lyin' to me," Inman had thundered.

Claudio wanted Inman and the others to know that he
was committed to creating an environment for them to
win. He would get them their very own engineer—the
young, talented Kettman—and start building a wall between Pontiac and Chevrolet.

But first he needed a dramatic gesture. Something to
show he was serious. That's when he grabbed a chair and
threatened to hurl it clear into their seats.

"If I hear one more motherfuckin' thing about that Jeff

Gordon," he screamed, "I'm gonna beat that bony kid's ass myself. From now on we stop bitching and start winning."

Later, as he drove alone back to the airport, he hoped they now felt they had someone watching their backs in the car wars.

7

FATAL TURN FOUR

Charlotte Motor Speedway: May 18 to May 26

Rat-a-tat-a-tat.

Two Kiowa Warrior attack helicopters flew in an even formation, spraying sheets of wind across the field.

"Sabre Three, this is Cougar Six. Spot report, over."

"This is Sabre Three, send. Over."

"Two enemy soldiers over watching from a building at the western edge of LZ Eagle. Request permission to engage, over."

"Cougar Six, you're clear to engage."

A rainstorm of fifty-caliber machine-gun fire descended from the Kiowa, landing on a lonely wooden barracks that collapsed instantly, as if it were just waiting for a hard wind. Two soldiers ran helplessly into the open, in time to be covered by the shadows of Blackhawk choppers landing nearby. As the chopper doors opened, thirty soldiers fell onto the grass, rolling as if they were trying to douse flames. One by one they fell into line with their M-16A2 rifles drawn.

Overhead, three more Blackhawks were arriving, their pregnant bellies full with M-119 howitzers. The Marines inside pushed the howitzers out of the galley bay, leaving them to float by parachute to the ground. As the antiaircraft battery landed, the ground troops ran to them and began pouring in computer codes. Soon, the control panels of the howitzers were blinking, ready to fire.

A shirtless man pressed his fatness through a Cyclone fence directly in front of one of the cannons. "Cool," he said.

Watching the action from a control tower 120 feet aboveground, Humpy Wheeler couldn't have agreed more. This was the fourteenth military maneuver that Wheeler, the president of the Charlotte Motor Speedway, had staged in his infield to precede the Memorial Day weekend race.

Listening to the crowd applaud as it got "fired" upon, Wheeler knew it was still the event of the season.

In a sport where prerace festivities usually mean putting a bunch of beer-soaked car salesmen on the track and letting them joyride for a couple of parade laps, Humpy Wheeler is the inventor of racetrack theater. His weird and wonderful use of white-trash car culture had spawned an oeuvre—one where cars painted as dominoes are tipped, the Grenada invasion is reenacted with Fords, and RV campers are launched Evel Knievel–style over 150 Porta-Johns.

He chuckles when he thinks about this, a light laugh that carries with it a continuing astonishment. At fifty-seven, Humpy Wheeler knows that NASCAR doesn't approve of him, his showboating, or the way he keeps topping himself. NASCAR is conservative, corporate, defensive. If it buys balloons, they are gray and black. Humpy's world is about spectacle, about a thousand red and white balloons. It is about a man who is still trying to colorize a boyhood spent in a drab cotton mill town called Belmont.

"I was brought up in this surreal middle-class family in a little town of five thousand people twelve miles west of Charlotte," he explained. "My mother was a small-town Southern Baptist and my father was the first Catholic she ever met. He was from the poor side of Newport, Rhode Island. But he ended up at Belmont Abbey College as athletic director, political science, hygiene, and history teacher—all for twenty-five dollars a week. So a typical dinner for us was like refighting the Civil War. My dad had spinach on his table side, and my mother had collard greens. I didn't like either one of them and I had to eat both. My primary exposure was to Benedictine monks and the people who worked in the cotton mills. The good thing about it was that we lived six miles from the old Charlotte Speedway on Little Rock Road."

He'd stand on Highway 29 and watch the brightly colored race cars on hitches pass by, and though he was built thickly, there was no question he would not work in the cotton mills. He was an honors graduate of the University of South Carolina, a journalism major, with a varsity football pedigree and a penchant for promoting races in his spare time.

To draw crowds, he'd invent personalities. For instance, Humpy had a childhood friend who'd been nicknamed Jungle because when they played in the woods around town, they pretended they were characters in the Tarzan serials of the day. When the friend started racing, Humpy dubbed him Jungle Boy and promoted him as a wild man. Another creation was Jim Dimeo, a local mechanic with a Saturday-night following. Figuring that everyone in the mill towns was Scotch Irish—and all they knew about Italians came from cheap Mafia movies—Humpy renamed him Jim Diamond and started a rumor that he was born in Sicily.

"Poor Jim," Humpy says. "He had no more idea where he came from than the man on the moon."

By twenty-five, Humpy Wheeler took a corporate job with Firestone, which was challenging Goodyear for NASCAR supremacy. At the same time, the Charlotte Motor Speedway was going through changes that would profoundly affect him.

Bruton Smith, an ambitious ex-paratrooper and promoter, built CMS with the driver Curtis Turner in 1960.

But two years later, it was $900,000 in debt and seeking bankruptcy protection. Ousted from its board, Smith went into self-imposed exile from stock car racing, traveling to Denver, then Illinois, then Texas, amassing a fortune selling Fords, and plotting a comeback. His opportunity arrived when a CMS board members asked Smith in 1975 if he'd be interested in buying 250,000 shares. Smith leapt at the chance, and with that wedge, began a yearlong acquisition of a majority of remaining shares. Now redeemed, he triumphantly flew back to Charlotte in his 747—the one he'd bought from the Ugandan dictator Idi Amin. Firestone had lost the tire war by then, and Wheeler was looking for work. Smith hired him to run CMS, setting the stage for a tense but unrivaled partnership that would use the speedway to incubate ideas years ahead of their time.

There are the apartment buildings built along the track's facade, one cream-colored, modeled in Miami Beach style, with white terraces, boxy windows, and a lobby done in mirrors and gold, the other added later in a more demure Fifth Avenue style.

There is the six-sided glass-and-steel Smith Tower, inserted like a wedge between the grandstands. On the ground floor, Smith ordered a marble piazza, an oak concierge station, and private brass-plated elevators that rise to plush office suites considered to be premier addresses in NASCAR.

There is the Speedway Club, with its deep red carpet, dark wood banisters, and oil portraits in the dining room and library.

There are the luxury boxes that go for $80,000 a weekend, the tent city of hospitality pagodas under whose canopies Texaco, McDonald's, and other bastions of the Fortune 500 spend lavishly to entertain prized customers. All of which makes CMS the biggest money engine in the sport. It also turned its parent, Speedway Motorsports, into a Wall Street darling when it went public in early 1995.

"About fourteen years ago," Humpy says, "I wandered into a library in Manhattan with three hours to kill. I came across this fantastic assortment of books on the Greek and Roman games. It really sent cold chills up my spine, because I found great detail about a hippodrome in Greece that had almost the exact height and width of our grandstand right here. They had VIP suites where the senators sat, their own refreshments, and they put on fantastic shows. We hear about the prisoners and lions, but there were other marvels. They had a chariot racer who was almost a carbon copy of Richard Petty. He won 405 races, raced until he was fifty, and had amazing communication with his fans.

"It was fascinating, and made me think that when you get too serious about this thing, you gotta think about two thousand years from now, when this whole place will have been forgotten and the archaeologists start going through the layers. They'll get to where the seats are, then they'll ponder these little chicken bones that we eat here, and they'll probably say, 'Hey, this is the same thing they did in Rome and Greece. But these people here were awful small.' " He smiles rakishly. Then Humpy gets up for a moment, leaving a visitor to look out from his glass office overlooking the fourth turn.

Since CMS first opened, turn four has been one of the most infamous corners in NASCAR. Built on landfill, it's rough and bumpy and beaten by the sun, tight and tricky in the best of times. If you stand beside it while the race cars are still far away from entering it, you hear something quite remarkable: The sound of the cars actually precedes them.

The sound travels along the 24-degree banking until it gets caught by an overhang, rattles around, and finally gets thrown back out at the exact moment the cars hit the corner. It is eerily affecting, because staring at the vacant turn filled by the sound of absent race cars, it's easy to imagine that you're hearing the ghosts of the nine men who died there.

Three of them died in Wheeler's darkest promotion: the sportsman division.

Humpy believed that Saturday-night racers needed a place to get practice on speedways, because the escalating, multimillion-dollar cost of Winston Cup racing was barring new stars from breaking in. So he created a race where Saturday-night racers could log speedway laps without the expensive inhibitions of the most current safety standards. Ironically, the series' existence was owed to the fact that NASCAR was heightening safety demands, leaving teams with a glut of old, outmoded cars that were perfect for sportsman racers who were limited only by the chances they were willing to take.

"It used to make us sick to cover those races," says a cameraman who still has nightmares about Gary Batson. In 1992 the forty-year-old bought a race car from a friend who had quit racing after being in a fiery Sportsman wreck. Unperturbed by the fact that the car he was buying was the same one that had been in the wreck, Batson entered it in another Sportsman race. Midway through the event, Batson got into a freak collision—again, in turn four. He went up on his left wheels while his right wheels rode the fence. Another car also went on two wheels, riding the underbelly of Batson's car like a circus elephant.

As the cameraman remembers it, "The booth tells me to go to One, which means they want a wide shot. But I'm on the car. And it fireballs. Now, NASCAR's had problems with safety workers getting killed, so it won't let the rescue vehicle go out until all the cars have slowed. This man is burning, and everyone's waiting [twenty-five seconds] for all the other drivers to slow down." Batson, who was conscious the entire fifty-seven seconds he was on fire, was crying when he was wheeled into the hospital. "He knew," his brother Roy told writer Bob Zeller. "You could tell he knew." Batson died about fifteen hours after the crash.

The last sportsman race occurred on October 6, 1995. The pole-sitter that day was Russell Phillips, a volunteer fireman and fabricator running his seventeenth event as CMS. Phillips led for the first two laps but soon fell to tenth. Then two cars spun ahead of him, causing another driver to brake and veer into Phillips's Oldsmobile. The Olds jumped onto its side, hitting the retaining fence roof first and skidding on two wheels for seventy-five feet until a caution light sheared off its top, as if it were cheap aluminum. Phillips, twenty-six, was instantly decapitated, his helmet sheared off at the shoulders. Skull fragments landed at the feet of photographers in the fourth turn. His hand was left hanging in the fence where the caution light lay. Track employees spent until nine o'clock that night hosing down blood in the fourth-turn grandstands.

It's hard to ignore severed body parts.

Humpy Wheeler, the great promoter, finally had had enough. After a drumbeat of criticism and pressure from NASCAR, he pulled out of the series, and it died soon after.

Humpy's world is built around events that send men over the edge, events that thrill, events that make him feel like he used to feel on those Saturday nights in Belmont. But in Belmont, cars weren't going 170 mph.

Humpy was chasing a memory. Prudence dictated it should have remained one. Yet even today he rues its demise.

"When we decided not to run the cars here anymore, there was a big outcry among the competitors who wanted to keep racing. There is too much distance between your Saturday-night short-track driver and the last-place car in the Busch circuit. It's a great tragedy for racing, but it's just the facts of life."

If Sportsman racing was Humpy's darkest promotion, his most brilliant is the Winston.

The Winston is an all-star race composed of winners from the prior year's races, Select champions going back five years and Winston Cup title holders. It has absolutely no parallel. Wheeler has mangled the rules so that every risk is magnified, so that the best and worst impulses of men with a pathological aversion to losing become fodder for a racing drama in three acts.

The first is a thirty-lap minirace whose winner earns $50,000. Act II is another thirty-lap duel, but in a delicious twist, fans get to vote about whether to reverse the order of the field so the first-place car is moved to last place.* The finale, Act III, is a ten-lap, balls-out dash.

If that was all, it would be show enough. But there is a prologue—a fifty-lap race where all drivers not invited to the Select claw and scrape for a handful of wild-card spots. It is called the Open. And for fans with a taste for watching desperate men do desperate things, there's nothing like it.

Certainly as the sun set on a beautiful spring evening, there wasn't a driver more desperate than Brett Bodine.

After North Wilkesboro, Brett had suffered through an eighteenth-place finish in Martinsville and a twenty-third-place finish in Talladega (he wrecked late and sprained his wrist). In the wine country of Sonoma, it looked as if he'd finally get some relief. He qualified well there and raced

---

*In 1997 the rules were changed to eliminate fan voting, since the field always seemed to get inverted and no one could ever quite figure out how Humpy managed to accurately poll 140,000 ticket holders in ten minutes.

flawlessly, making it to eleventh with eight laps to go. Then the heartbreak happened: A wreck in front of his yellow Ford made him spin into the grass and stop dead. By the time he restarted, he was shuffled to twentieth. The six-hour plane flight home was a torture, and to make matters worse, a baby was crying all the way. Showing the strain affecting the whole crew, one of his young mechanics screamed, "Hey, can't you stuff that kid in the overhead!"

In the thirteen days between his arrival back in Charlotte and now, he'd had a chance to catch his breath. Charlotte is considered the home track for many drivers, Brett included. All signs were positive. He'd won the pole there in 1993, and had gone over the car he was bringing here with a fine-tooth comb. In fact, he qualified third. Now, as the green flag fell to start the Open, he was determined to make this the place where he'd turn his season around and get one of the five wild-card spots.

Brett made himself part of an early breakaway, his yellow Ford pulling up the rear of a three-car lead train. When the gas pedal fell off of Dick Trickle's second-place car, Brett inherited the spot. Behind him he could see cars darting high and low, thrashing to lose their neighbors.

These skirmishes let Brett fortify his lead. But one car stayed in his frame: the blood-orange car, driven by Michael Waltrip. Waltrip's Ford kept eating up the daylight until it was right on Brett's tail, nudging its nose into his bumper, then pulling to his inside. Together they plowed into the front straight, each man carrying a train of drivers, like a pair of hot gamblers with their respective hangers-on.

Brett was in the more vulnerable spot. In the high groove, he'd have to hit the brake at just the right time to get an arc that would allow him to close Waltrip's exit lane. Barreling into the turn at 170 mph, Brett thought, *Not yet . . . not yet . . . not . . . Okay. Now. Brake. Turn . . .*

The car resisted with a push. It was the faintest hesitation, but at those speeds it was fatal. Waltrip went through the corner faster, carrying Hut Stricklin and Jimmy Spencer with him. In the blink of an eye Brett went from second to sixth, and took the checkered flag one behind that.

After he parked, Brett collapsed inside his transporter, emotionally wiped out. He nearly had a top-ten finish in Sonoma. Now he'd come *this close* to qualifying for the Winston. Wiping sweat off his red face, he stared at the floor. "I'm just getting so damn tired of this. It keeps happening. You think you have a strong car and . . ."

Bobby Hamilton also wasn't making it to the next level. The closest he'd come was when he pulled beside eighth-place Morgan Shepherd and they dueled side by side for a pair of laps. But like magnets, they suddenly separated going into the third turn, Bobby high, Shepherd low. Shepherd took the position. Neither advanced beyond.

Even if he won the thing, it's doubtful how much attention Bobby would have drawn. Everyone around the Petty crew was buzzing with the arrival of presidential candidate Bob Dole.

Actually, buzzing may be the wrong word. It was more like congealing. Since a presidential campaign carries its own mass, about two dozen tweedy reporters who'd flown with Dole from Washington, D.C., collided with the decidedly less fashion-conscious NASCAR press corps, forming a bubble around the candidate. He'd come for the same reason as Republican hopefuls since Richard Nixon: to have Petty introduce him to a captive audience of 140,000 friendly voters.

Yet Dole had difficulty making much of the opportunity. He stumbled through a halting and short speech, the crux of which was: "I'm for family values, country music, and NASCAR." After fireworks lit the infield and the

Phantom of the Opera theme blared amid cheers and pop-ping flashbulbs, Dole delivered his most animated line of the night: "Gentlemen, start your engines."

Humpy couldn't have asked for a better start. On the pole was Jeff Gordon, to his right Dale Earnhardt. Behind them were Mark Martin and Dale Jarrett. Gordon jumped out to the early lead, but Jarrett quickly swept under him, pre-viewing the dominance Fords would show all week. At the end of the first thirty laps he took the flag with a three-second edge.

Earnhardt's crew swarmed in the pits during the inter-mission, placing a rubber in the right front spring to stiffen it so the front wouldn't bounce through the turns as much. It worked. Thanks to the fans' vote to invert the field, Earnhardt started eighth, and surged to second behind Terry Labonte. With six laps to go, he powered up at the mouth of the backstretch, caught Labonte coming out of turn four, pinched him into the wall on the straightaway, and then fearlessly dove into turn one for the lead. They went one-two across the finish line.

And so it was that Act III started with the two coolest veterans side by side. As the green flag fell they took each other uncompromisingly through the turns, so close they could feel their eyes on each other.

Racing hard out of turn four, Labonte managed to get a nose in front of Earnhardt. But the black Monte Carlo shadowed Labonte's Kellogg car all the way back into turn one.

Then it happened.

Earnhardt's car shuddered, not a lot, but enough to send it sideways into Labonte, driving both of them into the outside wall, which recorded their dalliance with a thick black stripe. Michael Waltrip—the driver who squeaked into the race by taking the fifth wild-card spot away from

Brett—avoided the wreck and glided into first, continuing on to capture his first-ever Winston Cup victory. "I knew something was going to happen," he told reporters in Victory Lane later, more astonished than anything. "Heck, I'd seen it [before] on TV. Two cars get side by side and one gets loose. I knew they weren't going to give an inch, so I just waited for it to happen."

As Waltrip was talking, Terry Labonte parked his car by the gas pumps. Someone handed him a Diet Coke and he glanced at it. Then, considering Earnhardt's trailer thirty feet away, he hurled the unopened can with all his might. It exploded across the trailer, right on the larger-than-life portrait of the man who'd just wrecked him.

Over the next week, the politics of the presidential race and the pageantry of Humpy World were equaled only by the fireworks that were flaring between the carmakers.

The Earnhardt/Labonte dogfight meant more than either man losing $200,000. (Since it's an exhibition, the race doesn't affect the points championship.) It meant that Ford had been allowed to sweep the top two spots in the Select after winning all five wild-card berths in the Open. That it came on the heels of a NASCAR rules change that favored Ford didn't elude a single GM partisan. In the ten weeks since the March 11 wind tunnel test in Marietta, Georgia, Ford had been waging a massive offensive to portray itself as hopelessly hobbled by NASCAR's rules. Its publicists made sure high-profile drivers such as Dale Jarrett always said something about racing at a disadvantage. In private its racing chief, Dan Rivard, besieged Bill France with aero data.

"Dan was naive when he started," says an ex–Ford person. "He thought he was gonna teach us that if we were straight with NASCAR, they'd be straight with us. Then he started to spend tons of money on these aero tests to make his point. When that didn't work, he did what the rest of us did. He got mad."

By late May, Rivard had authorized a full-scale pullout of NASCAR racing, having in place an order that none of his teams be permitted to fly the Ford insignia. But at the last minute France came through with a partial concession. Rivard had been asking for an inch and a quarter off the roof—something that would make the air flow over the roof faster and then hit the spoiler harder, helping the cars stick to the track in the turns.

France issued a rule change for a quarter inch.

It was less than Rivard wanted, but it kept his finger from the dynamite button—for this week, anyway. Unfortunately for France, it was all that the Monte Carlo owners were talking about going into the Coca-Cola 600 on May 25, the longest race of the season.

In a tense meeting in Richard Childress's condo, Dave Marcis was among those who wanted to know what Herb Fishel, the head of GM racing, planned to do.

"Since we got this Monte Carlo, there have been eight changes to either hurt us or help the Ford," Marcis told Fishel. "It's killing us small owners."

Fishel nodded understandingly, but the reality was that the single-car owner no longer had any clout in NASCAR. With the exception of Childress, who received so much sponsorship money for Earnhardt's team that he could finance two lesser cars with it, the power in Winston Cup now rested with the multicar corporations, particularly Hendrick Motorsports.

Men like Junior Johnson always fielded a few teams at once. But when Rick Hendrick arrived in NASCAR in 1984 with his "All-Star Racing Team," it differed in one key detail: Hendrick tried to integrate his players and, he hoped, do away with the furtiveness and suspicion that is natural to rivals—even ones on the same team. His idea was so simple, it was almost utopian: Have all three teams share information, and run them as one.

But Hendrick had a problem finding the right mix of personalities to stoke his ideal. Tim Richmond, the flashy sex symbol, was too much for Geoff Bodine, the introvert. Bodine, a Yankee, grated on Darrell Waltrip of Tennessee. Ken Schrader and Ricky Rudd never became best friends. When Jeff Gordon joined the squad in 1993, he crashed so much he failed to finish a third of his races. By 1994 the conventional wisdom was that Hendrick never would make it work. But that year, GM gave Hendrick—who by then had become its largest single new-car dealer in the United States—a contract to debug the racing version of its under-wraps, new-model Monte Carlo. As a result, when the race car entered Winston Cup competition in 1995, Hendrick had a twelve-month head start. He also had three drivers who finally seemed to mesh: Terry Labonte, Schrader, and Gordon.

His dominance that year—Gordon winning the championship; the Monte Carlo winning twenty-one of thirty-one races—effectively killed the old order. This new world of advanced aerodynamics put a premium on expensive testing and technical support. An owner with three teams could afford so much more R&D than a single-team owner, the small guy no longer had a prayer of catching up.

So when it came to making the point that GM needed more proof that it was disadvantaged before Fishel could ask Bill France for relief, the head of GM Motorsports looked squarely at Hendrick. "Let's see how we do this weekend," he said. "Let's get some hard data."

In other words, Dave left thinking, *Let's get our ass kicked first.*

Frankly, Dave wasn't in the mood to take one on the chin for the team. Not with his sponsorship on the line. If he'd stopped to think about it, he might have compared himself to Dole—a midwesterner trying to salvage the worst, and maybe the last, campaign of his life.

After their tremulous trip through the short tracks, Dave started second-guessing Terry. In Talladega he stayed on the track during green-flag pit stops to take the lead, ignoring the caution that he was running out of fuel. Then he did run out, and got refilled in time to get caught in a four-car wreck, finishing thirty-ninth. The next week in Sonoma, he felt guilty and gave Terry free rein. But the rookie chief made a questionable call: After Dave ran a perfectly good qualifying lap, Terry made him requalify Saturday. Dave went slower and had to waste his second-to-last provisional to get into the race.

"I'm the laughingstock of the garage," he said in his trailer. "Earnhardt wanted to know what the hell I was thinking."

Now he wasn't sure whom to trust, and on top of all that, he had the sour taste in his mouth that Charlotte always gave him. Humpy Wheeler had the worst purse in the business. The richer Charlotte track paid a third as much as Dover for a twentieth-place finish, barely enough to cover a tire bill. Every year when Wheeler made his tour through the garage to ask drivers what they needed, Dave always managed to say, "A better damn purse."

This year, as if to add insult to injury, Humpy mailed Marcis a solicitation for a fund supporting Dole's candidacy, asking if he'd like to contribute $5,000 or $25,000 or $50,000. "That Humpy," Dave said, fairly spitting the words through his teeth.

After the military invasion ended, complete with the Kiowas spraying grandstands with attack fire as they began their ascent back into the sky, Dave and the other forty-two drivers waited for a summer thunder shower to end so they could get on with the racing. They knew their reflexes would be tested over the extra hundred laps— drivers develop body clocks to pace themselves through three-hour drives—and the waiting was making it harder. (Most hibachied under the awnings of their trailers with friends to pass the time.) By the time the rain ended, it was six-thirty—ninety minutes after the scheduled start.

Wheeler assembled an odd group to be onstage for the driver introductions: There was the lug-nut mascot of a car parts store, some local politicians, and James Garner, who starred in the 1966 film *Grand Prix* and was a friend of CMS's founder, Curtis Turner.

"I haven't been here in twenty-seven years, so I'm tickled to death, really," he insisted unconvincingly.

While the drivers made their way to their cars, the 82nd Airborne band played the national anthem, and then, in a first for Humpy World, astronauts from the space shuttle *Endeavor* appeared via satellite to say, "Gentlemen, start your engines."

From where they were in the back of the pack, Dave, Brett, and Bobby probably felt about as far away from pole-sitter Jeff Gordon as the astronauts felt from Earth. Dave qualified badly, and was in forty-first. Brett was on the outside of the next row, in fortieth. (Trying to make up for losing the Open, he pushed the brand-new Ford that his brother-in-law and crew chief, Donnie Richeson, built for him, crashing it in a spray of sparks during qualifying. The hollowness in his crew's eyes suggested the looks of people watching their homes burn with everything inside.) Looking diagonally in front, Brett could see Bobby, who was still suffering the effects of Pontiac's qualifying pains, in thirty-seventh.

If there was one thing they all had in their favor, it was that anything could happen in four hours.

In the opening laps Ricky Craven, Gordon, and Andretti

were dominating, but in the back a dozen battles helped the plotline form:

After dispatching Irvan in a hard-fought corner skirmish, Earnhardt was into the top ten. Rusty Wallace, who started dead last, was picking positions by the handful, as was Hamilton, who was behind him in fifteenth. Terry Labonte had moved into a slugfest with Gordon for the lead, but Jarrett was about to take it over.

Among the decliners, no one dropped off more than Andretti. From third he'd nosedived to twentieth, and was desperately trying to recover. Seeing Dave in front of him, the jockey-size driver banged the Prodigy car going into the fourth turn of lap 142.

"What the hell?" Dave said, looking in his rearview mirror. He'd just grabbed the wheel to correct his course, throwing his fist at Andretti, when a second, sharper hit made it futile. The bump spun him around and, with his left side facing traffic, Dave went smashing into the wall; the contact sent him repelling back down the track as sparks sprayed from under his folded hood.

"What happened?" Terry gasped into the radio. "John Andretti, that little bastard, that's what happened," Dave fumed. "Someone should put a cushion under his seat, 'cause he can't see." As his Monte Carlo was towed back to the garage to be buried for the day, a livid Dave had a new villain to add to his Charlotte honor roll.

"The purse back where I am won't pay the tire bill," he said, stripping out of his suit. "Damn Andretti, that little bastard."

The field barely had a chance to catch its breath when, not a lap into the next restart, trouble struck again: Bobby Hillin lost control of his car and spun in the middle of the track. Mike Waltrip's Ford couldn't clear Hillin's nose and collected Geoff Bodine and Ricky Rudd, drawing another yellow flag. After nearly continuous green-flag racing, the pits filled for a second time.

In the pit just beyond turn four, Robbie Loomis wasn't touching his STP Pontiac. Bobby Hamilton thought they were headed for a top-five finish, but Robbie was thinking bigger: They'd shot out of thirty-seventh place like a bat out of hell. He was thinking win.

As the green flag fell on the same restart lap they'd been trying to finish for twenty minutes, Bobby went out in fifteenth place, intent on chewing up more daylight. In a daring pass, he went into the untested, rain-washed high groove of turn four to pass the youngest of the Bodines, Todd. The two cars went through the corner as if glued at their doors, but they didn't come out that way. With Bobby breathing hard on his outside, Bodine couldn't nail his arc without veering a few inches off his line, just enough to send him sideways into Hamilton. The raging winds carried Bobby into the wall, where he crashed nose first, sparks flying, the day's dream dying.

Back at the trailer, Richard Petty put his hand on the car as if to get a pulse while his crew swarmed around it with whirring drill guns and mallets. It would limp on the track later and finish thirty-first, but for now, all a driver like Hamilton could do was boil.

It was more than a half hour since Andretti had bumped Marcis. The garage was filling with casualties. Nerves were beginning to fray. And then, as if to add incinerant, NASCAR allowed Ted Musgrave's Ford to line up ahead of Kyle Petty, though it was two laps down and Kyle's Pontiac had been lapped only once. Kyle's crew chief radioed to the spotter's tower, "Tell 'em to move," but word came back that Musgrave wouldn't budge. It was then that Petty said, "Don't worry, I'll take care of it," by which he meant he'd race to reclaim his rightful position.

Among the people who heard the remark was Gary

Nelson, but Nelson swore Kyle had said, "Don't worry, I'll take care of *him*." Sabates had fired Nelson three years earlier* and there was little love lost among any of the men, so Nelson watched with keen interest as the green flag fell and Kyle tipped the left edge of the Ford trying to pass on the outside. When Musgrave's Ford veered into the top column of cars on the restart line, front-runners began piling into one another as if part of a cheap comedy.

Smoke was everywhere. So was metal. Andretti's car was crushed. Rusty Wallace went airborne. And Nelson went ballistic. After Kyle escaped the wreckage to race back to the stripe and win back his lost lap, the Winston Cup director hit his former driver with one of the harshest weapons at his disposal—a five-lap penalty for rough driving.

A dumbstruck Kyle pulled onto pit road in time to see Sabates fuming, railing on their private channel, "NASCAR, you motherfuckers, I hope you hear this. If this is the Mickey Mouse way you run this sport, then you can go to hell."

Nelson heard it, all right. Well enough to have the inspector who was assigned to their pit stand in front of Kyle's car and hold two fingers aloft—a sign that two more laps would now be added to their five-lap penalty. Beside himself, Sabates stormed over to the NASCAR trailer and flung his credit-card-size ID badge inside. "I won't be needing this anymore," he said. "I'm not coming to any more races."

When the race was over and Dale Jarrett had won by a yawning twelve seconds, speedway officials directed four police officers to the Sabco trailer in the garage, ostensibly to protect Felix and Kyle from the media crush, though

---

*Sabates would later call the firing "one of the worst decisions I've ever made."

one wondered if they also weren't there to discourage a few hotheaded crew chiefs from visiting. When Kyle finally emerged to talk with reporters, he was asked what had happened on the track. He put the perfect period on the evening by pointing to the NASCAR trailer. "Go ask them," he said incredulously. "It's Kansas over there. That's where the wizard lives."

Actually, the wizard was standing in a control tower 120 feet above the action. Wheeler had to congratulate himself. He'd put on a hell of a show.

8

RUMORS

Dover, Delaware: May 31 to June 3

When Dover Downs was built in 1969, it wasn't designed to be a prototype suburban racetrack. In fact, it was put on the far edge of the city's limits—in the middle of a farm—because no one wanted to live near a stock car oval that had a horse-racing track inside of it. The city's treasury did very well from the two NASCAR races that were held there every year. But after a while interest in its harness racing waned, and by the 1990s its grandstands were virtually empty except on the spring and fall weekends that NASCAR came to town.

"To see this place turn into a ghost town was depressing as hell," the track's president told the New York *Daily News*.

The paradox was that all around Dover Downs, development was bustling. Shopping centers sprang up along U.S. 13, enveloping the racetrack in a Miracle Mile. Placed against that new suburban backdrop, Dover Downs's pink art deco exterior and high, wide arches lent it the look of an old Vegas motel just waiting to be knocked down.

Then, on December 29, 1995, the state legislature passed a bill that allowed gaming. Overnight its fortunes changed. Now you could see a race, shop at T.J. Maxx, and help Dover Downs generate $2.2 billion from a thousand slot machines—all without moving your car. Now, that was suburbia!

Friday, May 31, was a perfect time for the circuit to hit Dover, since everyone in the Winston Cup garage was gambling on which drivers would soon be fired. With more than forty teams to choose from, gossiping about drivers was hardly new. In fact, the arrival of the rumors is so predictable, it even has its own name: the Silly Season. What was different was how early the Silly Season was starting this year.

Mike Wallace and Steve Grissom, amiable drivers who hadn't yet distinguished themselves at the Winston Cup level, were the first casualties. Wallace's team was owned by the seventy-two-year-old racing veteran Junie Donlavey, Grissom's by the billionaire construction heir Gary Bechtel. For the back-of-the-pack drivers who could usually count on holding their jobs through Labor Day, the axings set a disturbing precedent. Suddenly, everyone was in the play, with the Greek chorus being the publicists and hangers-on whose fortunes rise and fall with the drivers they gossip about.

Some of the gossip was absurd. One persistent rumor was that Mark Martin, who seemed pale and gaunt, would be dropped by Jack Roush because he was dying of cancer. (He just had a cold.)

Some grew out of poorly concealed feuds between drivers and crew chiefs, like John Andretti and Tim Brewer. Pairing Andretti, a jockey-size computer nerd, with the rough-and-tumble crew chief was a recipe for disaster anyway, and the two had all but stopped talking.

Some wasn't concealed at all. After exploding in Charlotte, Felix Sabates rolled a car into Dover that was painted black, a dead-on copy of Earnhardt's car. He ordered the paint job without telling Kyle, leaving Petty to deal with scores of reporters who eagerly waited for him to fan the flames. Kyle, totally unprepared, wound up complaining about Sabates more than NASCAR, creating new (and ultimately true) talk that they would break up after eight years.

And some was old-fashioned peering-over-the-neighbor's-fence chatter. One of the juicier bits involved Ken Schrader's wife, who was reputed to have taken a Louisville Slugger to her husband's race car during a marital spat.

That's why the phone call a month earlier, on April 22, had jangled Brett's nerves. It came from the same Lowe's executive with whom he'd hatched the plan to muscle Junior aside the summer before. He was so cool and distant that every time he said "Have a good race," he made it sound like an ultimatum. The crew called him Tin Man.

Brett gave up looking for steady driving work to buy this team. The thought that it now might unravel made him nauseous. Surely Lowe's understood that the season had barely started. All he needed was some time.

Surely they . . . *How come they never followed up their promise to paint my race shop in Lowe's yellow and blue colors?*

Surely they . . . *Why hasn't anyone from Lowe's stopped by all season when their office is only an hour away?**

Surely they . . . *Now that you mention it, they've avoided making a single future plan with us.*

Brett was determined not to panic. He wouldn't put it past people to start rumors just so they could become self-fulfilling prophecies. He'd just call the chairman of Lowe's, Bob Tillman, and get it all straightened out.

Brett had met Tillman a couple of times during the 1995 season at luncheons in Junior's shop—precisely the kind of get-togethers Lowe's wasn't having with him. Brett was always gracious and could think of nothing he did to

---

*The executive they called Tin Man insists that he took a full tour, but on a day Brett was not present.

offend the man. But when he placed the call to Tillman, the CEO never called back. Instead, Brett was left to meet Tin Man at a Shoney's restaurant in Statesville. Brett looked nervous and had brought his briefcase, which Tin Man took to mean he knew what was coming. So he got right to the point. "We're eight races into the season, Brett, and frankly we're just not seeing any positives. We have until July to decide whether to renew our contract with you in 1997, but I'm telling you now to be up front, we're looking around."

The news stung Brett even though he'd braced himself to hear it. So after they talked some more, he let his pride put a period on the morning. "If you're going to make a change, make sure you get someone much, much better," he said. "Otherwise, I'm gonna pass you."

Brett wasn't the first Bodine to lose a sponsor. He'd watched Geoff lose Exide batteries just six months before. It was inevitable, frankly, and had its roots in the 1994 Winston Cup dinner.

Geoff, still at the height of his brooding over the divorce, went through a midlife change. He'd begun dating, most notably country music star Tanya Tucker, and decided to place an earring in his left ear. In a sport where people still think Armani sounds dangerously anti-American (men's fashion stops somewhere around Van Heusen), this was looked upon dimly. When the chairman of Exide batteries saw the new Geoff, he was said to have remarked, "I'll live with the beard, but the earring has to go."

As Cal Lawson, Geoff's ex-manager, remembers it: "Geoff was nuts. The next thing I know he's added a second earring. After that, the writing was on the wall. Exide's people weren't even speaking to him by the end of 'ninety-five, and our contract was so incentive-based that when we didn't do well, the money got tight. It wasn't a shock when they left."

Watching from afar, Brett just shook his head. The sign on the parts supply truck that Banjo Matthews brought to the track each week said it all: "Where money buys speed." If you want to buy speed, then you have to do what it takes to get the money. Junior Johnson saw that happening, and got out before it ate him up inside. But Geoff always left the business side to his wife Kathy. When she left, he was a race car driver in the rough.

The unraveling of Geoff's operation proved instructive for the younger brother. The idea of wearing earrings, let alone taunting a sponsor, was so anathema to Brett's makeup that any object lessons that part of the soap opera presented couldn't have been less relevant. But there were business lessons to learn. For one, a rookie owner needed the security of knowing his every race wasn't going to be scrutinized. That meant a three-year deal, nothing less. And because money buys speed, he couldn't afford an incentive-based package, a starter deal that paid a base of $2 million. He needed a $5 million package, guaranteed.

"I believed everything I read about NASCAR," Brett says. "I figured, 'Hey, this thing is booming. I'll put an un-baited hook in the water and we'll have to fight 'em off.' "

Where to turn first? At its heart, NASCAR is just one big collective of deals spinning around one another like planets in orbit. And figuring out who really knows their way around can be a dizzying exercise. A half-dozen companies do the lion's share of the deals. Everyone else is someone's ex-wife or brother-in-law claiming to have influence they don't really have.

"I get people calling me all the time," says David Blair, an Arkansas trial attorney who bought another of Junior's teams in the winter of 1995 and raced without a sponsor through the 1997 season, spending well over $1 million as a result of bad advice.

"There have to be a hundred guys running around trying to get that one lick, make that one big deal so they can retire on $500,000. They're teeming like ants. It's a very ill-defined business. I'm still not exactly sure what these people do."*

Knowing that he was racing to find a new sponsor, Brett reached deep inside himself on that Friday, May 31, morning and drove with abandon, almost losing his Ford in the corners as it circled the track in 23.5 seconds. It was enough to get him an eleventh-place start, his best of the year, and after the garage closed for the day, he and his wife Diane walked out through the grassy infield, up a glass-enclosed walkway that rises over the backstretch and leads out of the track, and to the pink arches that led them into the casino.

What Diane wanted for her husband was a return to their glory years, but on their terms. So, no, it wouldn't be right to say she was tingling from the thrill of Brett starting six rows back. But she was looking for signs that they were making it to the next level—and this was a good one. Seeking some distraction, she gathered up a chair and started feeding a slot machine to get her mind off racing. Of all the ones available, she chose the one called Lucky Lady.

As it turned out, Brett's race on Sunday was anything but. In the early going, Brett's Ford proved stout. Forty miles into the race, he was in eighteenth place, and he'd be

*Making things murkier, NASCAR, the umbrella organization in whose name all this happens, is also a player in the game. Just as these owners need sponsors for their teams, NASCAR hunts them to sponsor its races, events, and promotions.

there 140 laps later. Then one of his tires didn't get bolted snugly enough on a pit stop and he had to stop to fix it, going a lap down. Along the way, Donnie Richeson was growing puzzled by the fuel mileage readings. One set of numbers suggested a full tank would last seventy-eight laps; another showed ninety-nine. Unable to explain why, Donnie split the difference conservatively, telling Brett their tank was good for eighty-six laps. The Lowe's Ford started sputtering at eighty-four.

Clawing for what position he could in the next stretch, Brett complained "the back jumps out on the bumps." Gambling, Donnie decided to call him onto pit road before everyone else for the last stop of the day. He'd fix the back end, fill the tank, and send his driver out with plenty of fuel so when the others dove in for their last pits, Brett could stay out, winning his lap back and perhaps salvaging a top-twenty finish.

But just as he dropped into the box, Dale Jarrett plowed into the third-turn wall, drawing a yellow flag. There's no worse feeling than being caught on pit road when a caution hits, especially when the speed limit is 35 mph and you can't get out before the leader passes the start/finish line and you get lapped. Donnie gambled to erase a one-lap deficit. Instead he'd added to it. He let all his weight drop to his knees as he slumped by the tool rig.

What could get worse? He found out when a spring in the motor broke, killing the valve and making Brett run in a kind of no-man's-land with seven cylinders for the last hundred laps. He ended the day ten laps down.

It was a miserable Brett who went back to his hotel that night, and his brother-in-law wasn't much happier. Donnie kept his temper in check as he loaded the hauler and sent his men on their way home. Then he got into his rental van and hit the dashboard so hard he cracked the windshield.

The next morning, Brett hopped a short flight to Philadelphia and cabbed his way to an unremarkable five-story red warehouse on Thirty-second Street and Allegheny Avenue, the headquarters of the Pep Boys auto parts company, where he was scheduled to make his first official pitch.

"We're not a flashy company," the man from Pep Boys started.

Wondering if he'd made the right choice by wearing a stylish Banana Republic black suit, Brett answered, "And I'm not a flashy driver."

"So what's wrong? Why aren't you finishing better?" the man from Pep Boys asked. Brett launched into the litany. He wasn't ready for the season. He'd started late. The cars weren't uniform. His engine program wasn't up to par. "But let me tell you," he said, unveiling the line he would use so many times in the coming months. "This is my investment in a sport that's all my family has ever known."

Flying back home to Charlotte, Brett wondered if they'd read the story about him, the one in *Stock Car Racing* magazine that had said, "Today, one good run in a Busch car makes you a hot young name. Such is the power of television. Brett had won more Busch Series races than Jeff Gordon, Joe Nemechek, David Green, Ricky Craven, and the Burton brothers. But he did it when the only way to watch those races was to buy a ticket." Probably not. Sponsors had to be brought along slowly. They had to say no a few times before they said yes. Brett thought he had probably just laid the groundwork for someone else. Now he had to find a place where the groundwork had been laid for him.

It was June 3. The Olympics were about to begin, and most corporations wouldn't start finalizing their plans until September. He still had a long summer to go.

9

THE LONGEST MILE

Daytona: July 2–6

The early-evening light streamed through cracks in the garage bay doors and bounced off the concrete, bathing the purple Prodigy cars in a soft underglow. A half dozen of them lay in various states of undress, but the two that most mattered were already loaded like luggage inside the old hauler parked on the gravel outside. Dave Marcis shut the lights, locked the doors, and gave them a halfhearted endorsement on the way out.

"Nothin' much more we can do now," he said. In twelve hours they'd be heading to Daytona.

Flinging his Goodyear cap into the back of a mint '77 Caddy, he peeled out in a cloud of dust and rock salt, onto the tree-canopied roads that took him past his old garage—the one he rented for seventy-five dollars a month, with a sliding wood door that was heavier than cast iron when it rained, and with a wood-burning fireplace he used to have to wake up in the middle of the night to stoke if he wanted to work in the winter. Past the high school where he sent his two kids. By the twelve-by-fifty trailer he'd brought all the way from Wisconsin in a borrowed truck and lived in until he put those two kids through college. And to the mountain hideaway he'd recently built to retire into—a warm, secluded place where he could look out from his bedroom and see deer roaming contentedly.

It was Tuesday, steamed vegetable night, and *Wheel of*

Fortune was on the television. He pulled a frosted mug from his refrigerator just as an overweight woman from Ohio was winning a Hawaiian vacation.

"Helen, when was the last time we went on vacation?" he asked.

"You mean, besides going back to Wisconsin?"

"Yeah."

"We've *never* really had one, I don't think, Dave."

He picked up the *Winston Cup Scene* newspaper from his coffee table. The cover story was all about him. He glanced at the headline copy beside his photo. It read: *A mix of loyalty, friendship, perseverance, and hard work has brought Dave Marcis, the last of the independents, to his milestone 800th start.* "I wonder if Bill France appreciates that," he said. France could be a poker-faced figure, but Dave knew he read the sport's weekly bible, and was probably just now seeing the story.

"You know, us working eighteen hours a day, including holidays. Living in a trailer. Spending all our money to get to the next race." Helen arrayed the dinner dishes as he spoke: creamed potatoes, steamed vegetables, and cooked apples. The steam led him to the table. "All that kinda shit." Digging in, he said, "I don't think he understands the money. I've done more with less than any son of a bitch who's ever been here. And I'm the only one who's survived." On *Wheel of Fortune*, Pat Sajak was putting a lei on the overweight woman. "All our lives, we've done nothing but put back into it, put back into it."

"I know, Dave," Helen said.

"And for what? So we have a nice home. Big deal. We've had to wait for twenty-six years." He'd worked himself up, and let out a small belch, which seemed to distract him, though not for long. "That, after a lifetime of giving to the sport."

Dave had been thinking more along these lines as the

things he used to do weren't working anymore. He seemed more gaunt than he should have, and his eyes were starting to dance around distractedly. He always had faith in his ability to gut things out at the last second, but even that seemed to be going away on him.

Like in Dover. He drove too low in the second turn during his first qualifying lap, catching his wheels slightly in a trough, setting himself back yet again. In the garage, he looked into his engine as if it were the mouth of a muddy well. "I gotta find a tenth of a second in here somewhere," he said. But racking his brains through the next morning's practice, Dave managed to find only half that. As requalifying crept up, he looked into the engine again, waiting for it to talk to him. A piece of paper taped to the side of the fire-red NASCAR trailer announced that of twenty drivers who hadn't already won starting spots, six were exercising their option of trying again. Dammit, what should he do? Stand pat or take her out again?

"Do you have a tenth of a second in you, baby?" he whispered under his breath. It must have answered him, for Dave emerged from the hood moments later. "We don't got it," he said with surprising surety. "Put the race engine in. We ain't goin' out."

His crew chief, Terry Shirley, raised an eyebrow. "You sure, Dave?" Terry didn't think all six challengers would beat Dave's 23.827-second time and send him over the ledge into thirty-ninth place. But you never knew. After lunch, the crew huddled around the laptop in their hauler, watching each of the six times flash on their screen: 23.681, then 712, 740, 637, and 685. Brian Simons of Prodigy was there, and said, "I think I'm going to be sick." Dave was now in thirty-eighth place, the last spot guaranteeing a start.

It came down to Wally Dallenbach. Having grown up in Aspen, the thirty-two-year-old never entirely fit into the

NASCAR world. While his peers would be boating by their docks along Lake Norman, he'd be in Africa big-game hunting. He was one of the sport's best road-course racers, but his lackluster showing on the ovals led to nicknames like Wally Fallenback. Certainly he hadn't shown much on that hot Delaware afternoon. "Come on . . . come on," Dave said, sounding like one of the desperate gamblers in Dover's mirrored casino. Dallenbach hit the twenty-three-second mark on his exit from the fourth turn. By the start/finish line a sensor buried beneath the track waited to pick up a pulse from a transponder in his car. The pulse arrived .757ths of a second later.

Dave had been beaten by nine-hundredths of a second.

One by one each member of the crew walked out. Dave was left alone to wonder whether he couldn't somehow have found another tenth of a second from that qualifying engine. One good wind gust would have done it. A lucky twitch on a steering finger. Even a bit of cloud cover to produce a few degrees of cool on the track. He looked tired and, with tufts of white hair spilling out of his canvas jumpsuit, considerably older than his fifty-five years. In a small voice he said, "I don't know what to do. Now we're out of provisionals. Every race it's somethin'. It's never been this bad." Then he looked out from his hauler at all the people milling about. "I just don't got good people. That's the problem. Hell, I'm doin' it all myself. I can't baby-sit everyone."

He pressed his thumbs deep into his eyes with his reading glasses on his forehead. He didn't know that his crew chief was standing outside, listening.

At one time or another everyone who starts out seeing Dave Marcis as a true working-class hero comes to wonder if he's been out there alone for too long. They see a stubborn streak that's kept him from surrendering the steering wheel, from moving on to other things. To a new and richer life. As each year gets worse, those who care most about him get their hearts broken.

All week after Dover, Terry Shirley, Dave's crew chief, thought about quitting. The pale-eyed forty-six-year-old from Indiana had wanted to taste the big league of racing, and where better than Marcis Auto Racing, the Sam's Club of stock. NASCAR is a sport of ordinary people, not college stars or small-town phenoms. NASCAR is your local mechanic, box cutter, or delivery boy who finds a place as a tire specialist, gas guy, or truck driver, and is suddenly transformed by the uniform, the crowds, the life. Terry was no different. One moment he was in Seymour, investing the money he'd made from selling his gas stations and running a minor league race team. The next moment he was working the largest tracks in the country, the conductor of a weekly theater of chaos. He hadn't made so little money in twenty years, and he didn't care. It didn't matter to a man who was living a dream.

When Dave missed the races in Bristol and Wilkesboro, Terry took it personally, and told him, "I'm sorry I let you down." But after the overheard remark, traces of resentment started entering their relationship. "That tenth we got beat by in Dover? We had that in our qualifying motor," Terry said irritably. "If Dave didn't take it out, we'd have made that race."

In the Pocono Mountains, where the June breezes brought out weekend golfers in droves, Dave seemed to be second-guessing everything, fighting invisible enemies. He looked spooked, particularly when he started arguing with the computer. The readout claimed he posted the thirtieth-fastest speed, with a lap in 54.5 seconds. "No!" Dave screamed in a way that was startling. "We ran a three!" Then, huffing, he threw a shock absorber into a clamp on the wall and vented his frustrations by cranking the vise.

The pressure played on him behind the wheel. He entered the first turn on his qualifying lap too deeply, cheating himself of crucial speed on the exit. When he heard his time, he was almost defiant. "Now, I can't believe that," he said, as if challenging the lap to come back to fight him. "I had a hell of a lap, a hell of a lap."

Afterward, he watched the lady in the panama hat, who charts the finishes on the NASCAR tote board, move his wood slat from the twenty-sixth to the thirty-eighth slot. She was a friend of Helen's and gave Dave an understanding nod. Then a cheer went up from the grandstands, something like thunder. Jeff Gordon had just won his second consecutive pole. Dozens of TV cameramen and reporters trailed him all the way back to his trailer. Dave had his back to them, and one from TNN hit him in the kidney. "Watch it," he yelled, but the man was already deep into the crowd, trying to get Gordon's sound bite. Dave nursed his side, then walked off alone to his trailer.

The next morning, Terry led Dave to the roof of his hauler. Dale Earnhardt was going at full throttle by the wall, then dropped low into the first turn. "There, see that," Terry said, pointing to a black stripe on the wall where Earnhardt started to turn his wheel for the descent into the first turn. "That's your point."

Dave burned it into his brain, and when he went out and nailed the arc four-square, a wave of quiet relief swept over everyone. "Way to go, Dave," Terry radioed. "You picked up a full second. Do that when it counts and we'll be fine." When Dave climbed into his cockpit for the second-round lap later that morning, Terry watched him take the flag, then started walking back to the trailer, confident. Helen was inside, friends sitting with her, holding her hands. By the time Terry reached her, Helen's reddened face told the story. Dave had gone just 166.03 mph, thirty-ninth fastest.

This time there was no one else to blame. "I don't understand it," Dave was saying when he walked in. "I don't understand what I'm doin'. We had the third-fastest car in practice." No one answered him, because they were too exhausted, or dispirited, to try.

It took a few moments for the news to circulate around the garage. In the pressroom, one reporter looked at the results and said, "If you can't make it thirty-eighth here, you deserve to go home." Mechanics and other drivers poked their heads in Dave's hauler like rubberneckers at an accident, hoping to see fireworks. There weren't any. All they saw was a confused man in a green jumpsuit sitting on a cooler, saying, "I picked out my points. It's that same damn tenth."

Long after Dave had left to drive home with Helen, a fiftyish-year-old man was locking the hauler up tight. He had the weathered, sun-beaten look of someone who dug wells, which is precisely what Terry Beckley did before Dave Marcis plucked him out of nowhere, another ordinary man made special by the show. Beckley's world was a small one, consisting mainly of keeping the hauler running. He kept its old wood cabinets oiled so they wouldn't creak, and the heavy pull-drawers filled with tools. This was no small feat, since it had, by his own reckoning, nearly a million miles on it, a few hundreds of thousands put on by Beckley himself.

With the defeat a few hours old and no way to get the hauler out until the track cleared, Beckley was taking conciliatory handshakes from the other truckers. But his thoughts were with Dave, however far away he was now.

"Dave Marcis is my idol," Beckley said. "Dave's everything I ever wanted to be. It just kills me to see him going through this." He sat on the edge of the hauler and dropped his voice. "But the thing is, he won't listen to nobody. He has to know every second of everyone's day. I'll tell ya, it's gonna get serious. Hell, it already has. He's fifty-five, for Chrissake. He just can't do what he once done. And he keeps taking hard hits. He keeps a lot of it from Mrs. Marcis. In Charlotte, he hit the wall so hard he was limpin' for a week. His whole right side was sore. In Dover, he shouldn't of even been in the car. He should hire a kid like Cale Yarborough did. But you can't talk to him. You just can't get through to that man."

After every NASCAR race, a researcher in Ann Arbor, Michigan, sits before a videotape-editing console with forward and reverse knobs, and records every single logo he sees for four hours. The researcher, working for a firm called Joyce Julius Associates, then totals up how many minutes' worth of logo sightings each sponsor gets, and calculates the sum required to buy that ad time directly. If a sponsor doesn't do better with the car than he could buying airtime directly, the odds are he'll decide it isn't worth being with NASCAR for long. The economics of NASCAR work only so long as sponsors believe they are getting a bargain on television exposure.

Dwayne Leik watched those numbers religiously every week, racking his brains for ways to improve them. Once, on a frigid winter's day, he'd brought hot chocolate to the CBS cameramen high above the track in the hopes they'd train their sights on Dave a few extra times. But this year was a particular challenge. In Dover on June 2, where Dave went out early with a bad shock and finished thirty-first, Prodigy had forty-three seconds of exposure, worth just $70,165 in equivalent ad time. Jeff Gordon had thirty-two *minutes* of exposure, worth $1.9 million.

That's why Michigan was going to be so important. It was a CBS race, where a thirty-second ad cost $65,000—a third more than TNN charged in Dover. With Dave celebrating his 800th start, Dwayne figured his Joyce Julius number would go through the roof.

Seen that way, Dave's failure to make the UAW-GM Teamwork 500 did more than shake his confidence. Without the buildup to his 800th start, Dave had the camera on him for just six seconds in Michigan, netting a paltry $13,000 in equivalent ad time—nearly a hundred grand less than Dwayne hoped. As Brian Simons of Prodigy later said, "I love Dave Marcis. I really do. But from that moment, he was dead with us."

Daytona in July is an awful place. It's humid, and hot, and your clothes stick to you. And after the high-stakes Daytona 500, it doesn't seem to have the same magnificence, which may explain why Dale Earnhardt has won the July race twice, but never the season opener in February.

This time, though, it was decked out for the opening of the France family's much-anticipated $18 million interactive museum. It was the brainchild of Lesa France Kennedy, Bill Jr.'s daughter, who was considered the most forward-thinking France. This was, in effect, her coming-out party, and her father wanted all drivers there at six o'clock sharp in black tie.

Daytona USA was loud, boisterous, and, with its fifteen-foot-high STP balloons and a life-size museum exhibit of Bill France Sr.'s old gas station, the kind of self-congratulatory kitsch that proved that anything could be deified if placed in the right hands. Dave Marcis felt strange seeing the world he'd known since 1968 suddenly reduced to wax sculptures and newsreel films. Although Dave wasn't as prominent as Darrell Waltrip or Richard Petty—the truth be told, he was scarcely to be found at all—he knew that the weekend's celebration of history guaranteed that attention would be paid to the record he'd set tomorrow. That's what he was thinking as he sat in the museum's small theater watching grainy films that could well have been his home movies. It's what he was thinking the next morning when he flipped the ignition switch to bring Richard Childress's engine to life. It's what he was thinking as he headed into turn one for his qualifying lap. And it's what he was thinking when, all of a sudden, the oil pressure gauge went into a free fall.

Before he was even out of turn two, Dave shut the motor down to keep it from blowing and radioed, "It's the oil pump, Terry. Dammit! The son of a bitch busted before we could even get in our lap."

Childress was waiting, stunned and incredulous, as the Monte Carlo got towed back to its bay. The Thursday black tie gala combined with a sudden downpour threw everything off. Both days of qualifying had to be crammed into one—now they barely had two hours to get a new engine for the second round. Dave ran over to the NASCAR trailer, where the radar screen was projecting the weather for miles around. It was covered by a mass of green patches, showing a fast-approaching rain. If the sky didn't hold out, it wouldn't matter whether they got the engine in or not. The second round would be washed away, making the celebratory "800th start" paint job on his car a cruel tease.

Two dozen mechanics swarmed around the Seventy-one, drawing an audience for the dramatic emergency surgery. As the clock ticked down, they looked as if they might just make it. Then a NASCAR inspector threw them a curve. They did know, didn't they, that the rules required the new engine had to be inspected?

Dave dropped to his knees. There wasn't time for that.

"Forget it," Childress said, suddenly throwing up his hand. "Get Dale's engine. It's already been through inspection." Earnhardt had just qualified seventh. Now things were going to get interesting.

Dave waited out the transfer in his hauler. With some

time to kill, he'd taken out his hearing aid and, as a result, couldn't hear the loudspeaker call him when the time came to requalify. His crew went into a panic. Where was he? Simons found him reading an auto paper. "Come on, we gotta go," he panted, literally pulling Dave off his feet to start the mile walk down pit road. Above them, the skies looked ready to burst at any moment. As they got close, Dave noticed the fans in the grandstands were rising to their feet. He looked around, wondering what they were clapping for. Then it struck him. He was the only driver going out for second-round qualifying, the only driver taking that mile-long walk.

It struck him that they were cheering for him.

"I don't know how to put it into words," he'd say about what friends would later call The Walk. "It's moments like those that make you think the working people understand your struggles."

And then Dave Marcis ripped a 186-mph qualifying lap that was a mere five-hundredths of a second off Dale Earnhardt's pace. The oldest racer in the sport showed he could still run with a NASCAR points leader.

10

"JESUS CHRIST, HE'S DEAD"

Pocono to Pocono: June 16 to July 21

Bobby Hamilton allowed himself a moment of satisfaction as he looked out the window of his small Cessna over the green treetops of the Pocono Mountains. Five laps from the end of the race he'd just finished, Bobby was in sixth place, behind Morgan Shepherd. Pocono's best passing is done off the exit of a third turn that feeds onto a very long and wide front stretch, so Bobby had gone for the high pass there. Shepherd blocked him. Bobby tried again. Shepherd closed him off once more. The third time around the track, Shepherd's spotter said, "He's up there again." *Not yet,* Bobby thought. *Not yet.* Then, just as Shepherd jerked his Ford right to stop the outside challenge, Bobby threw his car left, jammed the shifter into fourth, and spilled low onto the straightaway past the cursing veteran.

Changing clothes in the back of his hauler, Robbie Loomis looked at him sideways and asked, "You set Morgan up, didn't you?" Peeling off his red, white, and blue jumpsuit, Bobby replied, "You bet your ass I did."

Bobby knew that even after a bang-up '95 season and his near win in Rockingham, Petty still had doubts about his ability to win. Which is why, despite being twelfth in the point standings, he was among the lowest-paid drivers in the Winston Cup. Pontiac claimed that his team was its flagship, but behind the scenes Gary Claudio was throwing all sorts of money at Joe Gibbs to entice his driver, Bobby Labonte, into a Grand Prix. Heading back to Nashville, Hamilton put them all out of his mind and thought instead about his crew. If a driver like him was going to make it, he had to make those men share his hunger.

"Look at me," he said, inviting a kind of naked, clinical observation. He held up his right arm, then winced when the cartilage in the elbow creaked. "I got this from a wreck a dozen years ago." He pointed to his left foot, where a hairline fracture runs through his ankle like a fault. "I can't play basketball, can't hardly run." His right knee is a trick one and occasionally pops out of its socket. He has a respiratory disease that causes him to forget to breathe at night and wake up choking. "I'm torn up. I'm all broken. And I ain't got no money, 'cause I've given it all away. I just don't got a lot of time left to make a future."

There was something about each of these scars that made the men around him believe that he'd give his damn life to run what they gave him. Why wouldn't he? He had no other life. And it wasn't just the road crew that felt that way, but the men back in the shop in Level Cross, North Carolina—men like Lenny Ball, an artisan who arrives at the white plank barn on Branson Mill Road every morning and, like a sculptor, spends hours kneading sheet metal over a fabricator's wheel to produce the race car's fabric-thin skin. He rarely visits a racetrack. Instead he waves good-bye to the road crew when it leaves in its chartered plane, and watches the race at home.

Ball says, "People like me, we don't get no credit. Not that we want a lot. The guys who go out on the road, yeah, they work hard and all. I ain't taking nothin' away from them. But they get to see the crowds, be part of it all. What do we get? 'Round here, lot of times, no one even says thank you." Bobby Hamilton understood such feelings. His words, like his driving, tend toward precision as he says, "I don't have but a handful of people who ever done for me."

After his grandfather's death, Bobby moved to Little Green Street, an invisible vein in the badlands of downtown Nashville where drugs are rampant and the police are frequent visitors. Literally a dead-end street, it's anchored at one end by a pawnshop and at the other by a junkyard in front of Martin's Wrecking Service. He lived in an old wood-frame home in the shadow of a billboard that jutted over the interstate. In the morning, he'd have his coffee, watching the commuters head downtown. Then he'd go to work at Martin's, towing the people he had just watched.

Now, at thirty-nine, he'd made enough from racing to buy a pleasant A-frame twenty miles away on a road dotted by modest farms that have brick gates and faux gas lamps. But in his mind he'd never truly left Little Green Street.

If his father, Bud, wasn't asking for money for medical bills (before he died), then his mother was pleading for grocery money that Bobby knew would be used to get intoxicated. The more famous he became, the more embarrassed his friends were to report back that she arrived at their homes in a stupor. His sisters were both wild, too. Put simply, Bobby had a past, and NASCAR doesn't like pasts. So he buried it. But not the hunger his past gave him.

"My dad had a black box that he wouldn't ever let go of. He had maybe four hundred dollars in it. He'd been so long with nothing, he thought it was a ton of money. If he hadn't had us, what would he have had? That's kinda how I feel about this crew. I ain't rich. But I told them, 'This is where I'm making my home.' And for a bunch of guys who hadn't had much to feel good about, that's been a kind of glue."

Robbie Loomis also wasn't a new face. Single and youthful, this son of a pool salesman from Orlando came to Petty Enterprises as a mechanic after its glory days were done. He was without a win, or even a pole, to his credit. As a result, he lacked the gravitas of the men a few years older whom he was in his own personal race to catch. Men like Andy Petree, who parlayed two championship seasons with Earnhardt into ownership of his own team, or Tony Glover, the diminutive poker player who had an uncanny knack for winning at Daytona and Talladega. They looked tough in the trenches, and decisive. Yes. That's what Loomis noticed. How they never seemed to doubt themselves. Robbie could still flush when he made a mistake, a sign he still had a ways to go.

Qualifying was a particular sore. It meant he didn't have all the pieces of his program nailed down. The engines had been spotty, and Bobby was starting to burn about always having to race from back to front. So Robbie leaned on his taciturn engine builder, Rick Mann, whose cropped beard and ordered appearance suggest a man tailor-made for such work. Mann had been tinkering with different changes over the prior months, and he dumped all of them into the motor for Michigan. Putting it on the dynamometer for testing, he could instantly see it took the changes well. He walked over to Loomis, who was toying with the engine they'd already installed, and said with a terse, staccato delivery, "This here's the one we need to be racin'." Robbie conveyed Mann's confidence to Bobby, who decided to push MIS's limits during Friday's qualifying.

Twenty-five thousand people turned out at the gargantuan asphalt oval forty miles out of Ann Arbor on Friday, June 21. The show, so far, was a good one. Derrike Cope was on top. But most of the stars, including Jeff Gordon, who was coming off three straight pole wins, had yet to go. After a warm-up lap at MIS, you hit the front stretch—a smooth, repaved rocket launcher—going 199. At that clip, the wall might as well be the Earth seen from the cockpit of a 747 dropping nose first out of the sky. Reflexes become abstractions, depth perception a mere guess.

Going into turn one, Bobby didn't even touch the brake. Keeping the Grand Prix in fourth, he feathered off the throttle for a second. The g forces pressed on his neck, but he resisted them, keeping his head straight up as he came through the second turn where the 2,242-foot backstretch opened before him. Bobby tested Mann's engine and it flung him decisively down the long flat. With so much power, the idea of going into the third turn wide open was seductive, but Bobby knew its pitfalls. The banking is so gradual, more than one rookie has been seduced into plowing into it, only to realize he's overshot his turning mark, causing him to brake and kill his momentum. Knowing what was coming, Bobby swallowed hard and lifted off the throttle just a touch as he went into a precision arc at 190 mph. In the heart of the turn, with terrific momentum, he kept his wheels low and waited for the exit out of the fourth turn to come to him.

This was where Mann was going to have to earn his money, down the fastest front stretch in racing. As the pistons fired, Bobby went WFO, flinging himself to the finish line. His heart was pounding so hard, it was all he could hear when the flag fell. Not Mann's engine. Not the wind. Not even the rumbling chant that was coming off the grandstands. Not until he saw 25,000 fans rising to their feet did he realize he'd run the fastest time. Robbie ran to the car, tore off the netting like a child unwrapping a wonderful gift, and said, "You smoked that, buddy."

Bobby knew he'd won the pole when, waiting out the rest of the runs behind the closed door of his hauler's lounge, he heard the stomping feet of his crew watching from the roof above. Back in Level Cross, the eight men in the engine shop listening to the qualifying on the radio let out a loud cheer, but Bobby felt neither euphoria nor depression. It was more like "It's about damn time."

Then something happened to remind everyone that NASCAR doesn't have rules so much as contractual obligations.

Anheuser-Busch sponsors a made-for-TV all-star race in Daytona called the Busch Clash,* which is composed of all the prior year's pole winners. To get into it, a driver must meet one prerequisite—his car must have a Busch decal. But churchgoing Martha Petty disapproved of alcohol since before Lee's moonshining days, and wouldn't let her son advertise beer. Busch's response was, thank you very much, we understand—but we're not giving you a dime. It meant that Bobby couldn't run in the Clash, where the lowest-place finisher would get $10,000, and he couldn't collect $5,000 bonus check for winning the pole.

Bobby downplayed his pique before the press. "If I was in it for money," he sighed, "I wouldn't be here anyway."

The next day he discovered something even more irritating than NASCAR politics: fame. No longer free to slip between his hauler and car like an everyman, Bobby got backed into corners and badgered for autographs. He became so ill-tempered, he actually fed Pontiac's press flack a quote for its daily press notes that read, "It bugs me when you're working on your car and people are in your window, standing 'round your pit stall." But the worst part of the day didn't come until its end, when a poor practice had Bobby convinced he wouldn't lead a single lap.

Driving to his hotel, he noticed a brown van shading him down dirt roads and the highway. Irked, he pulled into the parking lot of a Bob's Big Boy, leaving the van to shoot past him. "Could you put me in the back? I'm kinda

*In 1998, it was renamed the Bud Shootout.

trying to get away from people," he told a waitress. But no sooner had he ducked into a booth than the wide-bottomed, red-haired woman in a doily apron excitedly pointed him out to the very fans who'd followed him inside.

As Bobby got up and walked past them, glowering, one said, "Hey, you know your attitude really sucks."

Yes it did. And it didn't improve Sunday in Michigan, when he quickly fell off the lead and had to scramble to end the day in fifteenth place.

Robbie Loomis also wasn't glowing. But as he packed his bags, he tried to erase the day from his mind. He needed a clear head, because for the next three days they'd be testing in Indianapolis, getting ready for the richest race of the year.

From the outside, the Indianapolis Motor Speedway looks like an old-time ballpark, with steel supports casting shadows over the single-family homes that seal it in a suburban envelope. Inside, it's an oasis of greenery. A four-hole golf course covers its interior, a park tucked in the middle of a racetrack, which is in turn tucked in the middle of a city. Lest anyone get confused about where they are, the Hall of Fame museum at the mouth of the entrance announces that this is the "Racing Capital of the World."

The shrine of IndyCar racing didn't open itself up to NASCAR until 1994, but the Brickyard 400 became an instant sensation. Two hundred fifty television crews turned out to watch transplanted Hoosier Jeff Gordon take the checkered flag after Ernie Irvan cut a tire dueling for the lead with five laps to go. The legend of the storybook win grew when rumors started circulating that NASCAR rigged it by letting Gordon run an illegally light car. He hotly denied the charge.

All this intrigue merely added to the feeling that there

was much about this track that remained a mystery to stock car racers. That's where the black box recorder, also known as the Pi Data Acquisition System, came in. Robbie spent the early morning fastening it to the tray beside Bobby Hamilton's seat and running sensor cables through the penny-size hole in the black box to the motor. With each lap, the PDAS would record rpm's, speed, shock wear, temperatures. On Bobby's return, Robbie downloaded its memory into his laptop and then sent his driver out for more.

By Wednesday afternoon Bobby was exhausted. "Never mind five weeks. I'd be happy if I didn't come back here for five years," he said, ready to go home. Robbie was ready to let him. He just needed Bobby to run one last series to confirm how far they could go on a tank.

"Okay, run smooth now, driver," he said, making sure Bobby's head was still in it. "These are important."

Bobby knew the drill. Indy's corners are like giraffe necks, long and narrow, so you have to go deep into them, then turn sharply to come out in the center. Once you get there you can throttle down, since the turns have mini-straightaways, known as short chutes, inside them. The trick is directing the exit speed. If the car's pointing the wrong way, there isn't any banking to help carry it around.

The payoff of getting through the corners is Indy's straightaways. They're long, wide, and flat. At 200 mph, it's even possible to relax as you barrel down them. Passing the lap leader board—which rises like a sky-scraper over the start/finish line—Bobby let his thoughts drift to his nineteen-year-old son, and the test that the young racer who was trying to follow in his footsteps would be running in Nashville that weekend.

Most of the crew had already started back to the hauler. Robbie, Petty, and Mann, their engine builder, were in the grandstands waiting to see Bobby speeding out of turn four towards them.

With the backstretch now in his rearview mirror, Bobby went into the turn hard, the car pressing on the edges of its right tires, and used the throttle in the short chute. Then he felt something. It was the right front tire. Somehow, he'd cut it. It was losing pressure fast. He hit the brakes, but he was still going 140 mph. With no banking to throw him safely out of the fourth turn, he threw his head back and braced for impact.

As Bernie McCalister, then the Petty chassis man, remembers, "I was halfway to the hauler, and I heard the sound you never want to hear. There's only one way metal hitting head-on at that speed sounds. Like a bomb. I'd never seen a car wreck so bad. It took me a second before I could make it out as ours. I turned to Murph and I said, 'Jesus Christ, Murph. He's dead.'"

Mann remembers staring at Petty and Loomis, as if to say, *Did we just see what we think we saw?* "We were a mile away, but you could tell Bobby was knocked out because there was no smoke from the brakes. He wasn't even trying to control the car. He was like a rag doll riding inside."

The car hit so massively, it warped the dashboard. The roll bars by the motor caved in enough to poke holes in the valve covers. The transmission twisted. The front end was crushed into a V, no more than ten inches wide at its tip. The flaming undercarriage dug troughs in the track an inch deep.

Paramedics swarmed over the car. "Careful, now."

"Is he breathing?"

"Yeah, he's breathing."

"How about the roof? Do we need to cut?"

Bobby heard the words. But he couldn't open his eyes. Everything was black. He had a hard time breathing. That's when he thought, *Damn, I'm gonna die sitting in here.*

But fifteen minutes later he was emerging from the car on his own power. His chest was crimson red from where the shoulder straps burned into his skin, his face was ashen, and deep green bruises were starting to emerge around his face.

"I sure hit a ton," he said, laughing weakly.

"I'll tell you something," McCalister said much, much later. "That Bobby Hamilton's one tough son of a bitch."

From Florida on July Fourth weekend, the Winston Cup tour traveled up the East Coast to New Hampshire on Friday, July 12. By this point in the season, crews have to look at their plane tickets to remember where they are. But New Hampshire? There's nothing like a New England accent to set a redneck on edge. And Dale Inman was on edge.

Bobby reminded Inman why he still loved racing. Central casting's idea of a gruff-but-lovable old-timer, Inman had as much to do with Petty's success as anyone, but the two had drifted apart. Ever since Dale left Richard in 1981 to find an identity outside of Petty Enterprises (he went on to win the championship with Terry Labonte in 1984), things hadn't been the same. He came back in 1986, but by then Richard's glory years were behind him, and a long, fallow period for Inman began.

The silver-haired teacher began ceding day-to-day control over the cars to Robbie Loomis, and in a perfect metaphorical alignment for an éminence gris, took over the job as team spotter. Richard's last years and the parade of faces who replaced him as team driver hardly fulfilled a man who'd engineered more than two hundred wins. Then Hamilton arrived. He was a classic racer who just needed to be smoothed around the edges; and he was hungry enough to want to learn. After a year, Inman and Hamilton had become close friends. Inman never corrected the impression that this was Loomis's team. But when Robbie

briefly entertained the idea of taking a job elsewhere, Dale
and Bobby privately agreed that if it ever came to it, they
could go on alone.

Inman also knew something about drivers and crashes,
principally that drivers don't always show the effects right
away. So after Michigan, he'd called Bobby at home several times, and each time Bobby insisted he was fine. A
sixteenth-place finish in the Pepsi 400 in Daytona suggested he was right. But Inman still harbored doubts.

Friday afternoon's qualifying went a long way toward
erasing those doubts. Bobby blistered the track with a near-
record-setting lap. For the second time in three races, he
flew under the flag to see fans cheering for his first-place
finish. But this time the speed didn't hold up. Ricky Craven,
a New Hampshire native, bested it. Still, on Sunday the two
cars were starting side by side on the front row.

Outside the track, the woods were filled with campers,
and the air was thick with the steam of grills cooking steak
and eggs. A bare-chested man with a belly-length beard
sat by a sign that read, "Barber Wanted. Inquire Within."
Prospects were no doubt scared away by his buddy in the
front seat of their camper, who was crushing empty beer
cans on his forehead. About the only thing suggesting this
was New England was the infestation of mosquitoes that
followed Hurricane Bertha, which had forced the cancellation of practice the day before.

While fans were still streaming in, Bobby and Dale
walked the track together, alone. "I gotta take the lead
right there," Bobby said, pointing to the outside of the
rain-fresh front straight. Because the rain had washed
away the remnants of the prior days' practices, no rubber
was on the track, leaving the tires with nothing to grip. As
a result, Bobby knew that if he didn't pounce early, the
high groove would be too slippery to work in. And two
hours later the last of Inman's concerns dissolved as

ABOVE: Think of the Daytona 500 as a giant bazaar, stretched out over two weeks so everyone has a chance to jump on the gravy train.
© 1996 Ernest Masche

LEFT: Judge, Jury, and Jesus Christ: Gary Nelson (center), Winston Cup series director, with Mike Helton (left), its competition director, and NASCAR president Bill France Jr. (right).
© 1996 Don Grassman

The Old Man: Bill France Sr. helped start NASCAR, and was its "benevolent dictator" from 1947 until he handed its reigns to his sons in the early '70s.
© AP/Wide World Photos

After a series of B-movies, NASCAR went big-budget with Tom Cruise in *Days of Thunder*. © *Photofest*

The movie predicted the arrival of Cruise look-alike Jeff Gordon. © *AP/Wide World Photos*

Bobby Hamilton, a Nashville short-track driver, got his big break as Cruise's stunt car driver in *Days of Thunder*. He became a "name" driver after the bump with Dale Earnhardt (below) made headlines in February 1996. © *AP/Wide World Photos*

© *Mike Horne*

ABOVE: Junior Johnson with his new wife. "Now I'm just doing things that I like to do, like being with my family and children. The old dedication to racing is pretty much gone." © 1997 Don Grassman

LEFT: Flossie Johnson says that the men who worked at Ingle Hollow "were like our kids. I helped them with their lives and marriages. I guess mine is the only one that really failed in these walls." Courtesy Flossie Johnson

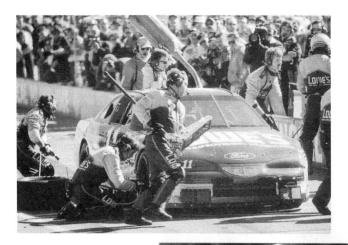

ABOVE: Brett Bodine went from being a driver-for-hire to owner of his own team with the help of the Lowe's company, which sponsored him in 1996. A year later, Lowe's left him. © *1996 Don Grassman*

RIGHT: © *Ernest Masche*

BOTTOM: Brett speaks to his brother Geoff, wearing the uniform of his 1997 sponsor, Close Call. When the owner of Close Call didn't pay his bills, Brett sold half his team to stay afloat. © *AP/Wide World Photos*

Dave Marcis in a treasured 1970s photo: from left, Darrell Waltrip, Dave, David Pearson, Richard Petty, and Cale Yarborough kneeling in front. *Courtesy of Helen Marcis*

© *1996 Ernest Masche*

ABOVE AND RIGHT: Dave in 1996, living and driving "digital" with Prodigy.

© *Dorsey Patrick*

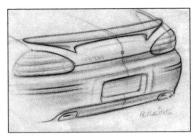

Pontiac's 1996 Grand Prix debuted on the heels of Chevrolet's successful Monte Carlo. But aerodynamic problems with the Grand Prix bedeviled its designers. An artist's rendering of the car's deck lid . . .

. . . and the front end of the production model.
Courtesy D'arcy Masius Benton & Bowles Sketch Courtesy Pontiac-GMC Division

LEFT: Salesman, spy, and seducer: Gary Claudio, an ex–New York cop and Pontiac's Motorsports Manager.
© *Kevin Kane*

ABOVE: Widely considered among the worst wrecks in Talladega history—Ricky Craven flies airborne during the 1996 Winston Select 500. © *AP/Wide World Photos*

LEFT: Rescue workers extricate Craven. Said Jeff Gordon, who initiated the fourteen-car pile up, "I just closed my eyes and kept hearing boom." © *Tom Whitmore*

BELOW: NASCAR's stringent rules regarding cockpit construction saved Craven from a more devastating injury. © *Mike Horne*

ABOVE: Jeff Gordon leads Dale Earnhardt out of turn three at the 1996 DieHard 500 in Talladega. By the time they reach the front stretch, Earnhardt, Sterling Marlin, and Ernie Irvan are inches apart. © 1996 Don Grassman

The ensuing wreck—the aftermath of which can be seen below—was the worst of Earnhardt's career. © 1996 Ernest Masche

Sterling Marlin.
© *AP/Wide World Photos*

Ernie Irvan.
© *Tom Whitmore*

RIGHT: The Allisons circa 1966, when Bobby was building the third most winning stock car record of all time. *Courtesy of Liz Allison*

BELOW: The Allisons in 1988, when Bobby was still at the top of his game. Later that year, Bobby was in a massive wreck. After emerging from a coma with brain damage, he lost his son Clifford in 1992 and Davey in 1993. *Courtesy of Liz Allison*

Davey at home with his daughter Krista. *Courtesy of Liz Allison*

ABOVE: This never-before-seen photograph shows how Gary Batson, an amateur racer, died at the Charlotte Motor Speedway on May 16, 1992. Batson is belted into the car that is pinned vertically against the wall (circled in photo). He was conscious the entire fifty-seven seconds he was on fire.

RIGHT: The Charlotte Motor Speedway. © *1996 Don Grassman*

Humpy Wheeler, right, general manager of the Charlotte Motor Speedway, and Bruton Smith, who built CMS in 1960. His company, Speedway Motorsports, went public in 1995 and is now worth more than a billion dollars.
© 1997 Don Grassman

ABOVE: Presidential candidates since Richard Nixon have sought out Richard Petty during election years. Here, Bob Dole is chauffeured by Petty before 140,000 fans at the Charlotte Motor Speedway. © *AP/Wide World Photos*

MIDDLE: Richard Petty with his wife, Lynda, on his own campaign trail, running for Secretary of State in North Carolina. He lost by eight points. © *AP/Wide World Photos*

BOTTOM: The King with Robbie Loomis (left), crew chief of the Number Forty-three, and Dale Inman (right), Richard's crew chief for most of his 200 wins. © *1996 Ernest Masche*

LEFT: Like a prisoner too long in solitary, Bobby Hamilton started to hear things when he took the lead of the Dura Lube 500. Was that the engine missing? Was there rattling under the dash, or a tire going down? © 1996 Ernest Masche

BELOW: Hamilton in Winston Cup's Victory Lane for the first time on October 27, 1996. © AP/Wide World Photos

ABOVE: As NASCAR's tracks become even larger, North Wilkesboro's brand of short track racing is becoming rarer.
© *AP/Wide World Photos*

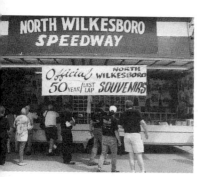

LEFT: In an era in which souvenir sales at large tracks can reach many millions of dollars on a single weekend, North Wilkesboro couldn't keep up as a small, family-run business.
© *AP/Wide World Photos*

BELOW: The Winston Cup drivers at the final race at the North Wilkesboro Speedway on September 29, 1996.
© *1996 Ernest Masche*

Bobby stayed true to his word, sweeping outside of Craven's Monte Carlo to take the lead and stay there for the next twenty-seven laps.

The first pit stop came and went with only six cars electing to stay on the track. Robbie ordered up four tires and a tank of gas, and sent Bobby out to reclaim first. "Whoah, I don't know what they did to that car," TV commentator Buddy Baker said, "but Bobby Hamilton's riding a rocket ship right now."

With his knee up on the infield wall, Robbie agreed. But then he noticed the kind of little thing that tended to chew him up inside. Bobby was starting to fade a bit in turn four. He watched warily as the condition got worse, and then as Geoff Bodine's Ford finally overtook their Pontiac on the exit into the front stretch. Chewing his bottom lip, Robbie diagnosed it as bad tires.

But what to do? He was handed an answer when Dave Marcis spun out just seconds later, drawing a caution. "Okay, Bobby," he radioed, "we're gonna get you some new tires." He said it so decisively,. no one bothered to question the call. But the second Bobby hit pit road, Robbie's stomach sank: The only cars pulling off the track were the six that hadn't pitted earlier. He'd failed to predict that all the others would stay out. Later, chief fabricator Doug Murph would bend down and pretend to take off his shoelaces when asked about that moment. "After that pit stop in New Hampshire," he laughed, "we had to put Robbie on suicide watch."

In the twenty seconds it took them to send him out on new tires, nineteen cars passed them by. Soon thereafter, Bobby came in for an overheating problem and rejoined the race *four cars from last*. He became cannon fodder back there when Geoff Bodine spun in a cloud of white smoke. Inman cried helplessly, "Hold on, Bobby. They're wrecking everywhere. Damn, I don't know where to go.

Hold on . . . *Oh no!* Morgan Shepherd just ran over us, Robbie. And no caution. Goddamn it! Our whole right side is caved."

His face flush, his eyes slightly wild, Robbie radioed, "Just hang in there, buddy. We're gonna get you out of this." He'd single-handedly taken a top-five car and turned it into a wreck. Now he had to bring it back.

His first chance to help came when the next caution fell. Jumping into the box as Bobby screeched to a halt on pit road, Robbie used a string to measure the distance between the front wheels, only to find the left was way out of whack. Grabbing a mallet, he started banging out the fenders so the tires wouldn't chafe against the metal, but the clock was ticking down. Needing to work in forty-second bursts so the pace car didn't pass them while they were stationary, Robbie sent Bobby back onto the track.

A minute later Bobby was in again. Robbie dove under the chassis to get to a small bolt in the tie rod, a threaded steel bar in the steering assembly that runs between the two tires and can be extended or shortened to keep the tires in balance. He tried prying it loose, but the bolt wouldn't budge. He sent Bobby back out again, knowing he'd have one last shot before the green flag fell.

As a furious Bobby sat idling, Robbie strained to get the bolt to turn as Inman counted the pace car's clicks over the radio.

"Pace car's in the first turn . . ." He strained, knowing Petty was furious. *"Second turn . . ."* He strained, feeling the wind of the passing cars, putting them farther behind. *"Third turn . . ."* He strained, feeling a hundred thousand pairs of eyes upon him. *"Fourth turn . . ."* He strained, knowing he'd killed his driver's comeback.

"It's close . . ." He was going to salvage this day . . . *"Closer, Robbie"* if it . . . *"Closer . . ."* killed him. . . . *"Rooobbbie!!!!"*

With Petty nearly pulling his legs out from under the car, Robbie dove over the wall and yelled, "Go! Go! Go!" as Bobby screeched out with his tire back in balance, just beating the pace car.

The temperature was supposed to be 85 degrees, but on the asphalt it felt more like 100. Robbie looked over his crew and saw their beet-red faces; half of them were lying on the concrete, exhausted. Their day would end with a twentieth-place finish, but Robbie knew the damage was a lot worse than that. As he later put it, "Shy of thirty-nine cars fallin' out, I knew I was gonna get spanked on Monday."

The only consolation was they were heading to Pocono, the site of Bobby's last good race.

"Andretti wrecked again last week."

"That give him most DNFs in the garage yet?"

"Dunno. But they should put that boy in go-carts. It's the only thing he's big enough to drive."

The laughter in the STP hauler drifted outside its closed doors. The rains washed out Friday's qualifying in Pocono, so with time on their hands, the crew sat around the trailer, bullshitting.

In the morning's *Winston-Salem Journal*, Mike Mulhern, a respected reporter, wrote that John Andretti was about to lose his job. Andretti was Petty's driver before Bobby, and the fact he stayed only a brief time belies how much the IndyCar racer actually did for them. They were a team with a lot of doubts when he came aboard. By qualifying second fastest at Michigan his very first time driving the Forty-three, John allowed them to start believing in themselves. But as powerful a present as that was, he cashiered it by quitting them eleven races later.

The Petty team watched the promise John showed with them utterly disappear as he left them to join the new Kmart team, owned by IndyCar veteran Carl Haas and

Ford's ex–head of worldwide racing, Michael Kranefuss. It was said that his contact lenses ruined his depth perception and he was too vain to wear glasses; that his roots—he was a nephew of the great Indy racer Mario Andretti—made it impossible for him to be comfortable in a 3,400-pound race car; that close contact made him go to pieces. Whatever the reason, he was crashing everything in sight. Coming into Pocono this weekend thirty-sixth place in the standings, he was exactly twenty-three rungs behind Petty and Bobby Hamilton.

On race Sunday, however, they were paired more closely than that on the starting grid. Andretti was starting thirty-sixth, and Bobby, thanks to a forgettable Saturday, was two rows ahead. Flipping the ignition switch, Bobby thought to himself, *Another damn Pocono where I gotta start in back.*

Ninety seconds after the green flag fell, Jimmy Spencer lost control, swiping the outside wall. Coming out of turn three, Bobby saw the smoke, and to alert those behind him that he was slowing up, used the standard NASCAR hand signal: a wave. From his spotter's tower above, Inman relaxed, waiting for Bobby to fall into a predictable line and race back to the start/finish line. But from a quarter track away, Andretti came plowing smack into Bobby, sending him careening into the outside wall, where a spinning Darrell Waltrip went back first into his left side, caving it in. "That damn Andretti," Bobby said in disbelief into his radio. "He came from six lengths behind me and ran me over. That guy ain't got no business being in a race car."

From pit road Robbie could see they needed a new radiator. In time he'd also discover front-frame damage, and spend the better part of the day trying to realign it with a huge hydraulic monster of a frame straightener.

Bobby watched for a while, face sunburned and sweaty,

jaw locked, eyes flaring. But after a while he just looked too pained to remain.

You could see the images of the past month flooding his head. The weekend in Michigan, which started so brilliantly and ended so sourly. The crash three days later, which, besides everything else, evaporated the car they'd gotten just right for the Brickyard. A top-five finish turned into a tortured twentieth in New Hampshire. And now this, John Andretti's very own get-well card, destroying another car and another race.

His breakthrough season was breaking apart in front of his eyes, and he knew that when it came time to explain the statistics, no one would care why. Would he add this to all the other messy years that he always seemed to be explaining away? His crew tried gentle pats. "You okay, Bobby?" Sympathy. "That damn Andretti's gonna get his." Encouragement. "Hey, it's still a long season."

Finally, Bobby just walked away and up to the roof of his hauler, where he watched another race unfold without him.

11

GOD POINTS THE FINGER

Talladega and the Brickyard: July 28 to August 3

*"Anytime you step on the gas hard, you're gonna
have your ups and downs."* —Ernie Irvan

There is no God-given reason why Talladega, Alabama,
should have anything that draws a hundred thousand
people. It's forty miles from Birmingham, ninety miles
from Atlanta, and hotter than hell in July.

But when Bill France Sr. was looking to build a sister
track to Daytona in 1967, and needed a place that twenty
million people could reach by car within six hours, his
friend George Wallace lobbied for two thousand acres of
soybean land on what was an airport used in World War II
as a naval flight training base. It is said that fliers became
convinced the base was spooked because it was built on an
ancient Indian burial ground. But that wouldn't have bothered Big Bill. A man who palled around with a rabid segre-
gationist like Wallace wasn't about to fret over the fate of a
few dead Indians.

Whether the old legend is true or not (a driver once
pulled off the track because he said he heard voices in his
head), the fact remains that spending a night in the infield
during race weekend is the closest thing you can get to ex-
periencing the Civil War in Sensurround. Between the
smoke from campfires and the fog, between the shooting
fireworks and occasional blast of a sawed-off shotgun, the

ground gets bathed in pea-soup air, making the flashing lights atop the patrolling police cars look like gaseous red clouds. To add to it, summer rains heave giant ditches into the ground.

It's not uncommon for hundreds of pickups to caravan around the outside of the track while women in the back happily flash their breasts. Someone usually tries scaling the track wall, and then more follow, leading cops on a drunken chase. The cops used to hoard the unruly ones (an admittedly relative concept here) into big school buses parked outside on the sweltering blacktop. But eventually business got too busy, and the sheriff's department built a nice new station with a pair of brightly lit cement lockups.

The drivers sleep in a guarded motor-home compound inside the infield while all this goes on. Since the only road in off Highway 77 is a two-lane, and most hotels are thirty miles away, it's easier to stay overnight and wake up at dawn right at work. None of them would ever entertain the idea of stepping outside the guarded chain-link fence, however. When it's dark, the fans rule.

On this night, the driving rain softened the red clay so much, you couldn't walk without having your ankles swallowed and calves caked. Those who were out were sticking to the main road, which runs through the middle of the infield. Fans milled aimlessly, eagerly, wearing their caps and shirts like armor, challenging anyone to duel over their favorite driver. Most everyone else was huddled inside yellow-lit school buses, vans, or campers, playing card games, having candlelit potfests, engaging in poorly concealed sex acts.

The reason these people were here had nothing to do with mud bogs, sex in a bus, or anything else that makes Talladega a twice-yearly redneck Mardi Gras. They came because they knew the longest, fastest track in NASCAR would be pregnant with disaster.

Ever since April 30, 1987, when Bill Elliott tore across it at an all-time stock car record speed of 212.809 mph, NASCAR has committed itself to keeping speeds down at Talladega. The reason wasn't Elliott's record, but the race the Sunday after, when Bobby Allison cut a tire while shrieking down the triangular front stretch at more than 200 mph. As the car spun wildly, gusts of air swept under its rear end, causing the spoiler to act in reverse. Instead of keeping the car down, it caused the front wheels to lift and the Buick flew nose first into the grandstand fence. The fence buckled and came apart, sending pieces of the chain link into the crowd and hospitalizing three fans. Facing panicked insurance companies, NASCAR's brain trust announced a slew of reforms, including using front skirts and curbing the horsepower of the engines.

For the most part, it seemed to work. (That is, if you don't count the incident eight weeks later when a part-time driver running an ARCA race swerved to avoid hitting a car spinning before him and flipped. Fans in the front row could hear his screams beneath the unreinforced roof as he was crushed to death.) Over the next five years there were chilling crashes, but they were the kind that served only to accentuate the track's mystique.

Then Talladega and its sister in Daytona became the stages for the bloodiest twelve months in modern NASCAR history.

The prologue was a plane crash on a cold and snowy April Fools' Day in 1993, when the ice-caked engines of a plane carrying NASCAR champion Alan Kulwicki stalled and the pilot, unaware of the proper procedures to restart the engines, crashed into a mountain outside of Bristol, Tennessee. Fourteen weeks later, on July 12, Davey Allison was killed piloting his chopper into the Talladega infield. Just like that, the sport lost a reigning champion and a future one. Davey's casket hadn't lain in the ground for ten days when Liz Allison, Davey's widow, started the July Talladega race with a prayer—and more bloodletting began. A seven-car melee claimed a Chevrolet piloted by short-track racer Stanley Smith, who hit a concrete wall with the right front corner of his car so hard that the back of his helmet cut into his neck, severing an artery. One of the drivers involved, Jimmy Horton, actually went sailing out of the yard. (In a bit of dark humor, Horton would say, "I knew I'd been in a bad crash when the first guy to reach my car was holding a can of beer.")

In the same race, another local hero, Hueytown's Neil Bonnett, went airborne in a manner eerily reminiscent of Allison's crash and ripped into the grandstand fence, causing the fans to be hit with a machine-gun spray of concrete chips. The somber mood was summed up by crew chief Steve Hmiel, who warned, "You cannot get in the stands with one of these things or you're going to put all of us out of business."

There wasn't a person in the sport who wasn't desperate to see that year end, and didn't welcome the fresh start that Daytona provided in February 1994. Then, in the first half hour of the first practice on Friday, Bonnett lost control of his Lumina in a wind gust and smacked the wall in the fourth turn. Soon thereafter, he was pronounced dead. (Though NASCAR withheld word until Bonnett's wife reached the track, a reporter got confirmation and ran with the story on a radio station to which she happened to be tuned.) In the cool wording of the autopsy, his skull was "remarkable in that there is a subgaleal hemorrhage associated with severe bilateral skull fracture [that] extends completely around the posterior aspect of the skull, where on each side . . . there is a gaping separation."

Bonnett was such a fixture in the garage that "we were all walking around like ghosts," says reporter Bob Zeller. "You get to know these people. They become your friends.

Most of us still hadn't gotten over Alan and Davey's death, and then Neil dies in the first half hour of practice. I hope I don't have a worse moment as a journalist than when I interviewed Bobby [Allison] that day. He'd just lost Davey. Then he loses his best friend."

The siege mentality was summed up by NASCAR's reaction in the minutes after the pronouncement. Its official publicist strode into the media center and announced that the cause was "driver error." Appalled that one of their own would be so callously blamed before his body was cold, Bonnett's colleagues filed a protest with NASCAR, and not long after a new publicist was named. Even Bonnett's friends, however, would come to admit he shouldn't have been behind the wheel, since doctors who treated him after the 1990 accident in Darlington had predicted that the odds of his surviving another major head trauma were slim.

As hundreds of reporters prepared to drive to Hueytown for Bonnett's funeral on the Monday after the crash, a thirty-one-year-old minor league driver named Rodney Orr was heading out of the first turn in practice. At 9:50 A.M., he lost control and hit the second-turn wall with such force, the caution light that sheared off his roof was found in the car—near his detached head. It took paramedics ten minutes to get both out. Racers and reporters thought it was a sick joke when word spread among them. That afternoon, they watched Bonnett's casket lowered into the ground.

After a pair of such seemingly inexplicable accidents, NASCAR desperately needed to deflect growing questions about its management. A nail-biting championship battle in which Ernie Irvan spent the summer at Dale Earnhardt's heels did just that.

Irvan was a dirt-track racer from California who followed his father, a promoter, east to Charlotte after his parents divorced. He raced on weekends and worked welding seats at the Charlotte Motor Speedway to pay the bills. As it happened, Earnhardt went to Irvan's fabricating shop to get a hunting trailer one day and saw a race car sitting unsponsored. In agreeing to lend it the name of his Chevrolet dealership, Earnhardt helped launch Irvan's NASCAR career. By the early nineties Ernie had landed with the hard-living Virginia men of the Kodak racing team, who make their home in the mountains near the Tennessee border. After seven wins and fifty-one top tens in 105 races, Robert Yates chose Irvan to fill Davey Allison's seat—then the most sought-after ride in the garage. In his first full season with Yates, in 1994, he looked as if he might win the title.

People still talk with hushed voices about the noise they heard on Saturday, August 20, 1994, when Irvan smacked the second-turn wall at the Michigan International Speedway doing 178 mph in practice after his right front tire failed. He hit on the passenger side, and though his harness kept his body still, his brain kept moving. It's called "deceleration syndrome." Doctors said his skull just "cracked like an eggshell" from the inside out.

While Ernie was lying unconscious with dilated blood vessels in his brain, and lungs that might collapse at any second, his doctors put his chances of living at one in ten. In the days immediately after, there was a palpable sense that the ambitious Californian would be the third Winston Cup driver to die racing in six months.

Earnhardt, having seen so much of this, made the trip to his bedside, the first time he'd ever been to a hospital for a racing accident. "Hey, this is Earnhardt," he said softly, leaning over. Ernie jerked and grabbed the hand, trying to make out Earnhardt's face through the blurred vision caused by his damaged left eye socket. He saw the outlines of the face, and that was enough. "You could tell he was real excited," said Mark Martin, who was there as well.

Ernie's wife had placed his newborn daughter's booty in his clenched fist when they'd first wheeled him into the emergency room. The first sign that the paralysis wasn't permanent came when he opened it five days later and the booty fell out. Soon he was talking—talking about coming back to racing.

"A lot of people look at me and say how'd ya do it?" Irvan said later. "I dunno. Your brain is a bunch of wires. I had a bunch crossed and they didn't know where they were supposed to be at." Here, he spread all five fingers on both hands, and then slowly clasped them together like teeth. "Every day new things just started to click. Like comprehending numbers. I'd try to dial 788-5555, and it was like 'Okay . . . seven . . . eight . . . eight . . .' " He let his hand hover in the air, shaking. "I had a real hard time making things go out of my mind and through my fingers. A lot of people have all these wires tangled up, and they're so twisted up, they never get back right. I just happened to be lucky. Everything just went back together."

This was a story that everyone could love, not least because it helped ease so much of the recent tragedy. Sixty thousand letters were received by well-wishers praying for his survival. But as Ernie advanced faster and quicker than anyone thought possible, the expectations he sold to himself and the public began doing unfortunate things.

Everyone in NASCAR walks around with convenient biographies that get in the way of history, and Ernie's no different. His wreck-filled early years earned him the derisive nickname Swervin' Irvan. In fact, many racers privately blamed him for Bonnett's head injuries. In only his second start for the Kodak team, Ernie was ten laps down yet went wide open off a restart, battling the race's leader, Ken Schrader. His crew was overheard telling him to go for the meaningless pass "to get us some TV time for our sponsors," but in doing so, he spun out Schrader and caused the spectacular eleven-car pileup from which Bonnett never completely recovered.*

In a dramatic gesture, Ernie apologized at the drivers' meeting in Talladega early in 1991, promising to tone down his act. And he did—on the track. Off of it, the fame and money led to a divorce with his first wife and, later, his team. When Allison's seat came open in the middle of the 1993 season, he did everything he could to break his Kodak contract. Owner Larry McClure refused to accept a buyout (he didn't have a midseason replacement), only to find his cars mysteriously crashing, blowing motors, and having problems they never had before. The disgruntled Irvan shrugged his shoulders until a few weeks of this eyebrow-raising misfortune convinced McClure to take a $400,000 buyout.

Robert Yates, the son of a minister, ran a more genteel operation, and Ernie matured there. In his first win in Martinsville, he unzipped his jumpsuit to reveal a Davey Allison T-shirt. It was a moment of respect and grace. But after Ernie's Michigan crash, a garage veteran who calls himself a friend says, "Ernie made himself impossible to like. He felt he had to throw time bombs at everyone. He was temperamental with fans. He just put a lot of distance between himself and those of us he'd been close with."

The fattest target was Dale Jarrett. When Ernie was recovering and unable to drive, Yates reached out for Jarrett, much as he had for Ernie two years earlier. Traveling with the team as part of his rehabilitation, Ernie openly questioned

---

*Bonnett decided to make a comeback three years later, in the July 1993 DieHard 500, where he crashed, finishing thirty-fourth. He didn't race again until the season finale in Atlanta, and went out after three laps with engine failure. His next appearance on a track was his fatal practice lap in Daytona.

Jarrett's talent, saying, "The guys can't wait until I get back so they can have a *real* driver in the car."

By midsummer Ernie's presence had become so corrosive that Ford nudged him into the Craftsman Truck Series, billing it as a planned part of Ernie's comeback, though it was really just a way to keep him separated from Jarrett. But the astonishing pace of Ernie's recovery made that a temporary solution. Come fall, he made a full return to Winston Cup in North Wilkesboro, astounding fans by leading thirty-one laps and finishing sixth. When he announced he was ready to return full-time in 1996, Ford helped Yates resolve the internal feuding. They gave Jarrett his own team, freeing the Texaco ride for Ernie.

But Texaco team, with Ernie back behind the wheel, struggled in the beginning of the 1996 season. Through thirteen races, their average finish was twenty-first. The fourteenth race, however, brought Ernie back to the scene of his crash. The closure did something to him, because he peeled off a pair of top fives and won in New Hampshire. Going into Talladega at the end of July, he was the hottest driver in the garage.

A sense of fatalism seemed to surround what had come to be called, without a trace of irony, the DieHard 500. Though one would have been hard-pressed to find a racer who'd admit to being scared, several privately dreaded making the season's second trip here.

The Winston Select 500 here on April 28 had effectively ended Bill Elliott's season, thanks to an accident where he went airborne and came down hard on his front grille, breaking his femur. Later, Mark Martin and Jeff Gordon sideswiped each other, igniting a fourteen-car pileup that sent Ricky Craven launching over Martin, catapulting into the retaining fence and spinning back out over the track upside down, where he bounced roof first over Ricky Rudd's Ford before coming to rest in the infield. It made every highlight reel in the nation, which was good for ratings and ticket sales, if not Craven, who awoke from a blackout with fractured vertebrae and painful head-to-toe welts. Gordon, who had never been caught in a pileup quite as jarring, remarked afterward, "I just closed my eyes and kept hearing *boom*."

On this morning, a bright sun was peeking through the clouds of the infield, and those who'd roamed the drenched darkness just a few hours before were sponge-bathing and hanging their laundry out on clotheslines.

Watching the morning break, a Californian named Guy, who'd moved to Tuscaloosa to sell bottled water, breathed the air as if it were sweet. "This is the infantry of the NASCAR wars, right here," he said, spreading his arms wide open to frame the sea of tents and campers. "There's no North and South here. There's just Chevys and Fords."

One infantryman was a baby-faced bus driver with a triangular face and a straw hat. He'd turned his psychedelic sixties ice cream van into an Earnhardt shrine, and was flinging his finger at all passersby, insisting, "There ain't one man on pit road who can outrun Dale. You cannot beat the man. The man has a plan. If the man is hooked up, he will win."

In the early stages of the race, Earnhardt's plan seemed to consist of little more than hanging in a five-car breakaway with Jeff Gordon, Sterling Marlin, and the Yates cars of Jarrett and Irvan. They challenged one another over the first hundred laps, but with suppressed horsepower could do little more than pull back and forth like busy elevators. Occasionally, a guest intruded. From nowhere, Andretti crept up behind Earnhardt, powering him into a large lead until Andretti lost the draft in the high groove and dropped back. Later losing his lead, he raced too hard to get back up front and drifted into Dale Jarrett, who went spinning down the track, igniting a twelve-car demolition derby.

With light quickly fading and the radar showing new showers nearby, the five leaders bore down for what was sure to be a shortened race. Earnhardt, Marlin, and Gordon raced off the restart and into a three-wide wing. Earnhardt squeezed out a lead, but three laps later Gordon daringly swept to his outside and the two dueled evenly to the flag stand. From their rearview mirrors they could see Marlin emerging from the backfield, with Irvan and Jarrett right behind.

Marlin's powerful engine brought him beside Earnhardt, but Irvan wasn't giving up. He stalked both, looking for a sliver of daylight to make the pack three wide. He tucked into the wind draft behind Marlin, then back down to Earnhardt, leaving Sterling high and dry. Desperately trying to keep from losing the draft, Marlin tried squeezing between them, forcing Irvan so low that his wheels were nearly on the grass. Then the worst accident in Dale Earnhardt's career happened.

Ernie's car skipped up a foot, nicking Marlin's Chevy, sending it into Earnhardt's machine. The black number 3 jerked right, taking Marlin's car on a ride into the wall. The hit peeled Earnhardt's hood up over the windshield, sealing him in near darkness as the Monte Carlo ricocheted over Marlin's crashing Chevy and went skidding along on its passenger side.

Cars scattered like seedlings thrown to the wind. "When there's so much smoke, all you see is shadows, so you look for a light and try to go there," Derrike Cope would say. "When the shadows became more vivid for me, it was too late." Cope hit the grille of Earnhardt's Chevy, which was lying on its side like a sunken shipwreck. Robert Pressley was the next one to see Earnhardt in front of him. He drilled his brake into the floorboard and said a prayer. Then he hit Earnhardt in the roof.

Sparks flew through the interior of Earnhardt's machine as it went airborne again, spinning completely around like a roaster on a spit. Its belly went upside down, then righted again, then hit the asphalt hard, bouncing off its left tires. Carrying too much momentum to stop, it slammed down again on its grille and skidded 180 degrees on its right-front tire alone. Through the mashing metal, Earnhardt felt his collarbone snap. Having already broken his sternum, he winced as the car ricocheted off its grille and onto all four tires just in time for driver Greg Sacks to hit it, jerking Earnhardt hard toward the infield. As he trailed off, the final impact was delivered by Ken Schrader's red Monte Carlo.

With smoke pouring out of the cockpit, Earnhardt flicked off the battery switch to cut the power as NASCAR officials raced to the wreckage.

Gripping his chest, he was helped to his feet and flashed a thumbs-up for the cameras. But struggling to breathe in the ambulance, he searched for some reason for what happened. "Why did Sterling get into me?" he wondered. "It had to be something broke on his car. There's no way he'd turn like that without some reason."

Marlin rushed into the infield care center to check on his health and answer that very question. As they watched the replay together, he pointed at the television and said, "See, Dale. It was Ernie pokin' his damn nose where it don't belong again." Still on the track, Irvan couldn't offer a defense.

Racers are remarkably quick to forgive each other for breaking one another's bones and mangling their cars. They forgive in the name of Christian charity, and of practicality. After all, they see one another every week, and circumstances can easily turn the victim into the victimizer. If you cause a wreck, you're expected to own up to it quickly and decisively. Nothing's worse than being known as someone who can't admit mistakes.

But as they keep to their haulers and motor coaches, or shuttle between appearances, drivers are growing isolated from one another. Months after Bonnett's death, for example, Earnhardt was still blaming Irvan for causing the original head injury. As Ernie tells it, it took his wreck to bring them together again, and on his first visit back to the garage in Rockingham, Earnhardt placed his arm around him and said, "I thought you were going to die before I could tell you I'm sorry for holding Neil's death against you."

So in the days after the crash, Earnhardt kept his own counsel, waiting for Irvan to call. But no call came. Then the heavily bandaged driver arrived in Indianapolis on Wednesday, July 31, for the first day of practice leading up to the Brickyard 400. To satisfy the media frenzy, a press conference was hastily arranged at the track's media center.

After spending a half hour describing the accident, Earnhardt was finally asked, "Have you said anything to Ernie, Dale?"

Looking over the packed room, he kept his answer curt. "No comment," he replied.

The mood of the press corps was hardly friendly to Irvan. Given his churlish behavior of late, his silence was seen as unimaginably callous. If Marlin was to be believed, Ernie had single-handedly ruined Dale Earnhardt's quest for an eighth championship. And even if he wasn't to blame, couldn't he find a minute to call and say "Sorry"?

Inside the Texaco team, Ernie's temper was boiling over. His return to the Brickyard—the race he nearly won in 1994—was supposed to be one of the highlights of his comeback. But now all the soft-focus testimonials to his courage and resilience were being replaced by the newly resurrected talk of Swervin' Irvan.

Around the speedway Marlin's partisans had filled the garage with eye charts that read, "Ernie, don't hit me, you one-eyed SOB." Earnhardt's crew had put a skeleton outside of their garage to show exactly where he was hurt. The question was whether he'd be able to drive more than a lap or two before giving way to a relief driver. Then, on Thursday during qualifying, the still-fuming Marlin passed by Irvan's checker-tiled garage bay.

"Come here," he snapped. Irvan approached slowly. "Took the whole fuckin' field out, didn't ya?"

"What are you talkin' about?"

"Talladega. Took the whole fuckin' field out and didn't give a shit."

"Look at the film," Irvan said, blood pressure rising. "You're as much to blame as I am."

"Bullshit," Marlin said, and threw a pair of Coke-bottle eyeglasses at Irvan, sneering, "Here, you can use these." Irvan started at Marlin, who looked as if he wanted nothing more than a clean shot at the smaller, more compact Californian. The Texaco crew broke them up.

By race time Ernie knew where he stood with Marlin, but he still wasn't sure about Earnhardt. In the driver's meeting, he'd approached Earnhardt to say hello. "He was real cold," Irvan remembers. Starting right behind the black Chevrolet, Ernie figured the odds were about even that Earnhardt would wreck him. But it didn't happen. In fact, when Dave Marcis was involved in a four-car spin-out, drawing a sixth-lap caution flag, Earnhardt dove into pit lane. It was jarring to watch him, a man whose image is wound up in his cool, choke back tears as another man got into his seat.

"Dadgum, it was hard to get out of there," he told

ABC's Jerry Punch, his gargoyle sunglasses reflecting the grandstands, which were packed with fans standing to give him an ovation. "This is my life right here."

In that moment Earnhardt's season would effectively end. He'd never get near first place in the point standings again, wouldn't win another race. But for now, the man who was getting all the blame had other things on his mind.

The Yates cars were strong all day, and after three hours of racing, Jarrett claimed the lead with thirty laps to go. Ernie, who'd hung around the top ten for most of the day, followed him into second, drag-racing Jarrett through the straights and hanging close through the corners. Seeing that he could run lower than Jarrett in the first two turns, he made a surgical pass for the lead with twenty-one laps to go.

The next fifteen laps were like watching something tee-tering on the edge of a shelf getting ready to fall. With an identically powerful engine, Jarrett hung on teammate Ernie's tail, never drifting back, waiting for him to make any mistake. "Ten to go," Ernie's crew chief, Larry Mc-Reynolds, radioed from pit road. "The only way he can get you is if he gets under you. Be smooth, babe."

It doesn't take much to make a racing tire skip on a smooth surface, and as Ernie went into the short chute be-tween the first and second turns—just one lap earlier than his 1994 misfortune—the faintest drop of oil left from a blown motor on Mike Wallace's car made his tires skip. That altered the precise arc he'd been using. Praying for a slip just like this, Jarrett slammed his wheel to the left. Ernie tried to dive down to box out the pass, but it was no use. Jarrett got inside of him. And then he was gone.

As Jarrett held the silver brick trophy over his head in Victory Lane, Ernie climbed out of his car by the fuel pumps in a remote corner behind the garage. His wife, Kim, was there to meet him. "It was a good race," she whispered in his ear as his blond-haired daughter, Jordan, pulled at his jumpsuit, trying to jump in his arms.

He didn't answer. Instead he waited silently for Jerry Punch to give the sign that his ABC mike was hot. When it came time, he started by saying, "It was a great battle and it was great that our race ca—" Here he stopped and used the word that had been giving him so much trouble. "Our *team* could finish first and second."

"Ernie," Punch said, "you have to think about how far you've come."

The driver answered sullenly. "This is a lot more heart-breaking than cutting a tire two years ago," he said. At that, Punch looked into the camera and told millions of viewers, "The voice is quivering, the eyes are moist. Boy, would he have loved to have this one."

But the truth was, Ernie went home not all that unhappy. "I gotta believe a lot of people looked at the Brickyard and said, 'What else can he do?' " he'd say. "That race was the turning point for me. It let people say, 'Ernie's back.' "

While Ernie was taking part in a champagne lunch Yates threw for his teams the next day, Earnhardt was nursing his sore bones. His condition had grown worse, not better, as had his disposition toward Ernie. He'd stayed silent, waiting for him to apologize, or at least acknowledge what he did. When he did neither, Earnhardt had just the way to get his attention. CNN had been pestering him for an interview, and on the Wednesday after the Brickyard he agreed to it.

The setting was serene, a plaza in front of a country club waterfall. Earnhardt, dressed in a polo shirt and slacks, struck the corresponding tone. He wasn't venomous. On the contrary, he was calm, almost professorial. "He makes tremendous mistakes," the legend started, "just like he did in Talladega. He caused the accident I was in."

This was what everyone had waited to hear: God had

pointed the finger. "His comeback is great," Earnhardt continued, "but then, too, I think he needs to be payin' attention and not make mistakes to hurt other drivers, like he did at Talladega."

Kim Irvan was flicking the channels when she came upon the segment. Though they both grew up in Kannapolis and her uncle lived beside him—"He used to call Dale the meanest little boy he'd ever seen," she says, laughing—Kim and Earnhardt rarely spoke. Certainly she'd never called him at home, even though their farms are only a mile from each other in Mooresville. But she was so irate at what she'd heard that she called his shop. A minute later she was being patched into the house.

"This is Earnhardt. What can I do for you, Kim?"

"You know why I'm calling, you son of a bitch. What you said on CNN was bullshit. After all my husband's been through, being at death's door, I woulda thought you, of all people, wouldn't accuse him of going out there to hurt people. You crash people all the time and no one says that about you. You've really disappointed me, Dale."

"Whoa, whoa," Earnhardt said. "All I wanted was for Ernie to call me."

Kim was taken aback by the answer. Is that what this was all about? A phone call. "People think Earnhardt is cold, but I think he's just learned to put up a good front," she'd say. "I mean, he's God and all, but that don't mean he ain't got feelings. It's just hard for guys to do stuff like that."

So she hung up and, as she puts it, "started fussin' with Ernie. I said, 'Put yourself in his shoes.' "

A half hour after Kim hung up with Earnhardt, Ernie was on the line, trying to explain his silence by saying he didn't want to bother Earnhardt when he no doubt had hundreds of calls.

"But that was probably the wrong thing to do," Ernie said finally.

"Yeah, it was," Earnhardt replied.

12

THE ALLISONS

"I don't know how I let this happen."

Bobby Allison was standing outside his home, staring at a For Sale sign. For Allison, it was an advertisement for the fact that he didn't have a cent to buy back the place where he'd raised his family; where Judy Allison, his wife of thirty-six years, had recently told him she wanted a divorce; where he'd built a dynasty and then lost it in the dim afterglow of brain damage.

It was late July, and the Winston Cup tour was back in Talladega, and so was Bobby, though this wasn't really home anymore, not like it used to be. Like so much in NASCAR, the sign at the mouth of Hueytown—"Home of Bobby Allison and the Alabama Gang"—seemed to have just a historical ring of truth. When he wasn't spending time in his condo at the Charlotte Motor Speedway, he was living with his ninety-year-old mother in her trailer across from the ranch-style suburban home that lay empty, void of everything the Allisons had collected in twenty-six years under its roof.

Judy told Bobby she needed to cleanse her life, and decided the best way to do so was to hold an auction. Though it wasn't planned as an event, hundreds of curiosity seekers streamed in for the day, cherry-picking belongings, from Bobby's old boots to yellowed news clippings about their deceased sons. Neither Bobby nor Judy advertised the auction in the NASCAR garage, and when it made the newspapers, it hit the racing community like a ton of bricks mortared with guilt and sadness.

He was born in 1937, and some could remember all the way back to when Bobby was a poor Miami teenager who broke into racing looking slick and handsome—a dead ringer for Sean Penn. He was a mechanical genius who couldn't keep twenty bucks in his pocket and became the epitome of the independent driver, shunning steady employment even from legends like Junior Johnson. He was churlish and self-involved and collected lifelong grudges like old parts. But he was a brilliant driver, and on his retirement Johnson said, "If I had Bobby all those years, we'd have two hundred wins, not Richard Petty."

Some could remember no further than 1988, when he was still cheating time by winning the Daytona 500. And some didn't even remember that far back. Those were the ones who knew only the man whose face was soft and hung loosely over his bones, the man who wore an air of befuddlement, like he was counting on you, a perfect stranger, to catch him if he fell.

The 1988 accident that caused this condition was one of the scariest in all of NASCAR. Not because of what it looked like on television, or even in the stands. Other crashes have been far more spectacular. It was the scariest because Bobby Allison outlived it in a way drivers weren't supposed to do, in a way neither of his sons nor his best friend, Neil Bonnett, did. It was the scariest because he recovered, but not completely, not in that feel-good way Ernie Irvan did, or in the walk-away manner in which others have left their wrecks. His recovery was incomplete. The auction was the perfect capstone. It made his life that much more incomplete.

The accident occurred in Pocono, four months after his Daytona win. It's been suggested, notably in a 1997 *Sports*

Illustrated profile, that he came into the race nursing a grudge against Darrell Waltrip, whom he is tied with for the third-most wins in Winston Cup history. The two had been in a wreck the prior weekend, and as Waltrip told the magazine's Ed Hinton, "Before the race started some of Bobby's crew came up to me. They said, 'Please watch out for Bobby. He's had a terrible week and he's crazy. He says he's gonna wreck you, and he's gonna wreck you big.' "

But Waltrip had nothing to do with the fact that Bobby cut a tire before the green flag fell. Because he was being passed by a train of cars below him on the track, he had to stay high. Bobby continued around hard, hoping he could get to pit road on the liner and that the debris thrown off by the tire would draw a caution, enabling him to avoid losing a lap.

The tire burst before he made it to the third turn.

As Bobby's Stavola Brothers Buick spun from his control, two cars were in his path: One swerved high and missed him; the other went low and clipped him, spinning the car completely around so its driver's side was facing traffic. A sometime racer named Jocko Maggiacomo barreled through the smoke and, before he knew what happened, T-boned Bobby Allison.

Unconscious for three weeks, Bobby awoke paranoid and delusional from surgery to lessen the brain swelling. He thought he saw bars on the windows and that he'd been kidnapped. He thought they'd tricked Judy into thinking he was dead. He feebly tried to prop himself up on a rolling table, but it slipped away, sending him crashing to the ground. Afraid the crash had tipped off his kidnappers, he dragged himself back to bed by his arms. Then he tried it again, only this time he hit the door. A doctor responding to the crash flung the door open and slammed it into

Bobby's head. The impact is reported to have cured one strange side effect from the surgery: cross-eye.

What can you say about a family where that is the closest one can come to a funny story? The Allisons have endured every pain that racing can exact. They also created risks for themselves, sometimes foolishly. Now they hover over NASCAR like ghosts, and when the wind rustles with their presence, it gives everyone in the racing community chills.

Racing people try desperately to forget the story of the Allisons. They'll curl their lips, ask why such intense tragedies must happen to good people, and then talk about "moving on."

Not so fast. There is much the Allisons still want to say.

"There's a lot about the whole picture I still don't understand," Bobby said as he stood in his empty home. "I said to myself, 'Why are we doing this? Why am I allowing this to go on? What are we going to achieve? What is the right thing to do?' But I agreed to it, because I didn't have a good argument not to.

"There are things I can brag about, and things I wonder about, and then I catch myself and say, 'Is that a brag, or am I identifying a weakness that I have?' I have won Winston Cup races in eight different brands of cars. I want to brag about that, because no one else has won anything close to that number. I have won for fifteen different race teams. No one else has come close to that number. Do those two statements mean that I was good, or that I was such a jerk that I couldn't keep a job? Why was I in fifteen race teams when Richard Petty was in one, when David Pearson was in three or four? Buddy Baker was probably the most traveled guy, and he drove for six teams.

"I probably can explain a little piece of it with one episode. I'd just gone to work for Cotton Owens, and we go to Augusta, and I win the race. Shortly after that, we came to Birmingham. Now, that's my home track, and Cotton ran Firestones. In those days you got there early and ran a lap of practice. So we mounted the tires, and I did really good. But I knew there was a better Firestone for that track. I still remember its name—a Red Dot 103. I looked around, and no one in the place had any Red Dots.

"Well, I had ten of them in my little shop, so I sent one of my guys for them. We put four on the car, and we were so fast we didn't even have to race anyone. Done deal. Then the Firestone factory rep comes by and says, 'Jack that car up, Bobby, and take those four tires off. I'm giving them to Richard Petty. When he wins tonight we want him on Firestones and not those damn Goodyears.' I said, 'Whoa, whoa, they're mine. I took them from home.' And he says, 'We didn't give them to you, we lent them to you. Take 'em off.'

"Cotton walks over and says, 'You give them the tires.' I said, 'How about you give him six and leave me with four.' But the guy wants all ten. So Cotton and I get in an argument, and I say, 'Cotton, this ain't fair.' Finally Cotton says, 'Do what you want, I'm outta here.' Well, I was mad as hell, so I gave up my Red Dots and mounted four Good-years just to show them. And I won the race. My Fire-stones finished second behind me. So I said to myself, 'I showed them. Ha ha ha.'

"But I got fired the next week. So what did I show? That I can't keep a job? What did I get myself? That's what I keep asking about my life.

"See, I should have a bank account. I have one, but it's pretty small. I can probably take you to lunch today, but just to the Iceberg," a greasy spoon down the road where the walls are covered with Allison family photos. "If I had been a businessman, I would have been able to capitalize on what I've done with the race car. I'm just not a good businessman."

Though Bobby cast a long, dominating shadow over his family, he often was little more than a shadow as a father. His brother Donnie told *Sports Illustrated*'s Hinton that "I coached both of Bobby's boys in little league football. He didn't." And he insisted that "Davey's first good race car, I gave him. I had told his daddy, 'Why don't you give that boy a car he can go race with?' Bobby said, 'He'll do all right.' That was it. That boy was at a stage where he needed help, and for whatever reason, he didn't get it."

Sitting in Davey's old office in their abandoned race shop, Bobby chose to remember their relationship more poignantly, saying that Davey would "ride in the truck and tell me, 'Dad, I know you're good, and you've won some races, but I'm gonna be the best ever.' It was really neat, because he'd say, 'What's my next step, Dad? What do I do?' How many fathers want to hear their sons say, 'Dad, what should I do?' "

It took some time before Clifford, who was younger by four years, came into his father's focus that way. Davey was always sure of what he wanted to do. Clifford, says a family friend, "was kind of just around." In later years, as Davey joined the Winston Cup circuit to trail his father, Clifford was left at home to work on his own cars. His closeness to his mother led to a convenient, if not entirely accurate, perception that Davey was Bobby's boy while Clifford took after Judy.

While Davey was working his way up in the Busch circuit, sixteen-year-old Clifford was running away with his girlfriend, who was fifteen. "They made it as far as Panama City, Florida, and found a guy in a pawnshop to marry them," Bobby remembers. "By then I figured, 'No use fighting this thing,' so we had a wedding here." The marriage didn't last. By eighteen, Cliff had moved home again, divorced and with custody of the couple's baby girl, whom Judy took in.

Davey, also married, was well into his career by then. He did not distinguish himself on the Busch tour, failing to win a single race, but he made the most of a handful of high-profile Winston Cup cameos. When the engine builder Robert Yates bought the Twenty-eight team in 1987 and took it to Daytona without a sponsor, he gambled that Bobby's boy would get him the attention he'd need. Davey became the first rookie ever to start on the outside of the front row.

He won two races in 1987 and two more in 1988, the year in which he finished second to his dad at the Daytona 500. But it also ushered in a period of intoxicating fame and self-involvement. Davey began partying hard, living the road life for all it was worth. He was realizing the dream of becoming his father, and it left him unprepared for the metamorphosis he'd be asked to go through after Bobby's accident at Pocono. It wasn't enough for Davey to be his father on the racetrack anymore. Now he had to become him behind the family's walls.

"The Allisons looked to Bobby for everything," says Davey's widow, Liz. "He called everybody's shots for them, and I think all of a sudden it was an awful lot for Davey to take. I think his hard driving in those years was his way of dealing with it. He wasn't sure how to take all the pressure."

The pressure was enormous as Bobby lay unconscious, pale and bloated from the compressors keeping him alive. "You weren't used to seeing him like that," says Clifford's widow, Elisa. "This man who was always so strong couldn't move. Bobby was the root of the family tree. We were the branches. When he was perishing, so was the tree."

Through the years he'd made, if not millions, then always enough to support his far-flung family—Kitty, the kids, their kids, and friends. But it left him with far less in the bank than seemed possible, and the medical bills ran through his bank account like acid. NASCAR didn't supply insurance, but it quietly stepped in to pay $50,000 of the bills. Bobby worked off another $60,000 with promotional appearances for the hospital, but that left $50,000 still due, and Blue Cross, calling his coverage inadequate, denied the family's claim.

"A lot of people have the illusion that tragedy draws people closer, but it didn't happen that way for us," says Elisa. "We held together as best we could, but we were all so tired." Davey's first marriage fell apart, and his sister Bonnie also went through a divorce. Davey remarried Liz, insulating himself in his new world. Clifford, who married Elisa in 1987, retreated to his new family as well.

Through 1989 and 1990, Bobby couldn't focus on much for long, so intense were the dizzy spells and medicinal side effects. His memory had gaping holes. His concentration was in tatters. Davey tried to stay close, but he was on the road, hitting the big time. Clifford, the one who was always the racing bridesmaid, became Bobby's road back to life.

"Bobby wouldn't go near the track. He'd lost interest. But then we took him with us to a track at New Smyrna," says Elisa. "I was off talking to someone and Clifford grabbed me. He said, 'Lisa, Lisa, look.' He was pointing to Bobby, who was leaning into Clifford's car, adjusting the carburetor. Clifford was so excited. He knew Bobby was coming back."

At the start of 1992, Bobby found Cliff a one-shot ride for the Busch race in Daytona. It was with a North Carolina race car builder named Barry Owen, who had a race-ready Oldsmobile that just needed an engine to run. Bobby agreed to supply it.

Clifford sped to tenth place in that race before his engine burned out. But the showing sparked them to run more races. What was to be a quickie ride blossomed into a full season as he kept posting solid runs. Heading into the fifteenth race of the season in Michigan on August 13, Clifford was twentieth out of seventy-one entrants in the Busch Series.

After so much misery, it was a wonderful time. Bobby, now on the mend, had both his boys competing at the same tracks—Cliff in the Busch garage, Davey in the Winston Cup one. The brothers were also growing closer. Davey no longer considered fame more important than family, and was making efforts to get to know the brother he'd kept at arm's length. For his part, Clifford felt more secure in his relationship with Bobby, who was playing patriarch again, talking about creating a superteam for both his boys.

As he climbed into his Lumina that afternoon, Clifford wasn't thinking about the frayed shoulder harness that was three weeks shy of its expiration date. He was thinking about winning the pole. His last words to his father were "We're gonna get 'em, Dad."

"He thought he had a chance for it," Owen remembers, "and in practice he kept pushing it and pushing it." Going into turn three, the Lumina shuddered and Clifford tried correcting it. The nose resisted him, and his car spun, hitting the wall, first in the rear, then flush on the driver's side, finally on the front. To fans and onlookers it looked like a minor version of more serious wrecks that drivers walk away from.

Not to Elisa.

"It's a sound and a moment I'll never forget," she says. "I ran straight for him. The other wives tried holding me back, but I ran straight at a twelve-foot fence. I was hanging on it, and they were pulling at me. They said, 'You can't do that, Elisa.' I said, 'Watch me.'

"When I saw them cutting the car open, I asked about his signs. No one would answer me. Then I noticed that as they were cutting him out, no one was hurrying. I knew in my heart that he was gone. No one had to tell me."

As the autopsy later explained, the loose seat allowed his helmet to strike the roll bar with sufficient force to cause a cranial fracture clear around his skull. He died instantly. But Elisa and Bobby weren't told until they'd followed the ambulance to the hospital. "I'll never forget the look that doctor gave me," Elisa said, sighing. "He said, 'We worked very hard with Clifford, and did all we could do. But he didn't make it.' I remember thinking, 'God help me.'

"Bobby collapsed on the floor. Then I collapsed with him. I said, 'What will I do with my life?' He just held me. Then Judy came into the room. They hadn't told her. She saw me and said, 'Oh my God, no!' Davey came in pretty soon after that. Everything was happening in slow motion, like a nightmare you're stuck in. Everything is pain and hurt. We stayed there awhile, but then I had to get home to the kids. On the way out, I pulled Liz aside. She and Davey were having problems with their marriage at that time. I remember telling Liz, 'Be good to each other, because you never know.' "

NASCAR's subsequent investigation came down to a single-page report notable for its calculating vagueness. Later, when Elisa asked questions about her husband's death, she says officials there made her feel that "if they ignored me long enough, I'd go away. They treated me badly, that's all I'll say." Ultimately, Elisa would file suit against the seat maker to get her questions answered.

The accident had a profound effect on the sport in some ways, and none whatsoever in others. It was the first of a tragic series of deaths that would turn the heat up on enhancing driver safety. Yet it didn't change the fundamental denial that drivers maintain about their sport's danger.

Judy Allison, more than anyone, loathed that denial. They call them racing accidents and talk about men knowing the danger. To hell with that. Clifford, her boy, wasn't killed by racing. He was killed by bad equipment. How could the question not be asked inside the Allison home about how that had been allowed?

After Clifford's funeral, Judy moved in with her sister, and Bobby spent time with friends in his native Florida. "I cried and cried and cried," says Bobby. "Somebody would walk up to me, and I'd cry. If anyone said his name, I'd cry. I'd been through the crying in my own recovery. If someone hollered at me in the hospital, I'd go sit down and cry. And that was a piece of recovery I had to accept. But then, with Clifford, it got to be that I couldn't tell what would cause me to cry. It got to the point where the least little thing caused me to cry."

The graves of Clifford and Davey are yards apart at the Highland Memorial Cemetery, just outside of Hueytown. Clifford's lies in the sun, a squat granite stone next to one reserved for Elisa, who's since remarried. Davey's is beside a shade tree, under which is a bench. A portrait of him cast in bronze adorns the twenty-four-by-thirty-foot memorial. A quarter lies in a gray stone vase, left by a fan who placed three pennies in orbit around it. (Cemetery workers save each twenty-eight cents and mail them to the family.) A black plastic bottle of Texaco oil with a pink ribbon tied around it sits on the well-traveled grass.

It's fitting that they are buried close together, though not beside each other. The two had always competed, but just as Clifford was settling down as a driver, Davey was settling down as a family man, thanks to a pair of bone-chilling crashes that occurred within two months of each other.

The first came in typically Davey fashion, as he barreled across the finish line at the 1992 Winston Select to edge out Kyle Petty by a nose for the win. The cars pinched under the checkered flag, and the contact sent Davey slamming, driver's side first, into the wall. Newspaper clippings the next day played down the bruised lung and concussion he received. Yates was quoted as saying, "His eyes kind of rolled back a couple of times, but he came around."

In fact, Davey's reaction was much more profound.

As Liz remembers: "We were up in the condo and the children were watching. He wasn't moving, they were getting the Jaws of Life out to cut him out. He swears to me that right then he died and had an out-of-body experience. He felt himself hovering over the grandstands, looking down on himself. After he came to, he said this was his second chance, that there were things that he needed to change in his life."

Two months later, on July 19—exactly twenty-five days before Clifford's death—Davey flipped his Ford eleven times at the same Pocono track where his father nearly died. Mark Martin, who was driving nearby, radioed to his crew that he thought there was no way Davey could have survived. He emerged with just broken bones. "Davey was a committed family man by then," says Brett Bodine, one of Davey's closest friends. "Subconsciously, I think he'd made his peace with the Lord and prepared himself for death."

In the summer of 1993, when Brett bought a Mooresville garage in the hopes of one day owning his own team, the seller asked if he knew anyone who wanted a Hughes 369 HS helicopter. Brett told Davey, who leapt at the chance.

Davey wound up using the helicopter very little. Though he was an excellent pilot just like his father and had 1,073 hours of flight time, only fifty-four were in helicopters and only nine of those were logged in the Hughes. His wife made him take lessons, and at the last one he promised his instructor that he was parking the helicopter and wouldn't use it again until their next appointment, after the Talladega race.

But on July 12, 1993, Davey lifted off from his home with his fellow Alabama gang driver, Red Farmer, to fly to Talladega. Flying guidelines dictated that he needed twenty-five hours of flight training to fly solo. He had three, and it didn't include instruction in downwind landings. The winds were blowing hard that day.

Farmer would later say that as they began their descent into the parking lot, "the ride became very violent and I did not know what was happening. I saw sky. I saw ground. And I said, 'Hold it, Davey' . . . I was scared and I didn't know what to expect . . . We went on the left side and hit the ground very hard. I was upside down and I yelled, 'Davey, let's get out of this thing before it catches fire.' I did not get a response. I looked up and could see Davey hanging in his seat unconscious." Actually, he was all but dead. The cause of death was familiar: massive head injuries.

In March 1995 the National Transportation Safety Board finished its probe of the crash. It wrote, "The probable cause of the accident was the pilot's poor in-flight decision to land downwind in a confined area that was surrounded by high obstructions and his failure to properly compensate for [a] tailwind condition. A factor related to the accident was the pilot's lack of total experience in the type of aircraft."

It was a cruel obituary for one who was brought up around speed.

At a store on the outskirts of town, a man who claims to be a friend of the Allison family is asked about Davey's widow, Liz. First, he demands his name not be used. Then, glancing at a wall of Allison photos taken from a distance, he twists his face and seethes, "Whore."

Davey received a hero's funeral in Hueytown. This is Allison country, filled with people who adopted Davey because there was and is nothing much else to adopt. The cemetery was thronged by drivers, well-wishers, and fans, many wearing black Texaco armbands. Davey's friend, the country music star Joe Diffie, sang one of Davey's favorite songs, "Ships That Don't Come In."

Not being from Hueytown, Liz had no one to turn to in the months after the funeral and began dating Diffie. She was either vilified or sanctified for this, called names at the supermarket or stopped on the sidewalk by fans who'd break down in tears. She tried to keep the children near Bobby, but in the end their lives were just too different. She left for Nashville, where she moved into a well-heeled development of gated homes on hills.

"I decided to move because I want my children to live a normal life," she said by the fireplace of her well-appointed living room. "I didn't want them to walk into a grocery store or anywhere and just be Davey Allison's children. People would come up to me and hug me and cry. It was just not a good situation for the children.

"Now I don't have any desire to go to the races anymore. Racing was hard that last year he was alive because of Clifford's accident and all of Davey's horrible accidents. The joy was taken out of it for us. It was very much a chore. I don't want to go. I don't want to know. The kids don't think anything about it either."

As she spoke, it was observed that none of Davey's trophies adorned her new living room. That was, she said, because they were all in a room down below. She hadn't been in it for some time—long enough, at least, that when she acceded to a request to open it, she noticed for the first time that water damage had ruined half a wall of framed photos. The room, she explained, was usually locked. It took her some time to find the keys.

Asked about her most prized thing in this room, Liz removed a folded American flag in a Lucite case from a bottom shelf. "The White House sent this after Davey died," she said. Then, surveying the walls, she settled on her favorite: Davey's beat-up old burgundy leather cowboy hat, which was resting in the corner. She held it for a moment. Then Davey's seven-year-old daughter, Krista, ran into the room.

Krista stopped for a moment, taking it all in. Brightening, she pointed to a portrait of Davey in uniform, holding her when she was an infant. "Look, Mommy," she said. "It's me with Daddy."

"Yes, dear, it's you and Daddy," Liz said.

Then Krista saw the hat, put it on her head, and began dancing around with an insouciant spirit. But Liz had a lawyer appointment, having to do with Davey's estate, and had to go. She took back the hat, closed the light, and then, gently easing her daughter out, shut the door.

Krista was still lingering outside the shut door when Liz was halfway up the stairs.

" 'Bye, Daddy," Krista said, her nose pressed to the closed door.

Standing outside the For Sale sign on his lawn, Bobby was asked about his future. After his race team's sponsor went bankrupt in April, he received temporary financing from a furniture company, but there were questions about how long it would last. He hadn't won a race with this team since its inception in 1990, and in his notebooks one saw scribbled recriminations about how he should have spoken up but didn't. He had similar regrets about the manner in which he handled the split with Judy.

"Why did I agree to allow everything to be sold that I didn't take personally?" he asked plaintively. "Because I didn't have a good argument. I found myself in a situation where confusion reigned. Why are we doing this? Why am I allowing this to go on? There were clothes I left in my closet that I didn't need that got sold. Now the place is so empty . . ."

Bobby let the thought trail off, listening to his voice echo off the empty walls and floors. Then he smiled weakly. "I have a lot of friends," he added, "and they'd like to see me have better days. So I'm going to try to dwell on the good."

13

BORROWED CHIPS

Michigan to Watkins Glen: June 21 to August 3

Brett Bodine had been on an emotional roller coaster ever since he'd pitched Pep Boys. First there was that awful weekend in Pocono. Ernie Irvan had spun out of nowhere and Brett barreled through a cloud of smoke right into the Texaco car. "I had nowhere to go," he said. He was watching his men work on the lost cause, his hands clasped tightly behind his back, as if he was afraid what he'd do with them if he let go.

Five days after that, on June 21, the Winston Cup tour moved on to Michigan for the GM Goodwrench Dealer 400. As first-round qualifying ended late in the afternoon, Brett passed Childress. It was the first time the two men had seen each other since Lowe's decided to defect to the new team Childress was starting in 1997. They ducked into an alley between two haulers so they could speak unnoticed.

"Look, I'm sorry about how that deal turned out," Childress said about Lowe's.

Brett thanked him, adding there were no hard feelings. "That's just racing, Richard. I understand," he said.

And he did. It would have done no good to get angry. "Lowe's walked into his shop and got its skirt blown up by the number Three car," Brett said in a moment of cool realism. "You can't fight that." Of course, it helped that a deal with enormous potential had been dropped in Brett's lap.

It came from a thirty-something deal maker out of

Indianapolis who said he worked for a Las Vegas maker of automatic teller machines. The ATM business is cutthroat, he explained, and the big players are the ones who can sign up national chains—pharmacies, supermarkets, video stores—which generate millions of transactions. The profit comes from the fee-per-transaction that ATMs charge, usually a dollar that is split between the store and the machine's owner. His client, he said, was a risk taker named Sven who wanted to make a big splash.

What made this snap lesson in the business of ATMs intriguing was the way Sven wanted to make his splash. He wanted to sponsor a Winston Cup team. As Mr. Indianapolis explained it, Sven would then woo large clients by promising them free exposure on the car.

Brett raised an eyebrow, his attention now fixed. The media liked to call Winston Cup cars rolling billboards, but that was too simplistic. They were integrated marketing strategies on wheels. Only a Jeff Gordon, Dale Earnhardt, or Rusty Wallace had the star power to lure a single sponsor that could cover their entire race budget. The rest needed to spread the cost among multiple sponsors, usually complementary ones that could be linked in cross-promotions. A dozen people might spend a year putting just one deal together, making sure everyone was happy.

This was where the times had really changed for drivers. In the old days, Richard Petty only had to worry about pleasing Andy Granatelli at STP. In the 1990s a driver might have a half dozen sponsors on his car—all wanting a piece of his time: an appearance in a luxury box, an autograph-signing at a store, a black-tie invitation to an executive function. Most drivers hated this part of their sport; they suffered the grip-and-grins through clenched teeth. Not Brett. He was smooth, smart, and telegenic. In the parlance of the garage, he was great at pushing product.

Brett was also shrewd enough to see Mr. Indianapolis for who he was—a small-time voyeur trying to gain entry into the so-called "glittery" world of NASCAR racing. That also didn't faze him. What bothered him was the manner in which Mr. Indianapolis began treating him as a partner cum social secretary. As the deal gained steam through the month of June, Brett tried to remain cordial, but his wife and her twin sister Donna were visibly chafing at the agent's gaudy, invasive presence.

The tension was infectious. On the June 21 weekend in Michigan, the agent admired a pair of sunglasses that Donna's husband Donnie was wearing. "How about giving me those?" he goaded the crew chief.

"Give me four million dollars and I'll buy you a damn case," Donnie snapped.

The next Wednesday—after they left Michigan with a disappointing twenty-second-place finish—an envelope from Las Vegas arrived with the usual mail at BDR Motorsports in Mooresville. It was a signed letter of intent from Sven. He was promising to pay $4 million to sponsor Brett in 1997.

Donnie ordered more sunglasses.

The Pepsi 400 marks the second half of the season, and the beginning of second visits to most of the tracks. As such, Donnie Richeson hoped the lessons of the winter and spring would serve his young team well.

A soft-spoken Owensboro, Kentucky, native who takes the racing axiom of never getting too high or low to a Bluegrass extreme, Donnie slept on his office couch at the beginning of the season, when he was so behind he could barely get cars to the tracks and couldn't afford to waste the twenty minutes it took to drive home. But now he'd caught up rebuilding their fleet, and the days were no longer thirteen-hour affairs. Small steps, maybe. But steps nonetheless. Hoping for a bit of closure, he brought to Daytona the car that had caught fire in February, thinking it might give his men a chance to reflect on how far they'd come.

Despite what Brett had said to the Lowe's people late the last year, Donnie knew their first year wouldn't be a top-ten one. Five, even three years before, they might have stood an outside chance with first-rate equipment and help from Ford, but not anymore. Not with the disparity between multi-car teams and single-car ones growing larger by the day.

Oh, how Donnie would have loved just a half hour of wind tunnel time. A wind tunnel is literally that—a long corridor designed for creating hurricane-force gusts. When giant fans at its base are set in motion, the air begins to swirl and starts building speed. Architecturally, it's like a theater, with the fans in a deep orchestral pit, and floors sloping sharply up to force the wind out of the dark, foreboding chamber and onto the main floor. The tunnel is jet black, but there is a wide metal plate in its center, illuminated from above by a spotlight. This is actually a series of concentric circles that hide weights running a floor beneath them. As the wind flies off its rise and hits the car parked on the plates, the weights move, sending readings to the control room.

From hundreds of flickering LED readouts, aerodynamicists can analyze the car as if it is a starship, producing exacting guides about how to make it handle better in the wind. The problem isn't the cost, though it is expensive: $15,000 per half hour. No, it's access. Unlike GM, Ford doesn't have its own tunnel. It leases time at one owned by Lockheed in Marietta, Georgia, and gives priority to its next-generation production cars first. If there's an open window, it might slot in a NASCAR team, but only proven winners like Jack Roush, Robert Yates, or Roger Penske.

That left Donnie entirely reliant on the test sessions that Winston Cup teams are allowed. Not to be confused with the normal practices held Friday and Saturday before a race, these are extended sessions held weeks, sometimes months, earlier. Ford will rent, say, the Charlotte Motor Speedway a month before the Coca-Cola 600 and invite all of its teams to test for three days. In that time, a crew chief such as Donnie may test a hundred combinations—bending, cutting, and reshaping the quarter paneling in fractional increments, trying different gear ratios and springs, hunting for any way to pick up speed.

But Donnie's ability to test was limited. NASCAR allows its Winston Cup teams only seven such sessions a season, and it is a severe restriction. Everyone needs to spend one date getting ready for the Daytona 500, and two more to prepare for the big-purse races at CMS and Indianapolis. Throw in a couple of dates at, say, Martinsville to test your short-track cars; then add a road course session. Now, what happens if you have an unfortunate year? Through no fault of your own, you've been in the wrong place at the wrong time, and an unexpectedly large number of your cars have been totaled. You must build new ones. Now it is July. You have half a season left, and an almost entirely new fleet of cars with no track record. You also have only one test date left. If you're Brett Bodine, you're screwed.

But not if you are Roush, who had a three-car team.* Roush got seven dates for each of his teams, twenty-one in all. If one of his teams ran out of test dates, he could send another to a session and report back the findings. So on top of the wind tunnel time Ford gave his top-drawer Mark

---

*By 1998, Roush had expanded to a five-car team.

Martin team, Roush netted three times the testing information of a Brett Bodine.

All this wasn't an apology for the performance of Richeson's team. It was just the reality of what Donnie awoke to
every day. So you had to forgive him if he wasn't unchar-
acteristically giddy on Friday night before the Pepsi 400,
when Brett gathered his crew for dinner at the Chart
House, a waterfront seafood restaurant in Daytona. Brett
hoped that by revealing the news about Sven and his com-
mitment to sponsor them in 1997, he'd reinvigorate his
crew. Donnie tried to look upbeat, even though he knew
the top ten would get more distant before it got nearer.

Brett, on the other hand, was more sanguine than he'd
been in months, and allowed that optimism to seep into an
interview the next morning with broadcaster Bill Weber
on ABC. Gently asked about his future before a national
television audience, Brett, dressed in chinos and a white
polo shirt, replied, "I'm really feeling good about our race
team. We're on the move, improving." He thought about
saying more, but without a signed contract, held back.
"We've got an awful lot to offer a sponsor" is what he
added.

As Brett was saying this, Donnie was helping push their
Ford onto the pit road. He'd outfitted it with a lower rear
gear ratio to give Brett more power through the corners
and a better hold on the low end on the track, where you
could go wide open without having to brake as much. At
least one other crew chief was also gambling on the low
groove—Buddy Parrott, the crew chief for Jeff Burton.
The two men agreed that their drivers should start out the
race drafting together down low. Maybe they'd power
each other out of their starting spots in thirty-sixth and
thirty-third place.

Brett had his early problems. He started inching up, only to have a jack break on an early yellow-flag pit. But in Daytona the cars run so closely together that it's possible to make huge back-to-front gains quickly, and with Brett pulling Burton through the corners, and Burton pushing him through the straights, they moved from the third pack to the second and then, quietly, to the tail end of the lead group.

The Eleven crew was coming up big when it counted this time, maintaining Brett's position with mistake-free pit work. When it came down to the last caution flag, Donnie looked up at the threatening blue-gray sky and played the weather. With the rain five miles off, he took just right-side tires on the gamble that the clouds would give way before his left-sides did. The two-tire stop took a scant eleven seconds on pit road, and an ABC announcing crew that hadn't noticed Brett all race looked up to find him suddenly in tenth place.

When the rain started soaking the faces of the Lowe's men, they threw up their arms in joy. They had their first top ten of the season, and a reason to believe again. Diane Bodine leapt off the top of the tool rig, hugging them. "I didn't want to be too happy," she allowed. "Yes, we'd been to hell and back, but I didn't want us to get to the point where we were thrilled with ninth."

Maybe not, but the effect on Brett was palpable. He headed north to New Hampshire the next weekend with a new confidence, and let himself rip off the banal veil of goodwill that remained with his relationship with Lowe's.

"I told them not to make a parallel move," he said in an *Inside NASCAR* interview. "They better move way up, because if they made a parallel move, I was gonna pass them."

But before long, a sixteenth-place finish in Loudon gave way to a twenty-seventh-place day in Pocono and a twenty-second-place showing in Talladega. The Bodines were becoming alarmed that things weren't advancing with the Vegas people as they'd hoped. Mr. Indianapolis told Brett not to worry, but an unsettling call made him do just that. It was from a salesman of Sven's who'd been on the road, trying to sign up clients. He was calling to let Brett know that if they could just get a few more big names, the deal would be done.

"You mean it's not done now?" Brett asked slowly.

"Well, no," he was told, and proceeded to learn for the first time that the letter of intent he'd been holding for a month wasn't what he thought. Mr. Indianapolis insisted that the $4 million was not tied to anything but Brett's final okay, yet it now seemed shakier than that. This man whom he'd never met, and who had no reason to lie, was telling him that the $4 million was contingent on whether Sven could meet certain sales targets.

What happened if they didn't hit those targets by the fall, when Brett would need to start ordering new engines and cars?

"Well . . ."

By the weekend of the Brickyard 400, "It was crazy," says Diane. "Brett would be getting ready to go out and qualify, and we'd get this call on the cell phone: 'Sold a hundred more. We're close.' We were qualifying in Talladega, worried sick whether this guy sold a hundred machines in Tulsa."

On the evening of Friday, August 2—the evening before the race—Brett and Diane made a dinner date with Mr. Indianapolis and Sven, hoping at last to nail down what was going on. When these people first came to him, they seemed bankable. Now, a month later, he couldn't get a straight answer. Driving to the restaurant address he was given, Brett was unnerved to find it wasn't a quiet place where business could be discussed, but a noisy pizzeria.

Inside, Mr. Indianapolis was joking with a half dozen of his friends, all invited to see a real-life driver up close.

Diane fumed, and Brett's stomach sank. Not only didn't anyone come prepared to talk business, the answers he tried to extract kept getting more murky. As the night wore on, he began to see these men as hustlers gambling his future with borrowed chips.

(Sven would later blame the incident on his counterpart, insisting that "my business partner in Indianapolis was handling the talks. When I had dinner with Brett that evening before the race, I realized he'd been given a greatly exaggerated picture of what I could do.")

It was now August, and most sponsors were starting to finalize packages they'd been developing for months. Brett hoped against hope that this shaky ATM thing would come together, but he also knew he could no longer count on it. He'd have to go back out. He'd have to start again.

Seeing a television, Brett sank into a corner booth and tried to tune in the Busch race that Todd was running at nearby Indianapolis Raceway Park. As luck would have it, the owner hadn't paid his cable bill. There was nothing but static.

So on the eve of the year's richest race, the one where Brett finished second in 1994—he and Diane took turns standing on a chair in a pizzeria, trying to get a picture on a fuzzy television with tinfoil rabbit ears.

Tomorrow night they'd be back at home, nursing a twenty-second-place finish that kept them twenty-fourth in the standings.

The road course named after the town of Watkins Glen, New York, offers a distinct change of scenery from the Brickyard, the track that it follows on the Winston Cup schedule. The Glen's eleven hilly and winding turns cut through this forrested section of the Finger Lakes like an asphalt stream, but more important to the Bodines, it's just an hour from their birthplace of Chemung.

Seventy-one-year-old Carol Bodine is something less than sentimental about Chemung. "Horrible, just awful," she says about the place that is little more than a fire department, a Methodist church, and a Baptist church with swirls of barren roadside flaring out from all sides. "The way it's changed, I'm ashamed to say I raised my boys there."

Carol and her husband, Eli, left Chemung in 1975 to be closer to Geoff, who hadn't yet made his Winston Cup debut when the road course went bankrupt in 1980. It lay shuttered until the nearby Corning company jointly invested with the France family to reopen it in 1984.* People around here will tell you that in its own way Watkins Glen is as much a part of stock car history as Wilkes County. Although nearby Chemung declared the reopened Speedrome a public nuisance, and the old Bodine homestead has burned, that history is still wound up in the Bodines.

Downtown Elmira closes early for a parade during the week of the race, as Dixieland bands and show cars fill the packed streets. On Friday night an annual reunion at Brett's uncle Duke's house draws as many as a hundred relations from all around. One of the family's acquaintances is Bob Kelly, who was public relations director at the Glen through the seventies and went on to stints with Ford and R.J. Reynolds before opening his own sponsor search firm.

Brett called him after returning from the Brickyard.

"I'm saying this as a friend, Brett," Kelly told him. "It's going to be hard getting you what you want for three years

*In early 1997, International Speedway Corp., the holding company for the France family's racetracks, bought Corning out to become the sole stockholder.

without your team being a proven front-runner." But that
night, Kelly decided that since "there are few drivers with
a better attitude, I'd develop this presentation with Brett as
Mr. Clean, from his demeanor, to his family life, to his in-
tegrity. I said, 'Here's the kind of person you can trust your
money to, who won't take it and run.' "

Ironically, one of the first companies to hear the presentation was the World Wrestling Federation, whose owner,
Vince McMahon, went through a very public trial—and
an ultimate acquittal—for allegedly distributing steroids
to his wrestlers. The WWF was in a pitched ratings battle
with Ted Turner's rival World Championship Wrestling,
which sponsored a Busch car. (The WCW crew was something of a joke in the garage for wearing lightning bolt
makeup around their eyes.) It made sense for McMahon to
follow Turner into NASCAR.

Brett and Diane understood the business sense in all of
this, yet they had a hard time imagining spending the next
three years with Hulk Hogan and his hoary band of ab-
dominally obsessed actors. So at the same time as those
talks unfolded, they pursued the clothing designer Tommy
Hilfiger, whose agents agreed to a meeting Friday night at
the Glen. That meant missing the reunion at Uncle Duke's,
but Brett counted that as a small relief. He wasn't sure he
was up to all the old friends and relations asking how his
fortunes were faring. No, better to stay low this year, as far
off the radar as possible.

Uncle Duke's also wouldn't be the same without his parents being there. Since Geoff had started his own souvenir
trailer and asked his folks to run it, they'd traveled the Winston Cup circuit with their sons. "People would come up to
us all the time," remembers Carol, "saying, you know, we
used to live next door to the Bodines. Of course, we'd
never have seen them before, but we never told anyone

who we were. We'd just say, 'Oh, really . . .' If the boys' fans wanted to feel special, that was fine with us."

Then Eli began ailing. No one used the word *emphysema*. Instead, they called it lung disease, a euphemism that suggested longer-term treatment possibilities. It forced him to give up the traveling in the early nineties, but this was the first time it kept him and Carol away from the annual reunion. Knowing their disappointment, Duke Sechrist had everyone sign a "Miss You" card for his missing sister.

On Sunday, as Eli and Carol gathered themselves in front of the television, about fifty Bodines were filling the grandstand behind turn one. This is their traditional place. They screamed here when Geoff and Brett finished second and third in 1990. (Brett could have passed Geoff, who cut a tire before taking the checkered flag, but instead protected him from behind.) And they cheered just as loudly when the brothers finished twenty-eighth and -ninth in 1994.

This time around, if asked who needed the win more, the Bodine clan probably would have voted with shrugged shoulders. Geoff hadn't won in fifty-five races. Brett was searching for a sponsor. Todd, who'd come in second in the June Busch race here, was subbing for an injured Kyle Petty and racing to land a permanent Winston Cup ride. Who needed a win more? Hard to tell.

And for much of the sun-drenched Sunday, it seemed an academic question. Brett was in twenty-fourth, radioing to Donnie about their car, "She's terrible." Todd was in twentieth, and Geoff was running where he qualified, in thirteenth.

But then, in the fifty-seventh lap, Rusty Wallace slammed into the eleventh-turn tire barrier, drawing a caution that beckoned the entire field to the pits to fill up their tanks. With five laps' worth of gas in his Ford, Geoff didn't leave the track. Instead he became the only car to stay and collected five bonus points for leading. Then, on lap sixty-two, he surrendered to his parched tank. Were the race to have continued under a green flag, he would have returned to the field as the last car on the lead lap, in twenty-fifth place.

But the race didn't continue. Just as he was pulling out, Ricky Craven's Monte Carlo sputtered and died. That drew a new caution, and an unexpected wrinkle. Every crew chief whose car was a few drops shy of lasting the final sixty-three miles, madly signaled his driver onto pit road for a gas-and-go. Nine drivers, however, stayed out, leapfrogging from back to front. Able to return to the field in ninth, Geoff looked ahead to find Todd in fourth and Brett in fifth.

Crouched on one knee in the Lowe's pit, Donnie scanned the green and black display of his laptop for the recalibrated running order. Terry Labonte, Earnhardt, and Gordon would come back fast. So would Geoff, who had the freshest tires in the field. With Ken Schrader and Bobby Labonte ahead, Brett might be able to stay in the top ten. The question was how fast his tires would fade.

"See if you can pass the Forty-two quick and save the tires for the end," Donnie radioed, using the number of Todd's car and not his name.

At the restart, Brett took the hard right into turn one, gearing down as he swept around Todd into three uphill turns, out of which lay the fastest part of the track. Hitting it at 180 mph, Brett tried grabbing second in a ballsy three-wide move that he backed down from only when he ran out of room speeding into a pair of hairpin turns at the end of the backstretch.

Shuffled back to third, now mired behind a lapped car, Brett raced back to the flag stand. But no sooner had they passed the stripe than the lapped car in front of him spun out of control. Brett rammed the wheel right, advancing unscathed. Meanwhile, all the braking in the backfield allowed Geoff to pick up three places and move to Todd's tail. Watching Geoff dispatch Todd behind him, Brett could feel his tires fading. And so it was that he didn't put up a fight as Geoff bridged the distance that separated them and spilled past him onto the backstretch, beginning his chase of the race leader, Ken Schrader.

Schrader and Geoff Bodine were drivers in similar straits. Like the elder Bodine, Schrader was a prolific racer, and still spent his off weekends on dirt tracks in the Midwest. And also like Geoff, he had a top-ten pedigree but had gone eons without a win—five years. To quiet the rumblings, Schrader's team manager, Ray Evernham, invented a motto for the season: "Revive the Twenty-five." Although they were tenth in the standings after nineteen races, they still hadn't found a way to win. That is, until now. Schrader took the lead two-thirds through the race. In seven more laps the monkey would be off his back.

But suddenly there was Geoff, stalking him from behind, riding him through a series of turns known as the "esses" for the way they run into one another. Geoff was merciless, and maybe a little out of control. Pulling outside of Schrader, he went for a frenzied pass that sent his Ford skidding inches from the red Chevrolet in the heart of the turn. It was an audacious, brilliant challenge, and it seemed to break the back of Schrader's Monte Carlo, which subsequently ran out of gas. The monkey was off one back, but still on another. Schrader finished twenty-fifth; Bodine coasted to the win.

As Geoff cried in Victory Lane, thanking "God for getting me through a lot of struggles in my life the last two years," Brett hurriedly changed in the back of his trailer. He didn't try to brave the reporters who were surrounding his brother or the autograph signers who kept Geoff tied up until nightfall. "That was his moment," Brett said, pausing before adding, "And, anyway, things were kind of edgy between us."

So Brett returned home to Mooresville with a fourteenth-place finish and the second hand ticking on the beat-the-clock game of keeping his team together.

14

SNAKE OIL & SALVATION

New Hampshire to Richmond: July 14 to September 8

A man on unsteady legs stumbled from behind the Baptist church. He wore a soiled undershirt, loose-fitting pants, and no shoes, which caused him to hopscotch on the gravel beneath his feet. Though Dave Marcis's garage was only fifty yards from the church—the two buildings being neighbors on a rural road off the highway—the man didn't walk the whole distance. Rather, he stopped halfway and took a break to lean against the eighteen-wheeler that was parked in front of two open garage bays. There, he watched a half-dozen mechanics busily getting ready for New Hampshire. Tools were clanging and there was the occasional sound of "Well, I'll be a son of a bitch," which was what Dave said whenever something annoyed him. After a few minutes of this, the man rubbed his eyes and walked up to the lip of the garage bay. He knew better than to approach Dave, but crew chief Terry Shirley was a softer touch. "Terry, my old friend," the cautious visitor said in a raspy voice, his words slightly slurred. "You wouldn't have a couple of bucks a man could get lunch with, now wouldya?"

Terry laughed good-naturedly. "Lunch? Or beer, Jack?" he said, pulling out a five-dollar bill.

"Well, I hadn't thought of it," Jack said, feigning surprise. "But now that you mention it . . ."

Two hours south in Charlotte, Hendrick Motorsports

maintains an office complex of gray buildings that have imposing signs like "Hendrick Engineering" and "Engine Development." Nearly two hundred people work there, and in the main building there is a gift shop with Plexiglas walls, behind which one can see the Budweiser crew. Like the crews assigned to Jeff Gordon and Terry Labonte—whose fleets of cars have their own buildings in the complex—the Budweiser team works on spotless floors with gleaming tools and crisp uniforms.

Dave Marcis's garage is not even as nice as a nice service station. Behind it are shack homes, where laundry usually blows on lines and children's toys share the crabgrass with piles of rusted metal. Inside, the shelves on its tin walls shudder with the weight of nearly every part Dave has ever owned, for he doesn't throw out a thing. This is also true of the attached wood-paneled office, where thirty years of ledgers are packed around the models of various cars he's driven. The Marcises work side by side, their desks joined into a T, Helen's near a proclamation from the mayor of Wausau, Dave's near a portrait of John Wayne.

It is a museum of sorts, filled with old pictures on the walls, like the remarkable shot of Darrell Waltrip with long hair and a high-water jumpsuit. But the artifact most impervious to time is Dave himself. There were those who could simply not fathom why he didn't quit driving and make real money; why he raced without a cent in the bank or a new part on the truck. But they missed his essential locus: Dave reduced a Winston Cup season to its barest, simplest form—a vehicle to keep himself driving by day, which allowed him to have some remarkable nights.

The New Hampshire race is one of the newer ones on the circuit, added in 1993. Dave wound up driving the old wooden rig to Loudon that first weekend, but he got there late and the track was closed. He was cursing, wondering what to do with the hauler, when he stopped at a red light and asked a local, "You wouldn't know where a guy could store a truck now?"

"Sure, my place," the man replied. And so it was that Dave found Dick Glidden, a thick-bodied jail guard with meaty hands and cresting silver eyebrows. The Gliddens were dumbfounded as they watched the race car driver sit at their table, scarfing their food and telling a few tall tales between servings. But they were even more surprised when he showed up the next year, the year after that, and now this evening, with a dozen tousled mechanics. Dick and his wife Germane promised an outdoor barbecue, but heavy rains ruined that, so Dave & Co. squeezed into their rustic kitchen, eyeing the sliced moose and caribou that their neighbor Ken had killed.

"Caribou, huh?" Dave said, raising an eyebrow, but he dove right in and was well into his third piece as Dick told an old jail story about a breakout and his granddaughter played at Dave's elbow. The Gliddens asked nothing until a zoo's worth of meat had been consumed, and even then they asked it tentatively. A bit embarrassed, Dick's daughter brought out a shirt, then Ken slipped a stack of trading cards out of his pocket and, well, as long as the kids broached it, Dick had a few model cars. Dave patted his stomach, reached into his shirt pocket for a marker, slipped on his bifocals, and gave the Gliddens their own personal autograph session until it was well past midnight. By then the beer was done, and he apologized but he had a race to run in the morning.

Unfortunately, a piston on their rebuilt engine blew on Sunday and they went out of the race early. But Dave came back to his shop no higher or lower than usual. He just resumed the shell game of juggling parts and engines so that one of his eight cars would be ready to leave Thursday, July 18, for Pocono.

The Pocono International Raceway is owned by Joe and Rose Mattioli, a dentist and podiatrist whose love of racing led to its construction in 1971. Among the last of the independent track owners,* the pair try hard to show their appreciation to all who come. In a lovely gesture, they host a late-summer picnic that is open to all in the NASCAR garage. Dave and Helen always made a point of coming, and on this night, as a barbershop quartet sang old-time tunes, Rose summoned the Marcises to stand. Dave had kissed Helen awake that morning and wished her a happy thirtieth anniversary. It was the latest in a series of things he'd done to celebrate their union, including buying her a grand piano, something she'd wanted since she was a little girl. (Of course, it was used.) But when put on the spot by the singing quartet and asked to remember what they'd done the day before their wedding, he went blank. Searching his memory, he finally, helplessly, said, "I guess I was racing."

The frustrated entertainers wanted to launch into "Bring Me to the Church on Time," and they looked at Helen, who shrugged. So, turning back to Dave, one said, "Remember the day *after*, then," to which Dave grinned even more broadly and said, "I'm pretty sure I was racin' then too!" The singers gave up, the quartet broke into their song, and Dave kissed Helen again. It seemed a perfect way to celebrate a NASCAR union based as much on perpetual motion as love.

---

*The 1990s have been a decade of consolidation for NASCAR. As of 1997, three corporations—those run by the France family, Bruton Smith, and Roger Penske—owned all but seven tracks. The last of the independents are: Richmond, Martinsville, Dover, Indianapolis, Pocono, Las Vegas, and New Hampshire.

Helen didn't go everywhere with Dave. Afraid to fly, she never went to California. And because of the heat, she stayed away from the DieHard 500 in Talladega, which is where the tour headed five days after Dave took the checkered flag in Pocono, in twenty-eighth place.

Spending a few days in their lakefront cottage near Wausau, Helen listened to the race by radio, and when Earnhardt's disaster was recorded, her heart stilled because no mention was made of Dave. As it happened, he was going into the fourth turn when he saw his friend's Monte Carlo go airborne. He thought about stopping, because if Earnhardt was unconscious "it might help if he heard a friendly voice," but on seeing the rescue effort, he drove through the smoke and on to an eleventh-place finish, his best of the year. Sitting on the dock by the lake, Helen tried to be happy rather than addled or angry. But after thirty years of this, her heart didn't have many more beats to skip. So she packed up, went home, and didn't say a word to Dave, because she knew it wouldn't do any good. A few days later they were back on the road, this time to Indianapolis and another strange bedroom.

Like the Gliddens in New Hampshire, Russ Dowden waited all year for Dave's arrival in Indianapolis. He was a big, portly man with Coke-bottle glasses and slurpy speech, and he lived alone in a suburban home a block from the speedway. A gear cutter by trade, he'd become a race fan long before when his mother suggested he needed a hobby. On Brickyard weekend you couldn't get a decently priced hotel room in the whole damn city, but all Russ wanted was a few bucks and a few stories, and he happily gave up his four-post bed for the couch. Included in the deal was his attic, which he'd loaded with beds for Dave's crew. The room was stiflingly hot and the cots were sandwiched too tightly for much leg-room, so this hardly endeared Dave to the men. The chief mechanic went to sleep with a flashlight lest a strange limb invade his space, and business manager Dwayne Leik bought himself a hundred-dollar steak dinner to bolster himself before retreating back to what he'd taken to calling "the cave."

Three years earlier, right there on Russ's porch, Dwayne had sat the chief down and put a $3 million contract before him. The sponsor wanted a kid in the cockpit, and he wanted Dave to shape him—much as Richard Childress had done when he gave up driving to recruit Earnhardt. Dave clearly had the tools—the savvy, the brains, the experience—to mold the next superstar. But staring at that contract back then, he couldn't bring himself to sign it. And he was no closer now. He knew that the news about Prodigy wasn't good, that it would probably drop out of NASCAR. He knew Dwayne had started calling every place from Centrum Silver to the Army in an effort to find new sponsorship. And worse, or at least more immediately, he knew he wasn't going to get into the Brickyard again. On Thursday he qualified just forty-fourth out of forty-six cars, and on Friday his second-round qualifying time was worse. The last-place finisher at the Brickyard earned nearly as much as other races paid to win. Watching his chief mechanic kick a stack of tires, all Dave could think to say was, "Well, I'll be a son of a bitch."

But then Providence interceded, starting with the way the qualifying times fell. After the usual thirty-eight positions were filled, Winston Cup regular Ricky Craven used a provisional to get the thirty-ninth position. That left a fortieth-place provisional slot to fill. The lucky part for Dave was that none of the other racers was eligible. They were all part-timers on the Winston Cup tour—people like the legendary A. J. Foyt, who was lured out of retirement by the purse—and NASCAR doesn't give provisionals to part-timers. Dave was the only full-time member of the tour left. Unfortunately, he'd used up his last provisional in Dover seven races before.

An identical circumstance forced Marcis to miss the June 16 race in Pocono. Everyone who wanted to make the race did, leaving a vacancy in forty-second place. And just like at the Brickyard, Dave couldn't fill it because he was out of provisionals. The sight of him packing up early to go home jarred many of the other racers, not least because they put themselves in his shoes. It was hard enough to make races as it was. If there was an empty space, by God, fill it! Don't make someone who puts their life on the line every week go home early due to a technicality. Bill France was moved by this argument. Like his father, he respects loyalty, believing that those who've helped grow his sport need to be watched and looked after. This was what people meant when they referred to him as a "benevolent dictator." So he issued what came to be called the Dave Marcis rule: If there's an empty space in the field, and only one full-time driver left to fill it, a lack of provisionals is no reason to send that driver home.

On August 3, Dave Marcis became the first to use the Dave Marcis rule, and was awarded the fortieth spot on the Brickyard starting grid.

Unfortunately, for all the trouble, Dave went out of Saturday's race with engine problems early, finishing in thirty-fifth. But he wasn't complaining. That paid $50,185, enough to keep the Dave Marcis Traveling Snake Oil & Salvation Show going.

Over the next six weeks it averaged a thirty-second-place finish as it raced across the tracks in Watkins Glen, Michigan, Bristol, Darlington, and, on September 7, Richmond. Then, on the morning of Sunday, September 8, it pulled up stakes yet again to head for a small Pennsylvania border town named Waynesboro, where thousands of NASCAR fans were gathering to pay tribute to their

favorite racer from Wausau, Wisconsin—even if he did
have the second-worst record in Winston Cup.

Midvale Road in Waynesboro lies past the grain silos,
cattle farms, and wheat fields of Route 64, beyond the
West Virginia border, just after the four-way stop by a
white farm. Dave turned right at the farm and drove for
two miles until he reached Midvale.

The street had become a magnet for thousands of
people who'd been cooped up for days by Hurricane
Bertha and were out to enjoy a sunny afternoon. A police-
man was directing traffic, and as Dave slowed to a stop, he
rolled down the window of his brown van and gave one
of his toothy smiles. That seemed to be all the identifica-
tion he needed, because the cop elaborately waved him
through. From there, he pulled beside a long, corrugated
building with a sign that read "Dave George & Sons Construction Company."

Dave George first met the Marcises in North Wilkesboro in September 1975. Dave was driving for Harry
Hyde then, and as George remembers, "His car came
through the fourth turn and I said to myself, 'There's no
way he's gonna make it.' " But he sailed right through,
and when George bought a photo to see what he looked
like, the picture man said, "Why doncha go up to him?"

It was that easy then. Crews weren't full-time employees with health benefits. They were your friends, and
occasionally perfect strangers who volunteered when you
needed it most—when one of your guys had left town with
a woman, or was in the car sleeping off a drunk. George
went up to Hyde to ask if he needed help, and in fact Hyde
needed a gas man. He told George to show up the next
week in Martinsville. It was Dave's 255th start and, as it
turned out, the first win of his career. George sounds pro-

prietary when he says, "I've helped him on and off ever since."

Dave Marcis Day started when a tiny grocer from Waynesboro invited the racer to sign a few autographs and Dave said, "Sure, why not?" But it became an event when Dave George took it over. With a disposition one EKG blip from frantic, and ten acres around his construction company, he turned a small get-together into a county fair.

Show cars were arranged around the white booths where men named Smoky Snellbaker and Ramo Stott sat under signs identifying them as "local dirt-track legends," while not far away folks were waiting to ride in the Winston racing simulator, which R.J. Reynolds delivered for the day, along with its blond Winston girls and cigarettes. The centerpiece, however, was Dave's old wooden hauler. It looked imposing out here amid the flat acres of gravel and weeds, and fans circled it as if it were a monolith.

George met the Marcises by the door and led them to his supply room, where there was a long table covered with plastic table settings and cups of lemonade. Dave took a seat on the far end, next to Elmo Langley, the thick-bodied ex-racer who drove the Winston Cup pace car. He'd agreed to come help Dave celebrate the big day, as had Kyle Petty. But Kyle hadn't shown up yet.

Between mouthfuls of Swedish meatballs, Dave became distracted by Kyle's absence. "Where's Kyle?" he asked George, but George had no idea. Hadn't Dave heard? Langley asked. Kyle was catching a flight to L.A. for a meeting with Hot Wheels about sponsoring his new team.

"You think we should tell those people he's not coming?" George asked, suddenly worried.

"Let's give him a while," Dave said hopefully, returning to his meatballs. They talked for a while longer, gossiping. Dave mentioned that Ken Schrader pissed off Bobby Labonte by racing him so hard from a lap down

that he cost him a position. "Shit," Langley said, chuck-
ling. "They shoulda let him go after Schrader. He woulda
shown the kid a thing or two about fightin'." But after a
while, as he kept checking his watch, it became evident
that Dave would have to go outside and face the crowd
without Kyle.

The line of autograph seekers had grown to at least fifteen hundred, curling into a pair of S's that looped well
down to the back of his truck. Dave walked past it like a
fighter checking out an opponent, unconsciously rubbing
his fingers. A helicopter appeared overhead, and someone on line screamed, "It's Kyle." But then the chopper
buzzed off. Dave took his seat behind the table, limbered
up to start signing, and put on his best face. With fifteen
hundred people staring at the empty seat beside him, many
having been there for six hours, it occurred to George that
a riot might not be out of the question. So he grabbed a
megaphone and announced, "Kyle assured Dave when he
spoke to him yesterday that he'd be here, but we haven't
heard from him today."

The first fans in line were two not-terribly-friendly-
looking teens wearing black Kyle Petty T-shirts. (One assumed they could easily have pulled Megadeth shirts from
the drawer that morning.) Their first reaction was, "Hey,
man, that's bullshit," so George thought quickly, invoking
the notion that the only possible thing that could separate
Kyle from his fans was death. Once again using the megaphone, though it created a counterproductive sense of
emergency, George added, "He said that he was gonna
drive his bike up. So let's hope nothing happened to him
by way of accident."

At that, Dave motioned the two teens over to get their
autographs, but having waited six hours to be the first to
greet Kyle, neither would move. "Where's Kyle?" the
taller one demanded with more than a hint of menace.

Dave shrugged helplessly. "Don't know. He said he'd be here."

They regarded him, he regarded them, and the situation wasn't so much defused as delayed. Eventually they moved reluctantly to the side, letting others past. For the next three hours Dave stayed out there in the hot sun, signing every single autograph.

One of the very last faces he saw was that of a girl of six with strawberry-blond hair and freckles. She studied Dave for a couple of seconds, as if she wasn't convinced the man who looked like her grandfather was an active racer. Finally she seemed to come up with a litmus test, and asked, "Do you know Kyle?"

Dave assured her he did and that he was a very nice man. Then he gently slipped a signed Prodigy card into her hand and smiled broadly.

One can only wonder what she made of the Kennedy-esque phrase on its back. It read, "We've done so much with so little for so long that now we can do anything with nothing."

15

"NO WIMPS HERE"

Indianapolis to Bristol: August 1–24

Robbie Loomis knelt on the checkered tile floor of his garage bay at the Indianapolis Motor Speedway, his face coated in sweat, burned by the early-August sun. The heart-stopping crash that nearly cost Bobby Hamilton his life on June 26 had decimated the car they'd spent all their time testing. Trying to duplicate it was like trying to re-paint a portrait stroke for stroke. You could come close, but never get it exact. He figured his best shot would come with the car he fitted for Pocono, the only other flat track on the circuit. But John Andretti had taken care of that when he rolled over Bobby just six laps into Pocono's July 21 race. Robbie kept his crew in the eastern Penn-sylvania mountains overnight Sunday, and on Monday returned to the flat speedway to break in his backup car—spending another of the seven test sessions that NASCAR permits per season to do it. He didn't want to. Using two of his seven dates to get ready for just one race was incredibly wasteful. But like an NBA coach reluctantly spending a precious time-out, Robbie had no choice.

The backup never took well to the Brickyard. Though the special silver paint scheme made it shimmer, there was little sparkling about its performance. Robbie massaged the skin under his neck, pulling it down in long, slow strokes as he tried to figure out what to do next. The usual adjustments weren't working, and Bobby's first-round qualifying lap landed him in thirty-ninth place; he improved only two more places in the second-round session on Friday. Then, late Friday afternoon during Happy Hour, Bobby was looking for ways to pick up corner speed when, coming out of turn two, the car leapt up and ricocheted into the wall. Richard Petty was in the trailer when Robbie stormed in with the news that they'd wrecked.

"Bobby okay?" the King asked.

"Drivers don't get no workouts except when they wreck," Robbie tried joking. "He ain't hurt none, except his pride."

Robbie watched the King take off his cowboy hat and rub his eyes in deep round circles. Deciding there wasn't much more to say, he walked outside to meet the flatbed that was dropping off his wreck. He let out a long, impressed whistle at the fenders, which were shorn up like raised eyebrows, and the deep crease along the right side. Then he motioned to his men to start removing the backup car from their elevated hauler bay. It was the car that won the pole in Michigan, but that meant nothing here. Not when it would be starting in eighteen hours on wheels that hadn't even tasted the track.

The mad dash to prepare it exhausted everyone, and by dusk Robbie was taking his first break, crouching on one knee, watching the sunset in his sweat-soaked clothes. Another Pontiac crew chief, Chris Hussey, walked by and softly asked how he was.

"Just because I'm smilin' don't mean I don't want to cry," Robbie said. "We wrecked three cars in five weeks." Then he caught himself. "But we're gonna win this bitch. I mean it. We're gonna come from behind. And we're gonna win."

Hussey smiled. You had to have that kind of bravado in hopeless circumstances. If you didn't, who would?

"See ya in Victory Lane," Hussey said, walking away.

"We'll be there," Robbie shouted after him.

He wasn't. In fact, Bobby didn't run higher than thirtieth all day, keeping him in fourteenth place, the sixth straight week he failed to gain. While Robbie set his sights forward to Watkins Glen, Bobby flew home to Nashville Saturday night preoccupied, though only partly because of their reversal of fortune.

A few weeks earlier, Kyle had come into the hauler and said, "Bobby, we gotta talk. You're gonna be hearing a lot of rumors, so I'm telling you first. I'm leaving Felix, but I ain't gonna take your car. I ain't comin' back here to take the Forty-three."

Liking Kyle wasn't hard. Despite his silver spoon country pedigree, he had been raised to be humble. When he was young, his father had visited President Richard Nixon in the White House, and his teacher had to read about it in the papers. "How come you didn't tell us?" she asked. "I didn't know I was supposed to," he answered.

Trusting him was even easier than liking him, especially when it came to Kyle's promise that he'd never race his father's car.

Kyle was handed the keys to Petty Enterprises in his twenties, and it nearly drove him from racing. Managing his fledgling career would have been quite enough without the added burden of overseeing his father's. As it was, neither Petty was well-served trying to run two teams out of the same old country barn. Richard wisely left first, taking a high-paying job driving for a Nashville record producer. He hoped that Kyle would flower if left alone back home. No one foresaw the ironic consequence. The King's absence created a vacuum into which Kyle, his uncle Maurice, and his grandfather, Lee, rushed in, feuding. Three weeks after Richard's 200th win on July 4, 1984, Kyle announced he was leaving the family business. "It was supposed to be a bed of roses," he said at the time, "but somewhere down the line I fell into a patch of thorns."

In the years that followed, Kyle became a racing version of Shakespeare's Prince Hal, carousing to escape the burden of expectation that one day he'd be the next King. First he went to drive for the Pettys' archrivals, the Wood brothers. He also dabbled with a country music career. When his racing career failed to take off, he chose as his Falstaff a man of appropriately ravenous appetites, Felix Sabates. With Richard at the very pinnacle of his public appeal and Kyle off finding himself with Sabates, Petty Enterprises shuttered its doors. For the first time since 1947 there wasn't the sound of engines buzz-sawing the silence around Branson Mill Road.

The rest is well-known. Richard came back in 1986 to rebuild the shop, and hadn't had a top-ten year since. Each year that Kyle had stayed away worked a little more on his father's ego. But now Kyle had decided to return to Petty Enterprises to start his own team—a piece to his inheritance of the entire operation. Bobby had to wonder where that left him.

That's why the call from Sabates proved so well-timed. "What would it take to get you back here?" Felix asked. Bobby wasn't sure. "How about $600,000 plus half of all souvenir sales and forty percent of the purse?" That was more in one year than he'd make in three with the King. Felix was shrewdly giving everyone a chance to make a clean swap. All he asked was that he be given an answer by Watkins Glen.

In a Holiday Inn room there, Petty was circumspect when presented with this denouement. When the King wants, he can be as direct as an enforcer, but when the mood strikes him, he can also be vague and elliptical, and now he was playing his cards very close to the vest. This was Bobby's fiftieth race for Petty, five times the number

Andretti had run, so Bobby suggested that it seemed only fair he receive roughly what Petty had offered Andretti: $450,000 a year. Bobby wasn't entirely sure what was said in the two hours that followed. All he knew was Richard hadn't said yes.

From the moment John Andretti came into the Winston Cup garage, he was viewed skeptically, first as an outsider from IndyCar, the sport long known for looking down on NASCAR racers as "taxicab drivers," then as a showboat. In July 1994 he didn't do much for himself in the Winston Cup standings, but he grabbed headlines by being the first to run the Indy 500 (he finished third) and then fly to Charlotte to take the green flag in the World 600 (he went out with engine failure). His rise from the desperately underfinanced Billy Hagan team to Petty Enterprises to the Kranefuss/Haas outfit in twelve months was, by NAS-CAR standards, meteoric. Kranefuss's links to Ford and Haas's links to the Andrettis in IndyCar made the pairing seem heaven-made. But if one thing kept it on a decidedly earthly plain, it was the partnership interest of Tim Brewer.

Junior Johnson's longtime crew chief is a wonderfully engaging man with a glinty-eyed gift for storytelling and a catalog of fifty-three wins. But he can also be stubborn, short-tempered, and, if some stories are to be believed, even vengeful with his drivers. "I don't know where all that talk got started," he says. "I've fired maybe three guys in my entire life, and they needed firing. The way I look at it, if you're with me, then you're with me, and if you're not, then you came to do to me the same thing I'm gonna do to you." Brewer had little patience for an IndyCar driver who pretended to know how a stock car worked, and less when that driver demanded that they acquire the latest data-collection gadgetry, only to start arguing with it. By late in their second year together, Brewer had come to see Andretti as a racer whose reliance on technology made him too easily intimidated on the racetrack.

By the season's twentieth race, in Watkins Glen, Andretti had piloted them to thirty-sixth place in the Winston Cup point standings. Thirty-sixth! It ate at Brewer as few things could.

The damned thing was, looking over the car he had built for the upstate New York road course, Brewer found it not inconceivable that Andretti, a talented road racer, might have a shot to win. In the early stages, Andretti held his ground in seventeenth, paying Hamilton, who'd started thirtieth, no mind. But on the fifteenth lap Bobby was suddenly on his inside. Heading toward the tenth turn, John had a slight edge and, this being early in the race, every expectation that Bobby would lift off the throttle to let him past. But when it came to Andretti, etiquette was the last thing on Bobby's mind. Not only was he still pissed that John never apologized for wrecking him in Pocono, he'd begun hearing that Andretti was floating trial balloons about wanting back into the Forty-three. One confidant of both men reported that John boasted he had "one foot in the car, and another on Bobby's back." It hardly left Bobby disposed to make things easier on John.

As Andretti tried slinging in front of him, Bobby refused to yield. Expecting an opening, John was caught unawares as Bobby's nose stayed inside him. Veering right, he hit Bobby's left front and spun 180 degrees, down the track and into a fence. To the untrained eye, it appeared the fault was entirely Andretti's, which was exactly what Bobby intended.

Nursing a twenty-sixth-place finish in his hauler after the race, Brewer finally quit, unable to take losing any longer. While Kranefuss was in the STP hauler screaming at Loomis, Brewer was giving Andretti one final piece of advice. It was the last time he'd speak to the slightly built racer, and looking at him squarely in the eye, he said, "Every once in a while you gotta make Christians out of a few of them jerks so the rest will know you mean business, John. If someone keeps banging on you, you gotta walk up to them and say, 'See that wall down there? The next time you touch me, you and me are both going into that wall windshield deep.' You have to earn respect in here, because if those guys know they can run you over every week and get away with it, it's open season. It's do unto others before they do it to you. And as long as you keep taking it, Bobby Hamilton's gonna keep dishin' it out."

Whatever scores Bobby might have thought settled, the satisfaction was short-lived. Not ten minutes after their contact, a timing belt broke in his motor and he spent the rest of the day behind the wall. Except for the Andretti-inspired thirty-ninth-place finish in Pocono, the thirty-eighth-place day at the Glen would be his worst all year.

The following Friday at the Michigan International Speedway, Robbie Loomis told Bobby that NASCAR officials were looking for him. Bobby wasn't surprised. He had known the talk about his feud with Andretti was getting too loud, and that Gary Nelson or Mike Helton would feel compelled to act. So he sought them out Friday morning. "If you're gonna ream my tail," he'd said, "bring Andretti in too. Let's clear some things up."

If NASCAR, as they say, is Judge, Jury, and Jesus Christ, then Nelson and Helton are the first two legs of the trinity.

Helton, NASCAR's vice president for competition, is an imposing presence, a tall burly man with a foresty black mustache who favors dark suits and carries himself like a small-town sheriff. His voice is low and rumbling and can still a room, but he is known as a particularly good listener—something that's invaluable in a sport where people love to blow off steam. As the court of last resort, he's well-respected for using his power judiciously. "You have a large family?" he asks in a tone that manages to be both dark and folksy. "Well, we're a large family, and sometimes we just need to sit around the table and hash things out."

That table is usually the cramped back lounge of the fire-red NASCAR trailer, better known as the Woodshed. It is filled with phones, computers and a fax, a leather couch, and a revolving easy chair. Now, as Hamilton and Andretti were led inside, Helton sank deep into the chair. Nelson stood by the door.

It is often said of Gary Nelson, a trim, silver-haired man with an easy California smile, that when Bill France wanted a Winston Cup series director who could police the cheating in the garage, he hired the best cheater NASCAR had ever seen. "I got quite a reputation for breaking the rules in my early years as a crew chief," Nelson, the son of an inventor, says. "But that was by design. I worked in the gray areas of the rules, and there were a lot more gray areas back then. Part of it was letting people think I was getting away with something. That way, they'd wait for me to get caught and wouldn't work on their cars as hard. It worked out well."

By going to "the other side," as crew chiefs called NASCAR's front office, Nelson saw his friendships with the colleagues he had to police grow inevitably distant. Still, he was the one who understood them best, and he started by saying, "What's going on here with you two?"

"I feel like a punching bag when I'm out there," Bobby complained.

"He's had it in for me since Richmond," Andretti parried.

"I'm losing all my best cars," Bobby said.

"He's got no class," Andretti replied.

"Class?" Bobby shot back. "If class had anything to do with this sport, Earnhardt woulda been a broke man."

"Stop now, both of you," Nelson finally interrupted. "I don't want either of you so much as *touching* each other's cars. Understood?"

"We mean it," Helton intoned. "From now on, we're making the two of you the poster kids for our sport."

As they were splitting up, the men shook hands guardedly, neither really convinced it would be the last time they'd trade paint.

Bobby went off to qualify fifth, Andretti fifteenth.

With all that had gone on, Bobby was dead tired. He fell asleep just as Richard Petty began warming to the subject of their future. So the conversation had to wait until the next afternoon, when the two sat across from each other in Petty's living-room-size Winnebago, with its long blue leather couches, spotless kitchen, and blinds closed to seal off the day.

Richard spoke about a good many things. About Andretti, and the fact that he now rued jumping to the highest bidder. About Kyle, and the uncertainties of picking up where they had left off a dozen years before. And, eventually, about winning. On this point the winningest stock car driver of all time grew animated, opening his eyes so wide that the crow's-feet around them expanded like fingers on an open hand.

"This whole deal is ridin' on *you*," Richard Petty said. "But you gotta get that block outta your head. Earnhardt wreckin' us in Rockingham is over. You gotta take control of this team. You gotta get them fired up." He went on for a while like this, came up with a new salary figure that was less than half what Bobby was seeking, and finally said, "Okay, we'll do a two-year deal and see what happens."

That was the part of the sentence Bobby wanted to hear. Not the part about how Pontiac said no to supplementing his salary the way it had for John, nor the part about needing only a handshake, not a contract. So he thanked Richard and went into the Michigan afternoon. With some time on his hands, he walked back to the famous blue and red machine that he had watched as a kid. It was still his. And perhaps the only reason it was had to do with the fact that his father had died with four hundred dollars in a lockbox and Bobby wasn't ready to be rich. Maybe Petty played him perfectly, knowing as much. But standing there before the crew, *his* crew, everything seemed perfectly ordered. In NASCAR, this is what people waited their whole careers for.

Bristol, Tennessee, is part of something called the Tri-Cities, one of those Chamber of Commerce names coined so that new businesses don't worry that they're moving into a cultural sinkhole. The buzzword in the Tri-Cities is regionalism, a civic euphemism for "If we draw a circle for fifty miles around we can collect enough taxes to build a zoo and maybe get a couple of research grants for the local college."

The Tri-Cities has one airport. It has three gates.

Johnson City is the most cosmopolitan of the Tri-Cities, owing to the shopping and restaurants around East Tennessee State University. Next is Kingsport, which houses Eastman Chemical and is more suburban. Bristol is the smallest and quaintest. Its brick-face main street is filled with flea markets, homey bars, and the famous dividing line of State Street that bisects Virginia and Tennessee. Not leaving anything to chance, the town's fathers have erected a bright white arch, which announces, "Bristol: a nice place to live."

On this bright Thursday afternoon, Bristol couldn't have been more inviting, as shopkeepers dressed in their Sunday best watched thousands of fans flock under the arch to meet the Winston Cup drivers who lined the street, posing for pictures and signing autographs. In the midst of all this a twenty-foot-tall shopping cart (no, really) suddenly roared down State Street. It had a monster-truck engine mounted where the cat litter usually goes, and a cockpit built into the fold-down vegetable tray. The cart belonged to Food City, a Winston Cup race sponsor. As it parked, Bristol took on the surreal look of some forgotten mountain town, where villagers all go to a Jurassic-size Food City for diaper wipes.

All of which couldn't have been finer with the local Chamber of Commerce, and it showed its appreciation to the man who made this day possible by putting up a billboard beside the speedway that said in big red letters, "Thanks Bruton."

Bruton Smith was considered something of a local savior for having bought the nearby Bristol Motor Speedway for $26 million that January. The seller was Larry Carrier, a local developer who'd built the tiny valley oval from plans he sketched on a napkin in 1960. Carrier also went on to found the International Hot Rod Association and World Boxing Federation, where his son Mark, a heavyweight, fought. At seventy-four he wanted to spend more time in boxing, not spend millions adding the necessary seats to pay for the growing purses Winston Cup was demanding. So Carrier quietly put feelers out about selling. Bruton Smith was the first one to the phone.

Smith immediately started building grandstands into the sky, and talking with German engineers about one day erecting a dome. Most in Bristol agreed this was a good thing, and not just because it might attract indoor sports. (Carrier once used the infield to host an exhibition NFL game.) Swarms of crickets usually descend on the Tennessee valley at night, flying right into the hot lights. Fans sitting in the top rows look forward to the time when they'll no longer be treated to a steady drizzle of crisped crickets.

And yet, when dark falls, Bristol's intimate size and defiant location make it the singularly most exciting place on the entire circuit. Eli Gold, the announcer, has observed that watching racing here is like watching jet fighters in a gymnasium, and that's about right. There are no moments when the cars disappear and conversation is normal. The noise is constant and deafening, and this is thrilling. It is the only place where you can watch a race unfold like the chess match it is, seeing every pass and parry from your seats. You are inside a bowl, so low in a valley that your knees ache just climbing up the stairs to get onto the grandstands. But once you get up there, you can sit back knowing you have the best seat to any NASCAR race all year.

As the fireworks shot high into the sky and the Rolling Stones song "Start Me Up" blared over the mountains, Scott Sharpe looked down from atop the tool rig where he videotaped the STP crews' pit stops and offered what should be the unofficial slogan of the Goody's Headache Powders 500.

"Strap yourself in," he said. "No wimps here."

Coming off a thirteenth-place finish the week before in Michigan, Bobby Hamilton was starting here in thirty-fifth place. Wrecks happen fast in Bristol: The track gives a crew chief low on car ulcers. So, pulling his headset over his ears, Robbie Loomis gave the tightly packed pit a once-over. "Everything looks good here, how about there?" he radioed into the car. Bobby checked his oil and water temperatures as he crawled through the 36-degree banking, the steepest in NASCAR. "Fine here," he answered.

The aim for the first couple of laps was getting into single file since an earlier rain had slicked the track, washing away the outside passing groove. Geoff Bodine proved the wisdom of that strategy. Trying to thread his way outside Jimmy Spencer in the first turn, he clipped him, causing a Spencer spinout. Geoff then got booted himself—by his own brother Brett!—coming out of the fourth turn. That drew a caution, and by not ordering a pit stop, Robbie vaulted Bobby into seventh place.

As the twilight turned dark, Rusty Wallace took the wraps off a setup that was nuclear in the low groove. Bobby receded to fourteenth, the last car on the lead lap. By now he was starting to feel the strain of the g forces, and it was easy to see what Elmo Langley meant when he once joked that the only reason Cale Yarborough won so much at Bristol was that he had no neck.

Searching for openings in the cramped corners, Bobby fell behind Earnhardt, Schrader, the Burton brothers, and Sterling Marlin in the line to break into the top ten. Before long, though, he was hearing, "Leader's three seconds behind you, Bud." That was only 160 feet. If Bobby lost his lead lap edge, he'd be trapped in the teens, where there was a real Wild West shoot-out. So he concentrated on rhythm—deep into the turns on the throttle, easy off to keep from spinning—which helped shave a quarter second off his lap times.

Finally finding a balance, Bobby wound up chasing Ricky Craven, who was running at an almost equal pitch. Patiently waiting for an opening, he edged his nose to the inside when the Maine native drifted high in the second turn. Though Craven was faster in the backstretch, Bobby dueled with him through the turns and throttled out hard enough to snare tenth place under the front-stretch lights.

Meanwhile, Dale Jarrett and Gary Bradberry had been bumping. Finally, Bradberry spun and a new caution was thrown. That gave the Forty-three team a chance to reload with fresh rubber.

On the restart, Craven dove under Bobby for position, but a dozen laps later Bobby was eyeing that same sweet spot in turn two. Robbie winced as Bobby went for an impossibly tiny patch of daylight, and cringed as Craven went spinning into the wall, his tires popping like fireworks as he locked the brakes. (Bobby tried apologizing in the caution period that followed when Craven pulled beside him, cursing and shaking his fist, but the message didn't get through. Craven was still railing in the garage after the race. "Did the stupid SOB give any explanation?" the exasperated racer said. "It wasn't like he just passed me. He just ran over me.")

In the pits, Robbie studied the nitrogen-filled tires that came off his car.* They looked like steaming manhole covers. Their 250-degree temperatures were well within range, and the wear on the inside of the left-sides suggested the concrete wasn't shearing them enough to require another pit. "You were hauling ass," Robbie radioed. "We're good for the rest of the day."

They were tenth, the second-to-last car on the lead lap. The car behind them was Bobby Labonte, but he was mired behind Mike Wallace. Though Wallace was hopelessly lapped, he refused to let Labonte pass, leading to an exchange of curses between their spotters and a frantic appeal to NASCAR by Labonte's crew chief to order Wallace to move. Frustrated after several laps of Wallace's indifference, Labonte finally tried passing him on the outside as they sped from turn two. But with all the distraction, Labonte didn't see Andretti and drilled him hard into the wall. Climbing from his own wrecked Chevrolet, its

---

*Winston Cup teams fill their tires with nitrogen, not air, because it lasts longer. But the nitrogen gets warm as the tire heats up on the asphalt. For every ten degrees of increased tire temperature, a tire's air pressure increases one pound, stiffening the sidewall. In a street car, it's nearly impossible to notice the change in handling that one pound of pressure causes. But in a finely tuned race car, that pound of change can wreak havoc on handling and performance.

radiator bleeding down the banking, Labonte let loose a furious kick to its door that nearly fractured his foot.

Half an oval away, Robbie paced the pit like an NBA coach on the sidelines of a playoff game. If they stayed out, if they could get by without another pit, Bobby could take the lead, maybe even win. But maybe they'd get spun out on their balding tires too. No, after two months of bad news, Robbie was going to play this one safe. He called Bobby into pit road with everyone else. In the closing laps, Bobby would be mired in lapped traffic and unable to put a run on Ricky Rudd. And Robbie would apologize to his peeved driver in the hauler afterward. He'd say he was sorry for "taking the race outta your hands." But as the checkered flag fell over them in tenth, he took a satisfied swig of Gatorade.

"Damn, we needed that," he said.

16

RAVENOUS FOR RESPECT

Martinsville, Virginia: September 19–22

A pair of elderly women looked through their curtained windows at the waves of people passing by the clapboard sign they'd hammered into their lawn, one side of which read, "You Will Meet God," the other, "Jesus Saves." It wasn't clear if the women intended on actually saving anyone, or if the sign was a kind of religious hedge being used to ward off those people who might do damage to their begonias. After all, the traffic to get to the flea market a few feet away on Speedway Road was brisk.

So many greasy food vendors and T-shirt sellers were trampling every available inch of front yard, one had to strain to notice that for most of the year this was a neighborhood like any other. But out of all the homes, one stood apart in its refusal to rent itself out to the zeitgeist. It was somewhat run-down, but a fresh coat of lime-green paint had been applied to the trim and doors, making it seem bright and even a bit regal. On a window ledge were five carved statuettes precisely lined up beside one another—two wooden drummers, a bride and groom, and a ballerina.

A bent-over black woman in a lively patchwork dress eventually emerged through the front door and started raking her front lawn, fifteen feet from a man hawking hats. They regarded each other for a moment, then went about their business. Like the statues standing guard in the

245

window, the woman seemed to be standing hers, trying against all odds to have a normal morning.

Though she was but a few hundred yards away from the Martinsville Speedway, which lay at the bottom of the hill like a river mouth, the notion of this woman's life ever intersecting with that of Bobby Hamilton, Dave Marcis, or Brett Bodine was inconceivable. As it was, the three drivers had disparate lives even in their own little world— although this afternoon those lives were intersecting. They had been randomly selected to follow one another in Friday's qualifying session.

Ever since Bobby had resolved his immediate future with the King in Bristol, he'd been on a tear. He shot out of Richmond like a rocket in seventh, and departed from Dover in tenth. For Brett, however, it was a continuing pattern of one step forward and two back. Solid runs were followed by uneven ones. He couldn't seem to find a race to build on. In Darlington a set of overheating tailpipes had blistered his legs and baked his arms, and he had to be replaced in the middle of the race. A nearly unconscious Brett was pulled from the cockpit, and while Diane caked him in ice, he whispered through shivers, "It feels like twenty below out here." The following Sunday in Richmond, he'd recovered enough to race but never broke out of twenty-fifth place, blaming an underpowered motor. In Dover on September 15, when he turned a thirty-seventh-place start into a fabulous fourth-place run, a bad set of tires caused a drift back to fifteenth. Trying hard to find the front, Brett went for a high pass of Ken Schrader, but with too little room he spun out and ended the day with a fourteen-lap deficit.* Now, five days later in Martinsville, he was fol-

---

*This spin would inadvertently create one of the most talked-about highlight clips of the year. Seeing Brett spinning, Jimmy Spencer checked up, causing a collision with Wally Dallenbach. Spencer became so irate that when Dal-

lowing Bobby onto the track for qualifying, but while the STP Pontiac circled the oval with a 94.12-mph pole-winning speed, the Lowe's Ford sputtered two full mph slower. It was a disconsolate Brett who radioed to his crew, "I'm getting sick of this," just as Dave Marcis's Chevrolet was pulling onto the asphalt. Dave had practiced well, and as he circled the track to complete his warm-up lap and begin his qualifying one, he sneaked a quick peek at the leader board, which showed a 20.77-second time. It was worse than anything he'd run all morning! As a result, he tried too hard through the rest of his lap, posting an anemic 20.554-second effort that placed him after Brett on the starting grid. They were situated thirty-fourth and -fifth in a starting grid that had room for only thirty-six cars. With the last four positions being provisional spots, neither racer was assured of anything. The cutoff for getting in on qualifying time was thirty-second place.

Because tracks have more oil on them by the time Saturday's second-round qualifying session starts, they tend to be more slippery. As a result, cars slide and lose time. Unless it's much cooler (cool air is like rocket fuel in an engine's carburetor), race cars inevitably go more slowly in the second round. That's why only desperate drivers avail themselves of the chance to try again. The rest stand on their first-round times, believing they'll be fast enough to survive a challenge.

But a thirty-six-car grid with four provisional spots made for a lot of desperate drivers. So at noon, fifteen cars piled onto pit road, the Lowe's and Prodigy ones among

---

lenbach came to rest at the mouth of pit road, he ran over and poked his fists through his window in a boxer's crouch. The sight transfixed the television audience, not to mention Brett's crew. Donnie had to yell "Stop watching the fucking TV!" to remind the younger ones who'd never seen such a thing that their own driver needed help.

them. Of the first nine, only three bettered themselves, moving the new speed-to-beat down to 20.494 seconds. Brett was next up. He needed to improve by just over a half second to make it. Helen Marcis watched his time flash on the leader board: 20.645 seconds. *Oh my!* That was almost a full tenth *worse* than Friday. Brett Bodine was going home.

Just like the day before, Dave was already on the track as Brett's time flashed. Helen kept her eyes on the woman who records each time on a wooden tote board. After the twenty-second mark came, she started filling in the space next to Dave's car number: a four . . . seven . . . and two. Helen held her chest as Dave's 20.472 second speed moved him into thirtieth place.

"You think that's safe?" he radioed to Terry Shirley, whose response sounded as if he were asked whether the sky was blue. "Yeah, I think so," he shot back. But even with a two-car cushion and four cars to go, Helen wasn't sure. In the next few minutes, Derrike Cope ran worse but Lake Speed improved, knocking Dave to thirty-first. Only Bobby Hillin Jr. and Gary Bradberry were left. When the woman started writing beside Hillin's name, *four* . . . *seven* . . . and after a pause that seemed interminable, *one*, the breath went out of Helen's lungs. That thousandth of a second was enough to drop Dave to thirty-second. Now Helen's eyes didn't waver from the board as Bradberry went wide open.

While the black woman outside the track was tending to her yard in the real world, in the NASCAR world time was standing still. Then Helen saw *seven* appear after the twenty, and time sped up again.

"It's a seven," she squealed, jumping up and down and singing the phrase as she ran back to the truck with a skip in her step.

"It's a seven. It's a seven. It's a seven."

* * *

Richard Petty dismissed the Thursday, September 19, edition of the Raleigh *News & Observer* and its page-one headline, RICHARD PETTY FACES HIT-AND-RUN CHARGE. "People pay millions of dollars for this kind of publicity," he said jauntily, walking with the paper rolled up in his hand. Referring to the traffic fine he had to pay, he said, "I got it for sixty-five dollars."

The voters who knew Richard, who loved him, did so because even now, at sixty, his face looked tanned and taut, rugged in the manner of Clint Eastwood the outlaw gunslinger. He still looked as if he could drive all day, stay up all night, and then deck any Yankee who got cheeky. It was that image that made the state's GOP come running to him.

After he'd retired from driving, the King grew restless. Though he'd served as a commissioner of his native Randolph County for sixteen years, it struck him as sensible that a man such as he should think about a higher mission. So in 1994 he volunteered to record a couple of dozen radio ads for the local GOP, stumped across the state, and formed North Carolina's first-ever individual political action committee, which raised $110,000 in nine months. Though Republican hopefuls since Richard Nixon had made Richard a whistle-stop on the way to the White House, it took that PAC to make them realize what he could do locally.

As Republican consultant Art Britt points out, "North Carolina was only starting to become a two-party state, and Richard was the first face we found to rally around." When Republicans picked up twenty-six seats in the statehouse in 1994 to claim their first majority of this century, Richard Petty, the winningest stock car racer ever, awoke to find himself the GOP's newest star.

After the legislature, the next target were eight statewide posts below governor that also hadn't gone Republican in the 1900s. The most senior of these positions was Secretary of State, an administrative job involving record-keeping and securities regulation. Richard was told it could be his for the taking.

It seemed perfectly natural. After all, Richard craved the kinetic bursts of contact that are the mother's milk of local politics. You can see it at the racetrack, the way he takes the issue of *Hot Rod* magazine you've handed him, the one that shows his '67 Plymouth or '70 Super Bird, and tells you, "That was one hell of a race car," making you feel you knew something more about him, something deep. Then he'll hug the wife, and tell the kid, "Howyadoin', buddy," as he settles down to sign. You watch his long, impossibly long, fingers. Somehow, you expect them to be gangly or scarred, and are surprised to find them perfectly manicured and smooth, which is a fair enough description of the man himself. His fingers grip the pen and then you notice his secret: He pushes it with his arm. That's why he can sign so long. His fingers don't tire. Each autograph is exactly the same. Fans stalk him like a zoo animal, jabbing him with autograph cards as if they are food pellets. And he always takes them. Always.

Why? "Look down there," he said one day on his private plane. "What do you see?" There was nothing to see beneath the clouds. "Exactly. Up here, no one is bigger than anyone else."

In intimate circumstances, it was easy to see he followed that philosophy. But in politics, he would prove naive, and slowly, that naïveté began to look like hubris— the very thing he'd strained for thirty-five years to hide.

He didn't help himself when he announced his candidacy before a skeptical press by saying he'd neither give up his racing interests nor serve full-time. When reporters questioned how he could be a paid pitchman for everything from Pontiac to Goody's Headache Powders and also serve the public interest, he looked earnestly into their faces. "I don't see what the problem is," he said. "I asked all my sponsors, and they don't mind."

There were other reasons to question how his good intentions would translate into public service, which is why polls showed that his early lead over a little-known lawyer had disappeared by September 11. That's when Petty came upon a forty-nine-year-old systems analyst named James Rassette.

The King was coming home from a business meeting at the Charlotte Motor Speedway on I-85 when he saw Rassette's Mazda ahead of him and began following a few inches behind. For Richard, this was no doubt a yawning distance, but Rassette found it less comforting. So at 70 mph, he answered with the universal highway fuck-you, a brake check. That caused Richard's pickup to bounce off Rassette's fender. Rassette changed lanes, expecting to stop to see if there was any damage, when the black pickup drove on. Rassette followed it for forty-five miles through three counties. Said the analyst, "I wasn't concerned with my property damage. My thought was, 'What's going through this guy's mind?' "

Rassette ultimately came upon a highway patrolman with the unlikely name Mickey Mantle at a rest stop. Describing what had happened, he led Mantle to flag Petty's pickup a few miles away. Richard's explanation was somewhat more subdued than Rassette's, along the lines that the cars merely touched, but he couldn't help adding, "If he were still in front of me, I'd knock his rear off the road again." Mickey Mantle duly noted this, but observing no damage on either car, logged a report that involved no tickets.

Which is where it lay while Richard went to Dover. He'd thought so little about the incident that he didn't even tell his wife Lynda. But on Monday, September 16, his lawyer called to say the matter hadn't died after all. It seems Mantle's report had been noticed by his superiors at the Highway Patrol, whose highest-ranking officer, Colonel E. W. Horton, was an appointee of Democratic governor Jim Hunt. Though the main prerequisites of a hit-and-run property damage charge—having an accident and having someone improperly leaving the scene—weren't supported by Mantle's report, something the local Republican D.A. made clear, the Highway Patrol gave the green light to file the charge. Word was leaked to media outlets around the state, and on Thursday morning, just as District Attorney Mark Speas was dismissing the charge for lack of evidence, everyone was waking up to the dubiously temporary "news" that Richard faced hit-and-run charges.

Few had more fun with him than *The Insider*, a Raleigh political newsletter that published the "Top 10 reasons Richard Petty was having driving problems." Among them:

6. Lost control of the car while doing the macarena.
5. Woozy from one too many BC Powders.
4. Brim of huge hat momentarily blinded me.
3. In a hurry to get to Raleigh, where Rufus Edmisten [the scandal-scarred ex-secretary] had fixed me up with a poofy-haired babe from the secretarial pool.
2. I didn't know there was a car in front of me; I can't see a damn thing in these sunglasses.
1. Was practicing notarizing bumper stickers.

Richard's campaign manager, a gentle, graying former U.S. congressman named Bill Coby, cringed while reading the list. He knew that non-Democrats had been out-registering Democrats six to one since 1990, but most of those new registrants were suburbanized transplants with Range Rovers, Panthers season tickets, and a taste for Thai food. Most important, they didn't think of themselves as southerners. To reach them, he'd have to fight Richard's redneck racer stereotype. The story undercut him in the worst way possible.

Richard had to leave for Martinsville, but when he came back, Coby decided to hit the road in the western part of the state, where the leaves were changing, and he hoped some Democratic minds would as well.

"This race is five hundred miles, all afternoon, gentlemen. That's *all* Sunday afternoon, no matter how you slice it. So work together when you're out there. Use your heads. Now I'm asking you. But I can tell you another way. That's with the black flag."

David Hoots, a NASCAR official, let the words he'd delivered like a Georgia prison guard linger over the concrete room packed with drivers who'd been on the road for twelve straight weeks. With just six races left, you could divide them into two groups: those racing to get on The Stage, and everyone else.

The Stage is the dais of the grand ballroom of the Waldorf-Astoria in New York City. NASCAR's year-end awards banquet used to be a boozy little affair held in a Daytona Beach hotel, but R.J. Reynolds moved it to New York in the 1970s when it renamed the series the Winston Cup. For a time there was a novelty in the hillbillies coming up north, barnstorming through the hotel's posh suites, but that time is long since gone. Today, the banquet is a dizzying two-day celebration of money and power. In 1995, Jeff Gordon was coronated with press conferences, an appearance on David Letterman's show, swings through trendy New York bars, photo ops in Times Square, and, finally, a three-hour ceremony in the gilded grand ballroom that was televised live over ESPN. The point of the evening is to award the top ten drivers, so this is what teams mean when they talk about "racing to get onto The Stage."

But the night really belongs to the champion. Gordon sat glazed and dizzy on the dais as óne tuxedoed bigwig after another rained praise and money on him. The evening ended with a midnight champagne dance in the Empire Room, where a billion dollars' worth of salaries boogied until the wee hours.

Now 76 points separated Terry Labonte from Gordon. And Dale Jarrett was only 21 points behind Labonte. At least a dozen others were in the thick of the hunt to get on The Stage, including the thirteenth-place STP team.

"Please, let's race each other respectfully," Hoots said, handing his microphone to the chaplain, who added, "I pray, my Father, we have a real forgiving attitude and a real respect. We ask it in Christ's name."

After the meeting, Bobby Hamilton stole some privacy in a narrow alley beside his team's hauler. All weekend his crew had been calling him Superman and King Kong, in deference to his stunning performance on Friday, when he won two poles. (An hour after he ran the fastest Winston Cup lap, he duplicated the feat by winning the pole for the Craftsman race in a Chevy truck he co-owned with the team's publicist, Chuck Spicer.) Richard, however, held back his praise. "How come you couldn't run faster?" he asked when Bobby got back to the hauler, only half joking.

"Hell, I woulda if I'd known I could run *that* fast," Bobby answered, throwing his helmet on the couch in the lounge.

Richard considered himself a fairly good judge of character, which helped him delegate authority among more than a dozen people in top levels within his organization (As such, he assumed running a state agency wouldn't be that different from managing Petty Enterprises.) But he remained perplexed by Bobby's inability to get past the block keeping him out of Victory Lane.

"What's the matter with Bobby?" Richard asked Debbie Hamilton as they stood alone in the hauler.

The remark took Bobby's wife off guard. "What do you mean?" she asked.

"Why won't he go to the front?"

Debbie started stewing but checked her anger and started out the door. "I don't think Bobby's got a problem," she said, leaving no doubt where she stood.

Richard nodded. They'd find out soon enough. This was a short track, Bobby's favorite. He was on a roll, finishing in the top ten in three out of the last four races. And he was being given a pole-winning car without a single obvious flaw. Now he'd see if his quarterback had that big game in him.

As the cars lined up for the start of the race, it was clear Richard wasn't the only one with doubts. The Vegas oddsmakers put Bobby at 28–1. ESPN similarly accorded him little respect. Its on-air introduction featured Gordon, Labonte, Jarrett, and Earnhardt, but not a single shot of the pole-winner. In the pressroom, a veteran reporter looked down at the Forty-three car and summarized the collective wisdom when he said, "I don't see the fire in Bobby Hamilton. He takes things too casually. He doesn't take chances. I just don't see the tension and competitive spirit of an Earnhardt in him."

Sitting in his bucket seat, it was almost as if Bobby had heard every single word, every inflection of doubt, and was determined to answer it all right here. Ravenous for respect, he came out like an animal, sideswiping Rusty Wallace in an attempt to get the lead. The attempt failed, however, because Rusty powered forward. On three straight entries to turn three, Bobby bumped, nudged, and nosed, like a boxer looking to turn a gash into a gusher. His combinations inside, outside, dead-on, were unrelenting and at times breathless. The reporter who'd doubted him gasped.

After thirty laps it seemed Rusty had finally opened a car-length lead. But suddenly Bobby was there again, right on his bumper. He dove to Rusty's outside, was blocked, swung low, then, unable to find a lane, swung back wide going into the corner.

"Draw back on your outside!" Rusty's spotter yelled. "He's there! He's on the outside!"

As Rusty sealed off the high side of the track, Bobby followed him on the outside to the next corner, lunging to get his nose past Rusty's rear wheels. He didn't get it, but he stayed outside as they spilled onto the backstretch. To neutralize Bobby's outside threat, Rusty veered sharply up, making a beeline from the apron to the wall. He rode in front of Bobby up there until they went once again into turn three. Bobby couldn't make his outside pass work through the third and fourth turns, so as they sped onto the front stretch together, he booted Rusty from behind. Back into the first turn, Bobby went outside yet again, but now Rusty's spotter was radioing, "He's on your outside! You better let him go or he'll wreck both of you!" Irked, Rusty stayed low as he went onto the backstretch, giving Bobby the high lane to pass. It had taken thirty-three laps, but Bobby showed the Vegas oddsmakers. "Great job, Buddy," Robbie said into his radio. Richard took his hat off and wiped his forehead. The boy was on a mission.

With his car drinking in the fresh air up front, Bobby wasn't challenged until Jeff Gordon made a run for the lead deep into the race. Working under the instruction "Keep pointing your nose inside and make him use his brakes," Gordon baited Bobby until he drifted high enough to take the lead. Then, a few feet ahead, Bobby dove into pit lane for a surprise stop. Under the pressure, the team's tire-changer bobbled a lug nut. On the next lap, Gordon's crew needed two fewer seconds to perform their pit stop. As a result, Gordon went to first, Bobby to third. Between them was John Andretti.

Over the next half hour the signs of a bad set of tires began to show on the STP team's Pontiac. Once so fearless, Bobby had to back off to keep control and he drifted to a distant fifth as lapped traffic tied him in knots. Richard watched with concern, then irritation, raising eyebrows among his crew by overriding Robbie. In a voice that laced impatience with panic, he chided into the radio, "Fifty to go! You gotta go from here on out, man."

Three laps later Sterling Marlin spun, drawing a caution. "Okay, this is our chance," Robbie cried. "Let's get the man a fast pit."

It was a whirling one, allowing Bobby to rejoin the field one spot up, in fourth. On ESPN, Benny Parsons looked down and said, "The question I have is can that Forty-three car find the magic it had earlier?"

It didn't. At least not in the next stretch, a thirty-lap interlude when Bobby kept looking at Andretti half a straight in front of him, but a caution would bring the race down to a final, three-lap mad dash for victory.

Andretti's new crew chief, Tony Furr, had been holding his driver back, but now he unleashed him. "Don't worry 'bout those brakes no more," he said. "We should finish at least third."

As the sprint began, Bobby tried getting around Andretti, poking his nose inside the Ford's right rear, then riding him side by side through the corners. John had the stronger car and powered past Hamilton. In the backstretch, Bobby rammed him from behind, causing the Ford to swerve to the next lane. With a stunning recovery, Andretti sealed off the passing lane before Bobby could get past. But Bobby wasn't stopping at just one try. Barreling through the corner, the most dangerous part of the track, he did it again, ramming John smack on the bumper.

Andretti fishtailed, madly trying to correct, but he was hopelessly high. Bobby poured through the daylight in front of him. With Andretti flailing behind him, having been punted two places back to fifth, Bobby took the flag in third.

In the pits, the crew was exultant. The third-place finish lifted them from thirteenth to eleventh in the standings, but the hard fact remained that they hadn't won. Debbie caught Richard by the hauler and asked him if the race had changed his mind.

"Nope," he said, shaking his head.

17

R.J. REYNOLDS TO THE RESCUE

Martinsville to Charlotte: September 22 to October 6

Brett Bodine let his answering machine respond to the well-wishers who called him on Sunday, the day he should have been racing in Martinsville. Ten years earlier he'd made his Busch Series debut there with a win. Now he was spending race day cleaning his garage, puttering around his garden, and, as evening came, driving through the leafy, colonial downtown alone.

One of his neighbors, the Busch Series owner/driver Phil Parsons, had thought about calling his friend but, as he remembers, "I made every bad excuse not to." So coming out of a local pizzeria at about eight, he was thrown off seeing Brett driving by in his Explorer. The two wound up talking for forty minutes.

"It happens to the best," Parsons told him. "It's just so competitive these days. It's a different sport."

Brett thanked Parsons and promised him as he drove off that "I won't beat myself up or run away from this." And making good on the pledge, he gathered his crew around Monday morning.

"I don't want any finger-pointing or blaming, and I won't have any head hanging or embarrassment," he said. "We had a good car in Martinsville and we would have had a good race. We just didn't have the motor. I'm gonna fix that as soon as we get a sponsor."

This, however, was becoming less and less an article of faith. It was now late September, and the news was getting grimmer.

"I personally pitched twenty companies and nothing seemed to be working," says Bob Kelly, the friend with his own search firm. "I'd find a guy on the inside. He'd get jacked up and pumped. He'd say something like, 'Yeah, I know I can do this.' Then we'd wait for him to have his ten o'clock meeting. They always called back about 11:45. And the line was pretty much uniform. 'Ahhh, it ain't happening. I'm the only one who wants it.' "

In the midst of all this, Lowe's delivered one last body blow, a letter per Brett's contract requesting the return of $103,000 for missing Martinsville. The company knew all their checks were going straight to Junior under the terms of the buyout, and that Brett's head was barely above water. "I was trying to save my team, using up every cent in my bank account and smiling through their appearances every week," Brett said later. "And they couldn't resist kicking me when I was down."

Brett called T. Wayne Robertson, whose company manages Lowe's racing, asking if he could help. T. Wayne promised to do what he could.

T. Wayne Robertson is a powerful man in NASCAR, and not because he manages Lowe's racing, or even because he's president of a company called Sports Marketing Enterprises.* He is powerful because SME is the special events division of R.J. Reynolds. Over their twenty-five-year association, RJR did much for NASCAR. But it was a two-way street. NASCAR helped RJR transform Winston from a moribund brand name into a synonym for the fastest-growing sport in America. And as the Clinton administration began its attacks on Big Tobacco, promul-

*On January 14, 1998, T. Wayne died in a boating accident.

gating federal regulations to bar cigarette makers from sponsoring sports events, NASCAR helped RJR with its grassroots political response. A T-shirt that said "Let NASCAR make the rules, not the FDA" became an instant best-seller. Pro-tobacco Republicans were frequently invited to join the prerace ceremonies and explicitly attack the White House. And drivers routinely supplied supportive quotes, though no one matched Rusty Wallace, who drove ESPN's standards-and-practices people up the wall when he said from Victory Lane in Bristol, "All those Democrats trying to mess with tobacco, you can tell them where to go. Vote Republican. Go, Dole!"

Robertson had been a key architect in all this. The dapper southerner with Jimmy Johnson's hair and Trent Lott's cordiality was barely out of high school when he took a job driving a Winston show car to the tracks in the early 1970s. His profile in NASCAR grew steadily, and by 1996 he was a senior vice president of RJR—a sign of just how seriously it took its NASCAR affiliation.

But with the increasing prospect that RJR might be forced out as series sponsor, Robertson moved shrewdly to inoculate SME from the shifting winds in Washington, D.C., by changing strategic course and involving RJR in the direct management of individual race teams.

Its first deal was managing the Lowe's account with Junior Johnson, and then supervising its transition to Brett. But when Lowe's wanted to leave Brett, T. Wayne was left in a ticklish position. On one hand, as series sponsor he was expected to deal with everyone evenly, particularly a tireless promoter of Winston Cup like Brett Bodine. On the other, he worked for Lowe's, and had a duty to replace Bodine if his client wished. This might have presented a conflict if Robertson hadn't turned it to his tactical advantage. If Lowe's wanted out, then he'd find Brett another sponsor, thereby increasing the drivers the tobacco giant managed by one.*

Through the summer, Robertson looked to be no more successful than any of the other agents Brett had on the street, but by fall he'd lucked into an improbable savior: a fifty-four-year-old millionaire with wavy gray hair, a fifth-degree black belt in karate, and an idea that had something to do with phone cards. Instead of just selling phone minutes like everyone else, he'd added a sweepstakes to each card. It was a gimmicky idea that needed a promotional hook, so in June 1996—the same month Lowe's was signing with Richard Childress—the entrepreneur, Carl Smith, walked into SME's offices and suggested they let him use the Winston Cup name to sell his cards.

"You know, we see a future for this product, Carl," he was told. "But racing is a fraternity. You can't play until you're a part of it."

"How do I become a part?" he asked.

"You really need to become a sponsor on a car."

Smith didn't need a trail of bread crumbs to the next question.

"Okay," he said as the July sun streamed in. "Who's available?"

On Saturday, October 5, Brett and Diane pulled up to a small Italian restaurant near their home to meet Carl Smith for the first time. It was race week in Charlotte, and it seemed everyone in town was having a news conference touting some new deal. In all, fifteen new cars had been unveiled; a few were surprising, most not.

The news that Ken Schrader would be moving from the Hendrick stable to Andy Petree's Skoal team was old.

---

* Besides handling the Lowe's account, RJR also managed the Camel car, repainted to advertise Winston.

Schrader didn't like the fact that he kept getting race cars built with Jeff Gordon's setups, and his crew chief, Phil Hammer, couldn't adapt them to his tastes. Moreover, the laid-back, partying driver chafed at the rigid regimen that his team manager, Ray Evernham, tried instituting. When Evernham said he was assigning Schrader a personal trainer and placing him on a diet regimen, reporters guffawed, wondering how long it would last. Not long, as it turned out.

To replace Schrader, Hendrick announced he was tapping Ricky Craven, a young New Englander. This, however, brought with it a new set of problems. Craven was behind the wheel of the Kodiak battery Chevrolet, owned by construction magnate Larry Hedrick. Kodiak had been with Hendrick in 1994, but was muscled aside in favor of Budweiser, which needed a new home after leaving Junior Johnson. Kodiak was irritated that it was kicked out of the Hendrick stable, though Hendrick helped find it a new home with the less competitive Larry Hedrick team. Kodiak hadn't really gotten over the affront, and wasn't happy to see Rick Hendrick stealing its driver. In the acrimonious fallout, Hedrick began intimating he might sue Hendrick Motorsports for tampering with a driver under contract.

It could have been the worst week in Brett's life, but just in the nick of time Robertson revealed the existence of the high-rolling Floridian. Now, sitting around a long table at the restaurant, Brett could see Smith was more garrulous than the button-down types from Lowe's whom he'd spent the year around. He kept his colorful shirts open a few buttons, and when he laughed a gold ducat recovered from a 1715 sunken treasure ship jiggled on a gold chain around his neck. Brett regarded the relic with interest, as he did a five-dollar turn-of-the-century gold piece that Smith had embedded in a gold ring. Smith, in turn, admired Brett's diamond-studded Eleven ring. After more than three hours of flowing wine and warm words, Smith suggested that the Bodines see his operation up close, and since they were heading to the Daytona condo after the next day's race, they agreed it was a fine idea. But following a map to an unassuming complex of low-rise condominiums a few days later, their unease grew. His offices, modestly appointed with only a couple of dozen people milling around, looked fine for a small law firm, but the Bodines couldn't imagine how it was going to support seven motorsports teams that would need at least $8 million over the next twelve months. Looking at her husband, Diane whispered, "Is this it?"

Brett wasn't sure what to say. In a month his line of credit would expire and they'd have to begin letting their crew go. Junior's other team, the one inherited by the trial lawyer David Blair, was also facing extinction, but Blair was skipping races to save money and working later nights to raise the money to keep it together. Brett didn't have those options. As it was, with less than $10,000 in the bank, he'd had to sell two fully loaded race cars for forty grand just to stay afloat. If their Mr. Smith turned out to be the real deal, it wouldn't matter. And if he didn't, well, it wouldn't matter either. Brett got a shooting pain in his mouth just thinking about that one. (The next week he went to the dentist thinking he had an abscess. Instead he was asked, "What have you been doing to yourself?" "What do you mean?" he replied. "Your teeth are nearly flat. You've ground them down to nothing." Waiting for Smith, he ground them some more.)

After spending a few hours reviewing charts and plans, the Bodines felt better, but still not quite good. "I don't know what I was expecting," Diane later said with a sigh. "Maybe a building with a big sign would have helped. In our business, sponsors have skyscrapers. It's not that we didn't think he could do it. We just couldn't see how he was going to be ready to start paying more than a million dollars of our bills in two months." But, out of choices, they went to Rockingham and prayed.

One of the ironies of their trip was that while Junior's team was disintegrating the year before, it still managed to win first place in Rockingham's annual pit crew competition, a highly anticipated event where anonymous crewmen get to step out from their drivers' shadows for an afternoon. Pulling his yellow jumpsuit over a muscular frame, Al Hyde, Brett's chief mechanic, announced he'd shave his thick red hair if they repeated as champs. As they walked onto pit road Saturday morning, past the clusters of crews eyeing one another like playground basketball players waiting for next, trying to psych one another out, Hyde ran his fingers through it as a subtle sign to the others.

Under the rules, crews are watched to see whether they stumble in any of a dozen disciplines, and as Brett pulled into the forty-by-sixteen-foot box, Hyde led the charge over the wall, diving hard for the rear wheels while his teammates emptied two eleven-gallon fuel canisters weighing eighty pounds each and changed the left-side tires. In all, it was a stout effort, a twenty-five-second pit, one of the fastest times to that point. But after the gas man threw up his hand to signal the tank was full, and after the tire changers peeled away and Donnie yelled "Go! Go! Go!" the front-tire man noticed something: He'd left his air hose lying out. He started toward it, but Brett was already in motion. Watching Brett run over it, the crewman looked as if he was about to grow ill. Walking back to the hauler, he was despondent.

"You don't think they saw that hose, do you?" he said hopefully.

Brett patted him on the back. "They saw it. They always do."

And so the mistake, with its ten-second penalty, turned an eighth-place finish into twenty-ninth place. Standing on the ledge of the Lowe's hauler, Hyde borrowed a woman's compact, and angling its mirror around his head, said with a sigh, "Guess I got to wait another year to see what I look like with a chrome dome."

The winning team was the one headed by Gary DeHart, the lantern-jawed crew chief whose rise through the corporate world of Hendrick Motorsports was one of the surprising stories of the nineties. A warm North Carolina native, the forty-eight-year-old DeHart had been an anonymous chassis specialist until 1990, when Hendrick added a fourth team to his stable, mainly to serve as a research arm. Though DeHart questioned whether he had the right stuff, Hendrick tapped him to run that show. When the crew chief of Hendrick's higher-profile number 5 car, then driven by Ricky Rudd, departed in 1992, DeHart was moved into that slot. He achieved seventh place with Rudd in 1992 and tenth in 1993. When Labonte replaced Rudd in 1994, DeHart got them into seventh again, and improved it to sixth place in 1995. Now he was elevating his game once again. With just three races left to this season, Labonte was only a point behind Hendrick-stable teammate Jeff Gordon.

It was no secret that DeHart and the crew chief for Gordon's team, Ray Evernham, had an uneasy alliance.* DeHart was a country boy who never strayed far from his roots. Evernham, a onetime short-track modified racer from New Jersey, had reinvented himself as a New Age

---

* Evernham wore several hats in the Hendrick organization in 1996. On race day he was Gordon's crew chief. But during the week he had the broader title of team manager over Gordon's Twenty-four car and Schrader's Twenty-five car. The hope was Evernham would be able to, in the words of the motto he coined, "Revive the Twenty-five." It never worked out.

motivational guru, intent on bringing pro-sport-style management to NASCAR. The two didn't socialize much, and if the talk was to be believed, didn't trust each other much either. But they did have one thing in common: They both dominated their sport with the weapons made available by the wealthiest team in racing. They had two hundred people at their beck and call, a staggering number out of which the most advanced research and development comes. When Hendrick, who owns scores of Chevrolet showrooms, wanted an aerodynamics expert, he went out and hired the best in GM. As a result, the chassis department at Hendrick Motorsports discarded more cars than other teams build, and those rejects are so good that rival teams began inquiring whether they can buy them to race as new.*

This Herculean investment upped the ante so much, only a few could dream of trying to match it. One of those who has tried is Felix Sabates.

After fleeing Cuba in 1964, and doing everything from stripping furniture for eighty-five cents an hour to selling cars, Sabates made a fortune in the early seventies when he was given an exclusive deal to distribute Pong, one of the earliest video games. In 1983, he bought his first race team—from Rick Hendrick of all people. "I was so naive that I thought I was buying the building, the tractor, the trailer, and all the equipment for $750,000," he says, laughing. "When we went for the closing, I realized all I was getting was four Monte Carlos."

But Sabates learned quickly. And as he watched his old friend outclass everyone in the garage, Sabates determined that he wouldn't lose by being outspent: He'd match Hendrick dollar for dollar. Toward that end, he announced in late summer that he was expanding from one

*In 1998, the Ernie Irvan Skittles team used Hendrick's used chassis as new.

team to three, and that he had hired his own driver named
Gordon to pilot the flagship one: Robby Gordon.

A telegenic Californian with a stunning blond girlfriend
who looked like the model Vendela, Gordon brought a
dash of San Diego to Charlotte. He'd quit a stalled Indy-
Car racing career because he sensed NASCAR was the
place to be, but after a handful of warm-up races, it had become evident Gordon's cocky attitude needed a bit of
smoothing, NASCAR-style. To help his young charge,
Sabates needed his own version of DeHart or Evernham,
and settled on a diminutive, poker-faced crew chief named
Tony Glover. Glover had been crew-chiefing as long as
Sabates had been in NASCAR, compiling the ninth-best
record among his active colleagues, with thirteen wins
since 1983. In all those years, he'd never seen a deal like
that Sabates was offering: $250,000 a year and a piece of
the purse.

As soon as Glover's employers—the owners of the
number 4 Kodak car—learned that their crew chief was
negotiating with Sabates, they kicked him out before he
could take any notes or secrets. So on Saturday in Rock-
ingam, he waved to his friends from the bay of Sabates's
hauler, a richer man by far. On a weekend celebrating
crews, his satisfied smile was a vivid sign of how the balance of power was changing. The era of the superstar team
had evolved to include the superstar crew chief.

Donnie Richeson, Brett's brother-in-law, greeted the
news with scarcely more than a raised eyebrow. Sabates
was sinking $8 million into that Gordon team, and another
$7 million into the two other ones under his roof. With his
head buried deep in his Ford's engine, Donnie would have
been happy just to have some notes on this damn Ford
he'd gotten from Junior. But somehow in the hasty transfer, every scrap of paper about its performance the prior
year here had been lost.

The corners at Rockingham were so narrow, you barely had time to turn the wheel before the wall was upon you, and since NASCAR had changed the rules again to mandate that the Fords raise their front air dam—causing more wind to sweep under the nose and lessening the downforce—he had to deal with a push. Add to that the fact that the winds blew sand all over the track, making it more slippery and difficult to throttle out of turns, and you had a wild card of a day.

Sunday morning, as Richeson walked to his pit in the shadow of Victory Lane, a friend yelled, "How's the setup lookin', Donnie?" His expression impassive, he blew into his clenched fist as if flinging dice.

In the opening minutes it seemed as if he'd rolled a seven. Brett picked up five positions racing to the stripe after a Robby Gordon spinout, placing him twelfth on the restart. But then, just as Donnie feared, their setup began resisting them in the turns, and so began an excruciating slide to thirtieth, where Brett motored for 250 hot and long laps. Brett would hang on—even as the race's winner, Ricky Rudd, lapped him for a second time with six miles to go—to finish sixteenth.

Scribbling some final notes, Donnie closed his spiral book. They'd picked up fourteen positions in the last hundred laps, digging, keeping Brett in the damn thing, putting in a hard day's work. It wasn't pretty racing. Hell, it was a mess. But stripping out of his drenched jumpsuit, having kept the patient alive for the last four hours, he knew he'd given Brett all a driver could ask for. Some days when you weren't winning, or even finishing well, that's what kept you going as a crew chief.

Unfortunately, it wasn't enough for many of his men. They'd been together twenty-eight races now, and as they changed in the hauler, at least four had already made up their minds to quit, figuring it wasn't going to turn around soon. And they were right.

Even Brett knew it. Which is why, when the FedEx envelope from Carl Smith arrived that Wednesday, he exhaled and sank into his high-back leather chair. All of his friends had been preparing to go to Vegas after the Phoenix race on Sunday, October 27, but Brett stalled booking tickets because, as Diane said, "How much fun is it going to be gambling money we don't have?" Now, leafing through the dozen pages of small type that spelled out a deal for $15 million over three years, it occurred to him that he might as well go and have one hell of a time because the gambling wasn't going to stop.

This contract that he'd waited on the edge of his seat for wasn't the magic bullet. In fact, the Bodines' worries about this slow-starting Florida businessman were painfully well founded. He'd have one problem after another getting his phone cards made, and when they were finally ready for shipping months late, he'd have a worse time selling them. Brett would exhaust the last of his savings making up the $1.5 million that this Mr. Smith would be late paying. Carl Smith wouldn't turn out to be a savior— just another wide-eyed moneyman trying to glom on to the biggest juggernaut in sport, the juggernaut Brett sold every time he left the house.

Brett had been behind the eight ball from the day he decided to give up living comfortably on a half-million-dollar annual salary to indulge the conceit that he could do better than all the other owners who'd failed to crack the top ten. He'd been behind from the day he called Junior Johnson at the mansion, the day the old man used him as a golden parachute out of the sport. He'd been behind since he'd paid top dollar for a team that needed to be rebuilt from the ground up, leaving him chronically under-financed. And when his sponsor bailed, when he couldn't find anyone to believe he'd turn it around if he could just catch his breath, he found himself back where he started, a driver with a target on his back. But Brett had gone anywhere, done anything his sport asked of him. And when he needed it most, it came through for him.

It's what you didn't see as a newcomer; what men like David Blair, the Arkansas attorney, had to learn the hard way as he tried to assimilate into the culture. It's what the folks at SME meant when they said "Racing is a fraternity. You can't play until you're a part of it." It's what keeps NASCAR, for all the talk about change, a closed world. It's what happens when a garrulous entrepreneur with an idea about phone cards wanders into the R.J. Reynolds offices and is told about only one available driver.

And so Brett was told for the first time about what Junior told a visitor back in February—that Brett didn't know what he was getting himself into.

Brett drummed his fingers on his black desk.

"Last year, when I was getting ready to toss in the towel, I wondered, 'Could we get it done in time? Or would it be too much to overcome?'" the owner/driver started. "Well, we made it through our first year. But did we overcome it, or didn't we?"

It's a hard call. For the first time in his career, he had fallen into the back twenty in the standings, and would finish the season in twenty-fourth place. But to look at him, to see the optimism, the energy, it was easy to see why so many friends in the garage were pulling for him. Finally Brett answered himself by spreading his arms in a manner that seemed to frame everything beyond his office door.

"I have a future now," he said, mustering a smile that was more hopeful than certain.

18

GOOD-BYE AND GOOD RIDDANCE

North Wilkesboro: September 27–29

Dave Marcis was angry, so angry his voice was cracking every tenth word. He and Felix Sabates were in his trailer, with Felix offering the first of many apologies for his golden boy of the moment, Robby Gordon.

Marcis had come to North Wilkesboro with a brand-new pickup, planning to test the waters of NASCAR's Craftsman Truck Series. The new spin-off that catered to America's fascination with pickups was selling 811,000 tickets a year, enough to put $6.9 million in purse money out there. Word around the Winston Cup garage was that the competition was so light, its drivers could make a killing.

So with a warm September 27 breeze blowing through the window, Dave eased the new Dodge onto the track, gently wearing in the brakes by pumping them as he rode the throttle at 40 mph. At the same time, Gordon was going into the first turn so hard, he completely lost it in the banking, hit, spun, and caromed into a certain fifty-five-year-old who was chugging along on the apron, driving like Miss Daisy.

Looking over the accordioned hood, Dave was livid. He hadn't even gotten a chance to get the damn thing up to speed, and now it was junk. He was considering everything in the penal code shy of felony murder when Sabates hurried by on a peacemaking mission. "Anything you want," the millionaire said. "How about I pay your tire bill this weekend."

Dave took the offer, worth about $8,000. After Felix departed, Dave looked at Gordon wading confidently into a pack of reporters. "Let's see how cocky that son of a bitch stays after he eats some concrete," he bristled.

There were more reporters than usual here this weekend, because the same economics that had lured Gordon into the sport were driving this little five-eighths-mile oval out. This would be the last Winston Cup race in North Wilkesboro. And the man most immediately responsible for that was parking cars in front of the speedway.

Jack Combs is a reedy seventy-year-old with shoulders made for ax swinging. They're slightly hunched now, a concession to age, but Combs still looks as if he could build you a house in a weekend and get the driveway graded before dark. On Friday morning he was standing by the roadside, directing race fans onto his prime property, five dollars for cars and thirty dollars for mobile homes (up ten dollars from the year before). He was a bit frazzled because rains had softened the ground; he'd had to shovel heaps of gravel onto the sodden grass.

Combs was twenty-one when his older brother Charlie and Enoch Staley, a square-jawed lumber hauler and moonshiner, started building a track on a hill in the middle of the woods where they hid their still.

"Back then, we heard tell of a man named Bill France and this thing he was callin' NASCAR," Combs said. "He was runnin' some race in Greensboro, so the three of us went to see him. I can remember the first words he said when we walked into his motel room. He looked us up and down and he said, 'Damn, they grow 'em tall in Wilkes County.' "

After some haggling, France agreed to promote their race for a quarter of the gate. He went to radio stations and papers in three counties, promising them that the brand-new track was something to see, and soon the word went out across to the Smoky Mountains. Enoch had built wood stands to fit three thousand people, but on May 18, 1947, four times that came streaming into the hills. Later that fall, France would come back to attach his new group's name to Enoch's race, making North Wilkesboro Speedway the first track to host a NASCAR event.

From Combs's back porch you could still walk up the hill and find a red-brick country house with a brown-painted North Wilkesboro Speedway sign that looked as though it should be hanging on a Route 66 diner. You could also find a tin barn with a sign advertising "Live-stock Exhibits" and neighbors so close that no more than 150 yards from turn one sat a trailer with a pink and blue swing set in the yard.

The 40,000-seat track was safe while Enoch Staley was alive, or at least no one openly talked about shutting it. But all that changed when he died in May 1995. His half of the track fell to his wife Mary. The other half was owned by the Combs family.

On June 18, 1995, the phone rang in Jack Combs's living room.

"Jack, Bruton Smith here," said the voice. "I was just sittin' around here wonderin' if you'd be interested in selling your half of the track."

"Well," Combs replied, "I hadn't thought that much about it."

Smith had. He was in the midst of building his gargan-tuan $160 million Texas oval. He had land in a massive development organized by the Perot family, the proceeds of an initial public offering in Speedway Motorsports to pay for its construction, and a long-term lease. What he didn't have was a Winston Cup date.

"What about me comin' up and talking to you to-morrow?" he asked.

Combs waited a beat and replied, "I'll have lunch if you buy."

The next day the millionaire and the gentlemanly giant met at a country kitchenette down the road. Smith got right to the point.

"What will you take for it?" he asked. Even with a night to mull it over, Combs still wasn't sure what to say. So the two talked, and two hours later Combs came around to his price: $7 million. Smith played with the salt and pepper shakers and offered half of that.

"I just don't think that'd work out," Combs told him.

The pair gathered themselves and drove back to the speedway, where Combs took him across the stone grand-stands and down to the asphalt. At Smith's Charlotte speedway, seconds could go by silently as cars disap-peared down the distant backstretch. He imagined race day here. The noise was deafening, because the screaming cars were never far from your ears. It would be ideal for an old-style Saturday-night TV hour. TNN or ESPN would love it, maybe even pay the purse.

Walking back to his black Cadillac, Smith said, "What about you calling me back at nine o'clock tonight?"

Combs called at the hour. "You know, Jack," Smith told him. "Seven million is really more than I can stand."

"Well, then, we'll see you later," an indifferent Combs replied. "Appreciate your interest."

"Hold on now, hold on now," Smith jumped in. "If I de-cide to buy it, could you have the stock ready for me soon? Like tomorrow?" Combs thought he could easily gather the stock certificates that legally showed he and his rela-tions held a 50 percent interest. He asked when Smith wanted to meet the next day.

"One o'clock," Smith said.

At one o'clock the next day Combs and his family were sitting on their back porch when the Cadillac with tinted windows arrived. Smith walked out, flanked by a lawyer in a dark suit and a black attaché case.

"You want to go in the house, Bruton?" Combs asked.

"No, out here's fine." Smith motioned for his attorney to examine the stock certificates. As each Combs signed over their certificate to Smith, they were given a check. Looking at his cut—$4 million—Combs felt the call to run to his kitchen cupboard, where several mason jars of moonshine resided on the top shelf. Choosing the one sweetened with cherries, the old moonshiner ran back out and, sipping right from the jar, sealed the deal with a wee taste.

Smith thanked them all and took his car the short drive to the top of the hill. Then he walked into the little red house and announced to a stunned Mike Staley, Enoch's son and the speedway's president, "I'm your new partner. I just bought Jack and his family out."

Mike's sister Marie would later call Combs a "skunk" for not giving them a chance to buy his stake first—especially "after all Enoch done for that man." But Smith assumed that once they accepted what happened they'd have no reason not to accept his offer of $8 million. Later, after all the trouble, he'd say, "Those two families were just like the Hatfields and McCoys. When the old man died, all their hate got transferred into those stocks." During the next several months, Smith made one proposal after another, telling Mike he could stay on with a fifteen-year, $150,000 annual contract—have anything he might want. He assumed Enoch's son would accept. What choice did he have?

Smith underestimated the forces aligning against him.

One of the ways Big Bill France kept iron-clad control of NASCAR was by making deals with men who were builders, not businessmen. All visionaries in their day, they built little ovals in the middle of nowhere, and like fields of dreams for race fans, watched the people come. They became big wheels in their small towns, making good livings off of Big Bill's word. He didn't believe in contracts that lasted longer than a year, but none of these men ever felt insecure.

Big Bill's paternalism was practical. If he kept his track owners happy and indebted, then he'd have stability. As a result, Bill's boys grew up treating the first generation of track builders—men like Clay Earls of Martinsville, Paul Sawyer of Richmond, and Enoch Staley—like uncles. When Bill Jr. was named president of NASCAR in 1972, how could he not respect the old traditions? After Bill Sr. added Pocono's speedway to the Winston Cup schedule in 1974, his son didn't add another new venue for fourteen years.* As recently as the late 1980s there were plenty of races to go around.

But most of these early builders were aging into their seventies and eighties by the mid-1990s. The modestly attended races that kept them in country comfort for much of their lives suddenly became highly rated events for ESPN and TNN. To keep up with the sport's growth, Bill Jr. began gently prodding his father's old friends to expand seating and upgrade the distinctly low-tech facilities. He wasn't threatening. He'd never do that to family. But they had to be realists. You couldn't ask a CEO watching the car he's spending millions sponsoring to piss in a trough. And you couldn't ask the drivers to come unless you kept increasing the purse money, and that meant new

---

*The only reason he made an exception for the Phoenix International Raceway in 1988 was that NASCAR needed a West Coast event after the much-beloved speedway in Riverside, California—a racing staple since 1958—closed because the owners wanted to build a shopping center on the site and there wasn't enough fan interest to dissuade them.

seats and skyboxes. Some owners didn't have the means or the energy to try, and who could blame them when these little concrete bowls built from sketches on the back of napkins had come to be worth tens of millions? Bill Jr.'s "uncles" started thinking about cashing out.

But whom to sell to?

Bruton Smith was the right man in the right place at the right time. He'd been around forever, had the gentle North Carolina twang that put people at ease, and could easily switch from seducing Jack Combs to selling the eastern bankers who were beginning to notice the spectacular profit margins at his Charlotte Motor Speedway. In a nine-month burst, Smith paid $26 million to Larry Carrier for Bristol, $7 million to Combs in June, started construction on his $160 million Texas oval, spent $5 million to acquire 24 percent of the North Carolina Motor Speedway, and leased the road course in Sonoma, California, for $40 million. With a portfolio already including CMS and the Atlanta Speedway, Smith's Speedway Motorsports had become the largest single track owner in NASCAR.

Smith called himself a friend, but France only had to look over at the world of IndyCar racing to see that Smith now had the chips to play a very dangerous game if he so wished.

In the spring of 1995, Tony George, the ambitious, thirty-six-year-old inheritor of the Indianapolis Motor Speedway, split acrimoniously with the sanctioning body that ruled his sport, Championship Auto Racing Teams. CART, like NASCAR, had presided over a period of rapidly rising costs for its competitors, something George thought was making it the province of ultrawealthy Europeans whom the average blue-collar fan cared little about. He argued for rules to keep costs down, and for more races to be run on American ovals. When he was rebuffed by CART's ruling junta, he formed his own league, taking his

Brickyard track out of the CART lineup and making it the gem of his newly formed Indy Racing League.

How could France not worry that the pieces were in place for Smith to make his own break? Like George, Bruton Smith owned a high-profile track. And like George, he believed the upward spiral in the cost of Winston Cup racing was discouraging the next generation of exciting drivers who didn't have access to multimillionaire sponsors. (What was the ill-fated Sportsman series that Humpy Wheeler brought to CMS if not a way to let unknown short-track drivers break into speedway racing?) But France had one key card to play: Smith had extended himself further than ever before to build his Texas showplace, and needed the power of the NASCAR name to fill its 150,061 seats. Just like his father before him, Bill Jr. set the schedule from year to year.

By buying out out Jack Combs to acquire North Wilkesboro's race date, Smith gambled that Bill France would allow him to move the race date to Texas. This was because Smith had got CBS to televise the 1997 inaugural, and network coverage is like manna for a sponsor. CBS charges two to three times what ESPN does for a thirty-second commercial, and if the television time is more valuable, then exposure their logos receive during a race is too. France would see that and know he'd have to accede to Smith's request.

But what if Smith bought out Enoch's widow, Mary, and won control of the other half of North Wilkesboro, and with it a second race date? Smith would surely want to move that date to Texas as well. What would France do then? His sponsors would be clamoring for the coverage, but could he afford to strengthen his wiliest, most unpredictable rival that much?

Enter Bob Bahre, the New England shopping center developer who, as owner of the New Hampshire Speedway, was one of France's most recent additions to the Winston Cup family. France expanded the schedule to give Bahre one race in 1993. But Bahre was hungry for another. So hungry that at the December 1994 Winston Cup banquet, Bahre approached Mary Staley. Not wanting to seem too pushy, he let her know that if they were ever of a mind to sell, he'd appreciate a call. And that's exactly what happened in December 1995, six months after Smith's buyout of Combs. Out of the clear blue she called Bahre and let him know she would take his $8 million buyout. There was just one condition: He must promise never to sell his half to Smith.

When asked if Bill France was involved in engineering the sale, Mary Staley snapped. "It was my speedway. Why would he have anything to do with it?" No matter. Smith was floored upon hearing the news. He'd been out-maneuvered. Without that second race for Texas, he stood to lose untold millions. He was on the phone to Combs immediately, yelling, "What in the world is wrong with the Staleys?"

Combs had no answer. "I can't hardly understand it neither," he said, not as surprised as he sounded.

Oh, there'd be hell to pay.

The Staleys were naive about the fallout from their actions. Just because their two Winston Cup races were being removed, that didn't mean that the track would have to close, did it? NASCAR sanctioned two thousand different events outside of the Winston Cup. Surely Bill France could find a few dates from his Craftsman or Busch Series, or one of NASCAR's eight others, to move to North Wilkesboro. Surely no one wanted racing to disappear entirely from this historic town, the first ever to hold a NASCAR race.

But here Smith had the upper hand. The Staleys had screwed him, and poured salt in the wound by making

Bahre promise never to sell him the track's other half. They could go to hell. Of course, he didn't put it quite that way. He invented a pretext that he knew would bind the Staleys in a catch-22. "Our assets are our people," he said, "and we're not going to invest our most precious assets unless we own it all."

As the race weekend began Friday, there was hope that a bold, last-minute compromise might be reached. A front-page story in the local *Journal-Patriot* newspaper reported that Bahre had made the first move, offering to sell his half back to the Staleys for a dollar and, playing on public sentiment, challenging Smith to do the same.

Smith, however, had his own offensive. Junior Johnson, the paper reported, had also jumped into the fray, beseeching the two sides to sell to him and an "investment group." Smith publicly announced he'd sell to the local hero, but Bahre, suspicious of who controlled the group, refused.

By race morning all of this intrigue had left Mike Staley shell-shocked and exhausted, sitting behind the desk in the little red house by the livestock barn that still bore his father's nameplate and pictures from forty years of racing.

"I just can't believe this is really happening," he said. "I can't believe after all these years they're just going to let us go away."

Dave Marcis went out of his way to find Mike and Mary. In the years when track owners paid the Pettys and other stars appearance money to attend their races, Enoch never would, believing that all the gate receipts should be applied equally among drivers, not skimmed to benefit superstars. That helped Dave in the lean years, and he shook his head in a manner that suggested the world was going to hell when he said, "Any of these motherfuckers around here would stab anybody for fifty cents. All I can say is this sport better be careful it don't forget the work-ingman, which your father was, Mike."

Mike agreed, though the millions in his bank account now colored his status as resident victim.

In fact, besides Dave, it was hard to find anyone who felt particularly victimized. A threatened picket never materi-alized, and the prevailing sentiment seemed to be one yawn away from indifference. And so it was perfect that after "Auld Lang Syne" crackled through the loudspeakers and the race itself started, Jeff Gordon would string to-gether his third win in a row, completing the track's journey from NASCAR's old world to its new one.

As fans were taking down the spray-painted bedsheet banners wishing the little track well after all those years, and as Gordon was saying something about owning a piece of history, Bruton Smith was at Tavern on the Green in New York, enjoying oysters Rockefeller and a fine slice of fish. As for the new millionaire he had created, Jack Combs was where he'd always been, running from one mobile home to the next on the wide lawn between his house and the track, making sure everyone was getting their thirty dollars' worth.

19

THE KING'S CAMPAIGN

October 8–9

It was a drizzly Tuesday afternoon when Richard Petty stepped onto his Winnebago to begin the two-day swing into the far west part of North Carolina, deep into the Smoky Mountains.

Two other men were joining in for the ride. Mike was a dapper blond with a crooked smile who looked as if he was probably the most popular frat boy in his day; now he wanted to become insurance commissioner. Tom was a round man with an exceedingly well-developed ability to look concerned; he wanted to replace an agriculture commissioner who'd been in office so long that constituents called him the Sod Father. Along the way they would pick up a candidate for state treasurer named Ann, who boarded the bus wearing a mandarin jewel-neck jacket and black skirt, and who carried on at great length about her husband's problematic urethra, causing Mike to look horrified and Tom to be deeply, deeply concerned.

Petty studied these politicians quietly, wondering what it must be like to be so anonymous, so little known. Earlier, he'd offered a confession on his private plane that shed light on the sheltered life of celebrity he'd led. "Man, if I wasn't Richard Petty, I couldn't do what those cats do," he said. "I mean, if no one knows you, politics is hard work."

After a stopover for sleep, Wednesday began with a new guest—Jim, a local legislator whose job was to introduce Richard at the first handful of events. With an American flag tie not quite as loud as his voice, Jim spent the better part of half an hour dropping factoids such as "All our land is on its side. If it were laid flat, we'd be bigger than Texas." And: "Ya'll know how New York has the apple dropping on New Year's Eve? Well, I invented the possum dropping." By the time the bus pulled to its first stop at seven o'clock, the National Guard armory in the farm town of Murphy seemed like a relief.

The crowd was composed of housewives, hired hands, and children with eyes as wide as full moons. They were thrilled that anyone more famous than their water commissioner would wander by, and when Petty appeared, there was an audible gasp. Richard stayed in the back of the gymnasium until Jim finished his overcaffeinated introduction, thinking about the notes his campaign manager, Bill Coby, had typed for him.

> Richard should emphasize his public servant background in addition to the business experience he will bring. He may also allude to his five-point plan, which will: restore integrity; promote economic development and tourism; protect investors from securities fraud; modernize the office; advocate for working men and women.

But somehow, by the time his mouth started moving, that had turned into this: "Y'all think'a me as a race car driver. But I run seven different businesses. I've been a county commissioner for seventeen years. The whole family has been out there doin' that kinda stuff. . . . Ya know, racing brings in $80 million a year. It's all, like, a big round deal that the Secretary of State connects. It's a job-related situation. We do a lot of things as far as copyrights. Well, um, 'cause, the thing is, it's not really that complicated, but it's kinda hard to explain."

Coby rubbed his eyes, and the crowd clapped politely, waiting to fall in line, like schoolchildren in a lunchroom. For the better part of another hour Petty signed their pictures and cars and shirts.

Next, the Republican riders made their way through the hollers of Shooting Creek and up Chunky Gal Mountain, where patches of cloud hung between the orange peaks, to Macon County, a tourist area where the chief cultural debate seemed to be whether the Yankee sandbirds from Florida should be allowed to import opera. A lawyer buttonholed Petty with a meaty index finger and said, "Around here, people have opinions about three things: dogs, the land, and women." The King obligingly asked about his dog.

Before the bus had stopped, Coby was reviewing a stack of recent campaign clippings, many of which hit Richard hard for his refusal, if elected, to give up his racing interests. "Here's what I think we should do, Richard. If it comes up, just say that whenever I'm somewhere, I'm there full-time."

Richard nodded, but as he climbed up to the back of another flatbed for yet another speech, he decided to make a joke of the potential conflict of interest. "I won't mess up the office completely because I won't spend all my time there," he said, mock seriously. Then he waited a beat. "I'll be at the races."

Coby bit his lip, then, hearing the laughter, decided the line worked.

If this campaign featured one of the starrier candidates in North Carolina history, it didn't necessarily always know its bearings. En route to the next event, Coby's advance man arranged a stop at a lonely mountain road gas station, where a dangling sign said it all: "Welcome to Clay's Corner, Possum Capital of the World." Ten men stood open-jawed as the Winnebago stopped and men in suits and cowboy hats piled out. "Howyadoin', buddy," Richard said to one with particularly poor teeth. The leathery men nodded, still staring at the Winnebago as if it were a vision. Inside, Richard chatted amiably, smiling as the proprietors gave him a bumper sticker that read, "Possum, the other other white meat." Walking out, he was reminded by the leathery man, "This here is God's land."

Drinking in the lush greenery, he smilingly replied, "Looks like the Lord knew what He was doin'."

By midday the bus was full and the mood was festive. Tom, Mike, Ann, and Jim were joined by a thirty-five-year-old first-time candidate named Lyndon, who looked as if he'd dyed his golden temples gray. Lyndon was the most dynamic one of the lot, and certainly the least likely to leave a detail untended. But as the bus pulled up to a rally he'd organized at a paper mill in Sylva, his face turned the color of the budding dogwood trees outside.

His mother, acting as an advance woman, had been alerted to the King's imminent arrival and was giving the invocation of her life. "We need our land healed, my friends, and God will heal our country if we elect Republicans," she was thundering, shaking to her soul. "Satan stole our country, and we have to steal it back. The devil, people—I said, the devil, people!—is in the Democrats."

Petty arched his eyebrows so that they peaked above his sunglasses, wondering if all that Satan-repelling would cause the woman to keel over before he even left his bus. "She sure gets into it, don't she?" he said politely. Lyndon smiled apologetically and signaled someone to stop his mother by running a finger across his throat.

The gravel square in front of the paper mill was lit by bright sunlight and someone had the foresight to bring the song by Alabama, "Richard Petty Fan," written for his 1992 farewell tour. It was the kind of syrupy anthem that gave a perfect backdrop to a country fair atmosphere, and with buck-fifty hot dogs, a bright yellow fire truck escort, and the mountains in the background, Richard grew inspired. "I've never won a single race," he said, testing a theme he'd continue refining. "But my *team* won two hundred races. Now, if you send Richard Petty to Raleigh, hey, I don't wanna be down there by myself. I brought my team members with me. These are the people who'll make it all work. Send them with me."

Three mill workers listened by the dogwoods.

"He's got to be a pretty good feller to come this far. I believe he'll get it," said one.

"I think he will," said another.

"I hope so," said the third.

When the rally was over, the candidates reboarded, positively jazzed. Mike believed he had won votes with his smiling promise to lower car insurance. Ann had found someone who also had problems with his urethra. Tom heard about a new crop disease, and was very, very concerned.

Richard dug into his tin of chew and layered it between his lower lip and teeth, spitting in a perfect arc. As the bus passed cattle lands and his new friends cluttered the silence with wonk talk, the King good-naturedly listened from behind his shades, nodding when someone struck an agreeable note. When he decided to weigh in with an opinion or anecdote, his guests fell silent, like MPs at a high tea when the general decides to speak.

"I went to Langhorne, Pennsylvania, in 1950," he intoned at one point when the talk turned to drinking. "A boy my daddy knew well there had a race car and we went to his house. It was the first time I'd ever seen a TV. The men were drinkin' beer and then their two wives came outta the kitchen, in their aprons, with cans of beer in their hand. Well, I'd never seen such a thing. When I came home, the first thing I said was, 'I seen two women drinkin' in the house, Mama!' It was a whole new society."

Ann, Tom, and Mike nodded gravely, then went back to their talk, leaving Richard to stare out the window and think more about these small towns that had made him a household name before Ann or Mike or Tom could even vote.

There was one last event, in an old baseball field in the western city of Asheville, and one last guest, a local legislator named Whilma Sherill. A cross between Martha Stewart and Martha Mitchell, Whilma had spent the better part of the week selling fifteen-dollar tickets for what she called a victory celebration. Predictions of torrential storms left her in a snippy mood, but more than two hundred well-heeled Republicans were waiting for them at the park. It was a spectacular evening, and the brick arches, boardwalk slats, and wood billboards framing the field against a sloping green mountainside lent it a pristine, old-time feeling. As well-coiffed ladies balanced plastic plates of barbecue on their arms and the hoi polloi danced beneath the burnished arches, Richard stared at the outfield.

"Daddy didn't come to my first race in 'fifty-eight 'cause he had one here," he said. "Lot of times they didn't have enough cars, so we'd go rent some. Finally, it got to where the rental car companies put it in their contracts that we couldn't race them. The field's the same, but . . ."

Here he paused, as if rerunning a thirty-six-year-old race.

"There was tires all around. Every time some ol' boy flipped up over 'em, the owner went after him, shakin' his fist 'cause it messed up the grass."

This was a perfect chance for him to sound sentimental, but he disappointed. "Eighty percent of the tracks we ran on are gone," he said, "but the only people who care are old-timers, and hell, they can't see anyway."

With that bit of pragmatism hanging, Richard stepped onto a platform in front of home plate and launched into a speech that was surprisingly seamless. Gone were the stumbling references to the office as "this whole big deal," or to the Democrats as "those cats."

Instead he began to articulate a case for himself, his voice measured and certain. He talked about his grand-children, his business interests, his yearning to give back to the state that had given him so much. He said, "We have to do what needs to be done to shake up Raleigh," and got applause. Then he said, "Vote for Richard Petty and the Republican party," the band played "God Bless the USA," and he disappeared into the crowd, signing autographs for another hour.

It was near midnight when his bus finally pulled into Level Cross. The hat and shades were off, his long legs were sprawled on the leather couch. "This was a good day, Richard," Tom said. "Real good," said Mike.

"We got it won now, boys," the King said.

After they'd left he was asked if that was the way he really felt, or if the endless shots he was taking in the press weren't getting to him. He was told that at so many ap-pearances he looked as if he was halfhearted, a man pushed where he wasn't sure he wanted to go.

He thought about this and spit his chew into a plastic cup, missing the Italian tie. "It's a funny thing, but I don't know what I'll say until I get up there," he started. "Really I don't. But the good Lord put me here and looked after me for a reason. All that stuff I got into on my own, all those wrecks, all them near-death situations. He kept bringing me back and putting me back there so I could go at it again. Somewhere, there's a grand plan. I don't know what it is. So I gotta do different things. I gotta see where the good Lord wants me to go."

Then he got out of the bus and said good-bye. Because at least for the moment, the good Lord wanted him to go to Rockingham.

20

WIDE OPEN

Rockingham to Atlanta: October 20 to November 10

Bobby had seen this movie before.

In 1995 he was in tenth place, three races away from a breakout season, when a crash in Rockingham dropped him to eleventh. Moving to Phoenix, it looked as if redemption was close. He was running in sixth place and only getting stronger when the distributor in his motor broke. That kind of breakdown was so rare, no one could remember it happening before. Ever. Watching them go twenty-three laps down as the crew dug deep inside the motor, Bobby knew it was over. They left Phoenix 240 points out of tenth place. With only one race left to the season, the most Bobby could earn was 185 points for a race win. As if to underscore its futility, he cut a tire six laps from the end of that last race, finishing seven laps down.

Over the long winter of 1995–96, another off-season where he had to listen to people talk about his potential— God, he hated being thirty-nine and still having to hear that—he thought about little else other than getting back to where the team had been on October 21, 1995, the day it started going south in Rockingham.

And he did. He finished third in Martinsville, and salvaged an eighth place in North Wilkesboro, after Kyle shuffled him from the lead with a fourth-turn spinout.

Now in eleventh place in the points standings, he was coming to Rockingham more assured and positive. But the race would still prove bedeviling. Bobby struggled in the teens for three hundred laps before Robbie finally hit on the right mix to bring him to the edge of the top ten. Derrike Cope was the last driver in Bobby's way. Flinging himself high on the narrow backstretch, Bobby tried to get an angle when . . .

Inman's voice sounded like a newsreel voice reporting a disaster. "Oh no! We hit the Twelve car. Aw, damn, we tore ourselves up to hell."

Racing hard to erase the memory of the year before, Bobby had succeeded only in summoning it. He was the twenty-eighth car beneath the checkered flag.

The Phoenix International Raceway lies a dozen miles outside downtown, past the county jail and the flatlands, where there's little besides scrub and telephone lines, inside a valley hidden by stubby foothills that were once a part of Mexico.

The scenery might have let the STP team believe they'd left their bad luck in the purple hills of North Carolina if a freak forty-mile-an-hour sandstorm hadn't blown through town, depositing dust and rock on the oval. Bobby thought he was fast enough to win the pole on Friday, but qualifying had to be canceled for the first time ever due to sand, and he managed only seventeenth on Saturday.

The delay was a gift to Terry Labonte, whose gas pedal stuck a half hour into the first practice, causing him to smack the wall and ride hard against it until he came to a spark-filled stop. The Winston Cup leader arrived at the track Saturday with a cast on the forefinger of his driving hand, and if his thirtieth-place qualifying effort didn't rise to the level of Earnhardt's heroics after Talladega, it was enough to suggest that it would take more than a broken finger for Labonte to loosen his thirty-two-point grip over Jeff Gordon.

Earnhardt was barely a footnote to any of this. Since Talladega, he'd finished out of the top five a very un-Earnhardtlike ten of eleven times. As a result, Richard Childress was meeting reporters Saturday afternoon, telling them that, yes, he was replacing the top leadership of the team, but no, he wouldn't say with whom. "We'll have another crew chief," he allowed, "but that's all I can tell you."

Once, working for Earnhardt was the best job in the garage. But at least one available crew chief had already turned it down, believing that Earnhardt's age and injury presaged a period of slow decline for the team. When Childress asked Robbie to take the job, the Petty crew chief sought advice from a small number who could be trusted to keep it quiet. Ray Evernham, for one, counseled against it. "The Three is proven, but you may only be three years away from a championship at the place you built," he said. Robbie was still unsure. So on Saturday night, as he sat with Bobby for their usual prerace talk, Bobby lobbied hard, reminding Robbie of his own words: "We need another year to finish what we started." Bobby had based his future on Robbie's assurance that he felt that way. Now, searching his crew chief's eyes, he wasn't so sure.

The next morning, the Valvoline-meets-Versace fashion show of executives' wives and big-haired groupies lingered in the 85-degree sun, clogging pit road. You could always tell the drivers' wives from the others, since they had chaise lounges and beach umbrellas set up for them on top of the tool rigs, and didn't flinch when a car flared its engine a few feet away.

Debbie Hamilton didn't like going out to pit road before a race. Though she supposed doing so was a sign of support, she felt like "too many people did it to be seen. Plus, when I go out there I get real choked up. There's just something about going out there and it being so final."

No. Better to stay behind. So while she puttered in the hauler, Bobby spent the final few minutes before the race as he always did, standing with Robbie looking over the track. Thousands of fans had dragged lawn chairs up to the parched hills, and the grandstands spread out like the wings of a cactus wren. Bobby closed his eyes for a minute. While the sun baked his face he thought about the drivers around him. Directly ahead was Sterling Marlin, his best friend. John Andretti was in front of Sterling, who cared no more for John than Bobby did. How long before they traded paint?

As it turned out, not long. Within five laps of the green flag falling, Andretti had come down on Sterling when Marlin tried passing inside along the backstretch. With no banking to hold him down, Marlin went flying into the outside wall, where Brett Bodine plowed into him, effectively ending Brett's day. Bobby picked up some ground there, but still he lay back, following Jeff Gordon to the door of the top ten. Gordon had been struggling with his handling all weekend, and the problem was still vexing him. Once they cleared traffic, Bobby took tenth from the kid.

The normal groove in turn three is a car width and a half off the apron. But Robbie had worked hard on setting up the car to have a gluelike grip on the lower lane. As Bobby made his way to Ernie Irvan in seventh, he figured this would be the first test of the day. And when he began his advance in the backstretch, waiting until he got to the sweet spot inside turn three to pass, the ease with which he did so—gliding underneath as if on a soft cushion—told him that he was heading right to the leader, Mark Martin.

Martin was strong, but Bobby noticed that in practice the Fords shuddered when the Pontiac's sloped grille came behind them. Past the hundred-lap mark he inched to Martin's tail; then, just as he started his arc into the first turn, Bobby slipped his nose right underneath the Ford. On cue,

Martin's backside broke loose, sending him right into Derrike Cope, who was trailing on his outside. As he watched Cope carom off the wall, Martin made a mental note to apologize later. For now he dove on and off pit road, taking just right-side tires so he could reclaim the lead.

Dale Jarrett followed him out and forged into the lead within five laps. It would take twenty-four laps before Bobby could take another run at first, and when he did, he used the same trick—pulling right to the Ford's tail, watching it break loose, then ramming the wheel left to take the lead. The words "Way to go, buddy," were barely out of Robbie's mouth when they were replaced on the radio by "Watch out, Bobby, they're wrecking everywhere!!!" A multicar spin-and-slide changed it all. Not only did Bobby get passed again by Jarrett and Martin on pit road, but a new collection of names leapfrogged to the front. Geoff Bodine and Terry Labonte were among them.

Lining up in tenth, with a row of lapped cars beneath him, Bobby measured his aggravation. A driver couldn't wreck in Phoenix without taking a half-dozen cars with him. He'd made two runs at the lead without even pushing. Now, as the leaders mixed in with the lapped cars in a side-by-side free-for-all through the track's flat corners, he could just imagine some idiot trying an Earnhardt move and taking them all out. Over forty of the longest laps of his life, Bobby drove defensively, until he was back where he started, on Jarrett's tail. Bobby could hear that the wheels of the Robert Yates Ford had started spinning out of the corners, so he waited to pass until he could get under Jarrett coming out of the third turn. Now he was behind only Bodine and Labonte, who, broken hand and all, had forged into the lead.

Across sixty more laps and two high-pressure pit stops—one a green-flag series where Jarrett lost considerable position, the other under caution—the casting stayed the same. Except for one twist. Geoff Bodine opted to stay on the track as Labonte and Bobby pitted for the final time, gambling that this desert oval had one caution left in it.

Since Rockingham, Bobby's answer to anyone who asked when he'd get that first win was "It's just a matter of time." But when it became clear that something was wrong with the tires Labonte had just taken on, that it was easier than it should have been for Bobby to dive low out of turn four and pass the Winston Cup points leader, he looked toward Bodine's balding Goodyears and thought, Damn, it's time.

In the hauler, Debbie was laying out three drinks— Pepsi, Dr Pepper, and a bottle of water. Pepsi was a sponsor, so plenty of cans were on hand in case he raced well enough to be interviewed afterward. Dr Pepper, his favorite, was for the times he didn't. And the water was for when the race aggravated his ulcer. She also carefully laid out three wet washrags for his face, his shoes, and his clothing. She did these things watching neither the TV nor the track.

TNN was on a commercial break when Bobby passed the lapped car of Mike Skinner to pull to Bodine's tail. Watching with intrigue, racer-turned-broadcaster Buddy Baker realized Richard Petty was close to winning his first race as a car owner and told his producer, "Get a good shot of the bleachers. If he wins this baby, they'll tear the place apart."

Using the grip on the low line that got him here, Bobby tried diving under once, twice, three times, but Geoff shut him down fast. Then, barreling across the starting line with Labonte on his tail, Bobby bumped Geoff. In that second they both wavered, Terry swung wide under him, forcing Bobby to drop to cut him off. Richard couldn't look. Robbie's face went white. But Bobby was racing with all the frustration that had been building over the prior twelve months—hell, over his whole career! And so it was that as he sped into the backstretch and around the tri-oval, Bobby Hamilton pulled under Geoff and rode him all the way to the lead coming out of turn four.

Watching Bobby barrel out, Petty dropped his head and stared at the asphalt. "Ten to go," Robbie radioed, his face impassive. The legs of one crewman shook. Another went behind the tool rig and dropped on his knees in prayer.

Like a prisoner too long in solitary, Bobby was starting to hear things. Was that the engine missing, rattling under the dash, a tire going down? Watching Marlin pull into third to tie Labonte up in a dogfight, Dale Inman wasn't remembering the times Petty won, but the times he blew up taking a white flag. When he saw Kyle having motor troubles, he nearly passed out. "Tell Kyle to get the hell off the track!" Inman screamed.

About then it was occurring to Debbie that she didn't know where Victory Lane was and she was afraid to look for it. "I'm not gonna run up there and be standing around if something happens on the last lap and it ain't Bobby who pulls in," she said, trembling. "Everyone's gonna be laughing at me." But as the white flag fell, no tire cut, no engine exploded, no car was close enough to do damage. Martin put his final run on Labonte, but they were 1.23 seconds back.

It was 3:08 P.M. on October 27, 1996, and Bobby Hamilton would never again have to answer the question about when he'd win his first race.

From his seat he thought about the man whose voice and advice was always in his ears, and said on his radio, "This one's for you, Dale Inman."

Pulling into Victory Lane, Bobby was kept from jumping out of his car by Bill Brodrick, the Unocal public relations director who managed the weekly celebration and knew enough to save the shot until TNN came out of its commercial. So with adrenaline still coursing through his system, Bobby watched his own party from the fish-bowl of his cockpit. When Brodrick finally signaled him and Bobby sprung to the roof, rattling his fist in the air, he scanned the crowd for Inman. Where was he? Later, Debbie would swear she found him walking out of the men's room with his eyes red and puffy, as if he'd been crying.

Petty was still on pit road, sitting on his tire, head down, the winningest stock racer in history tasting the win on dry lips. A reporter asked him for a comment, but Petty waved him away. He'd spent years telling his people they needed to know the feeling of winning, only to discover *he* didn't know what he was feeling now. Relief? Pride? Envy? When he was told to go to Victory Lane, all he said was, "No, it's their time." Eventually he relented, only to wander around it like a stranger.

As for Bobby, he meant what he said about "being glad for the guys." But later, when all the commotion died down, he leaned into the question about how it felt and gave an answer that made you realize there's really no such thing as a storybook win in NASCAR.

"I'm happy for the people around me, but as for myself, I'm just glad to win one so I can tell everybody to go fuck themselves. I mean, there's this TV person who thinks he knows a lot about racing. He asked a good friend of mine, someone he didn't know I knew, when Richard Petty was going to quit putting up with mediocrity. I'm waiting for that son of a bitch. I've got his name burned in my mind like a damn computer chip. You get so much pressure these days to perform, and you hear so much stuff, that when you finally do it, the crap that everybody put on you just ruins the first win for you."

The celebration went on into the evening, but Bobby and Debbie weren't a part of it. As soon as the last question was answered, they bundled into their charter and went home.

"Hey, Bobby," she asked, leaning over to see her husband blankly reading a newspaper, depressurizing. "Did you think about your daddy when you won?"

He looked out the window, because this was the first time he'd even thought about Bud, and that made him feel a little guilty. "Nope," he said, looking down on the clouds. "Not until you just said it."

Over the next few days their lives were a blur. Bobby was out early the next morning, having promised his son he'd help him at the Nashville Speedway. And things didn't slow down after that. It wasn't until Wednesday night that Bobby even had a chance to watch the race.

Debbie came out of her bubble bath and found him in their bed, propped up on the pillows. Wrapped in her towel, she slid to his side, and he put his arm around her.

As they settled down to watch it together, she noticed he was smiling.

A Georgia state trooper with traffic-stop shades and a desk-job belly spread his arms wide, using his girth to try to move back the crowd that had massed below the scoring tower. The last drivers' meeting of 1996 was breaking up upstairs, and as Terry Labonte walked out the door and down the long stairway to the garage, the trooper's admonition to "give 'em room" was drowned out by shrieks of "Terry, Terry." He flashed a smile that could well have been caused by the fact that this insane publicity juggernaut was about to end.

The last time Labonte had won the points championship was in 1984, when a young mechanic named Gary DeHart worked on the crew run by Dale Inman. So as Inman walked past the crowd now, he made a point of seeking out his student.

"Nervous?" Inman asked.

"I don't remember you being like this," DeHart told him.

"Wanna know how I was?" Inman said, walking DeHart to the edge of the Kellogg's trailer. "It gets so bad that you want to throw up. That's the way I was."

DeHart nodded appreciatively and disappeared into a pack of his people. Inman walked briskly into his own hauler, where one of the crew was spraying air freshener.

"What the hell's that?" Inman asked, taking a deep, dissatisfied breath.

The crewman pointed to a certain flatulent driver in their midst.

"Hell, get the boy to a hospital, then," Inman said without breaking stride. "He's fartin' perfume."

The STP crew broke up in laughter, which was desperately needed. Today was going to be one hairy day. It was the last race of the season, and all their work had brought them to tenth place in the standings. Tenth place probably would net Petty another $100,000 in prize money, a few thousand of which might filter down to the crew. That was certainly nothing to sneer at, but it wasn't the big payoff. Being in the top ten meant no longer having trouble luring top talent, selling more merchandise, getting looked at more closely by new sponsors, and, most important, having your team believe in itself. Sweet mother, it had been a long time since anyone strutted around Level Cross!

The points situation could break either way. Petty's crew was eighty-eight points behind eighth-place Ernie Irvan. Unfortunately, they were precisely the same number of points away from Jeff Burton, who was in fifteenth. Moreover, everyone ahead of them in the standings either had won Atlanta or finished second. Bobby's best was twelfth, *a lap down.*

Nervous? he was asked. Bobby answered with a noise

that caused the crew to break out the air spray again. Passing with his nose buried in his STP jacket, Robbie walked out into the morning and said, "I'll be at the car if anyone wants me."

Robbie had been strangely depressed since Phoenix. He'd spent eight years working toward just one thing—a win—and now that he'd done it, well, he felt empty. "Whenever it came up, I used to tell people my dream was to win one for Richard Petty," he'd say later. "But when it happened, I got the wind knocked out of my sails. I didn't set my goals high enough."

He almost wished Childress had never called, because the more he thought about it, the more natural it seemed to take the Earnhardt job, especially since he'd just fulfilled his goal with King Richard. Looking over the Forty-three, Robbie thought the shame of it was that this was probably the best speedway car he'd ever built.

Richard Petty was in his bus, talking about the election day.

He'd waited out the returns five days earlier in Republican headquarters on Sunset Street in Asheboro, a small Mayberry-type town a dozen miles from Level Cross. The headquarters was really just a storefront between an antidrug center and a kung fu shop. Inside, the walls were covered by huge precinct maps, the ceilings by balloons, and the tables by homemade spreads in Tupperware. The night started with ritual campaign optimism, but as the tallies got worse and food was picked apart, it began feeling like a party gone on too long. Richard walked out before the final numbers were in, before he wound up losing by eight percentage points. He left through a back door, which was kind of the way he got into big-time politics in the first place.

But instead of being contemplative, exhausted, sullen, he was bouncy in his bus. "Only three men got more publicity than me," he said, grinning, "and they were all running for President."

As he tended to a flurry of last-minute deals—most of them having to do with Kyle, who was starting a team under the Petty Enterprises umbrella—one could see that Petty was more than a little relieved things had worked out as they did. Four years after he retired, he was finally figuring out a post-driving place for himself in the sport he'd built, with his flagship team finally coming together and his son finally coming home. And though the people of North Carolina had shelled him at the voting booth, Richard, at fifty-nine, would make sure they'd shell out big money for his ever-expanding empire. Walking out of the bus into the cool, 50-degree sunshine, he had to admit it wasn't a bad denouement.

A circle of fans trailed him to pit road, and though he found it sealed with even more people, they parted politely for the King. He tipped his cowboy hat and sat down on a sideways tire, his office for the next three hours.

Bobby had retreated to his car after going through the drivers' introduction, where he was lauded for his Phoenix win by the television star Craig T. Nelson and the Mr. Lug Nut mascot of a car parts store. All weekend he'd kept examining his weaknesses, comparing them against the weaknesses of the men ahead of him in points: Marlin, Irvan, Wallace, Rudd, Martin, Earnhardt, Jarrett, Gordon, and Terry Labonte.

He also kept a wary eye out for the men who'd be breathing down his neck: Ken Schrader in eleventh, Bobby Labonte in twelfth, and then Mike Waltrip, Ted Musgrave, Jeff Burton, and Jimmy Spencer. Things were so fluid, anyone from Schrader back to Spencer could steal his position.

The thing was, he couldn't find any weaknesses in his car's handling or horsepower. He was passing as well high as low. His cornering was superb, something that would be critical in Atlanta, where half-mile turns and quarter-mile straights meant he'd be forever turning. And he had motor. Hot damn did he have motor. After what happened last year—the random misfortune of having a flat tire that sent him six laps down—he was the last one to be over-confident. But on the heels of Phoenix, he honestly believed this silver Pontiac was the best car in town.

Robbie leaned in, took a look around the gauges, and then as he was about to walk off, remarked, "Just do like you done all year." Bobby nodded, connected the tube that carried clean air into his helmet, and after the anthem was sung, flipped on the ignition switch.

The early going merely confirmed what he'd suspected. He passed quickly and easily in the first forty laps, pulling to fifth. By then the fickle fans wedged into the narrow lane behind the DuPont pit were gravitating to the Texaco and STP stalls next door, bored by the fact that Jeff Gordon had gone two laps down with tire trouble. The Petty men drank in the spotlight when the first caution flag flew and pit road opened, and the race moved into their hands. Ernie Irvan sped off pit road first, then Jarrett, then Andretti. Just as Earnhardt was gearing up to pass from several stalls away, Robbie yelled, "Go! Go! Go!"

Bobby didn't see the Goodyear tire that Irvan's crew left outside the painted yellow line of their pit stall. A race tire weighs seventy pounds, and punching the throttle, Bobby went full force into it, smacking on the left side of his nose assembly, which is made of thin plastic. The nose is the first thing that meets the wind. If its curved contours are dented, the wind splays everywhere but smoothly over the car.

"How bad?" Loomis asked Inman.

Looking through binoculars from the spotter's tower, Inman saw a dent about two feet wide and half a finger deep. "Bad," he answered. "It beat the shit out of the right front."

It's that easy to go from fifth to thirty-fifth. One tire left out of the box, and the next thing you know, you're wasting a green-flag pit to tape up a dented nose. If a tire is left out intentionally, NASCAR has a range of penalties to impose, including directing a driver to drop back several positions. Irvan wasn't fined, however, because the act was unintentional. Looking at his crew's funeral-ready faces, Robbie would later describe himself as being "sewed up so tight, you couldn't put a pin in my mouth."

In his cockpit, Bobby was neither angry nor flustered. When he raced the day after his father's funeral, he said he'd found a feeling he'd been waiting for as a driver. What he meant was that he hadn't completely cleared his mind in a race car until then. Drivers go to pieces. It's a fact of life. What Bobby had learned was how to be cool in a coal-hot race car. Thirty-fifth?

"Hell, let's win the bitch," he said.

Keeping radio silence over the next two hundred laps, he patiently waited for the race to come to him. Running as fast as the leader and growing more confident with each pass, he brought himself to the door of the top ten. His crew began mimicking his moves with their body language, and when Atlanta's 180-mile-an-hour airstream began shearing up the damaged front skirt and he had to pull onto pit road, they riveted on an aluminum brace quickly enough to keep him in the top twenty.

With ninety laps left, he'd motored all the way up to ninth, going nose-to-tail with, of all people, Earnhardt. Watching Hamilton try to keep his line, and Earnhardt powering past him on the outside, Robbie narrowed his eyes, knowing how much his potentially new boss wanted this win, and how much his current driver wanted to ruin it for him.

Not long after Earnhardt had wrecked him in February, Bobby had sat on the couch of his Winnebago, blinds drawn, and said, "One day I'm gonna wreck the mother-fucker and it's gonna be over with. Oh, I'll be a sorry son of a bitch in everybody's eyes and NASCAR will fine me $10,000. But I'll write the check and it will be done with, that simple. NASCAR is never gonna fix this. It'll take five of us with the balls to wreck his ass. He can't run all of us off. And I guess I'll be the one to start it. The next time he jacks with me, I'm turnin' his ass."

As Bobby fell behind the black Monte Carlo, he thought, Oh man, it would be so easy to take care of business right now. He was keeping himself close—so close that all he had to do was throttle a little harder and he'd punt the son of a bitch into the wall. "I made up my mind that if he bulldogged me, there was gonna be trouble," Hamilton would say. "But if he raced me clean, I'd leave it at that."

And, to Robbie's great relief, Earnhardt stayed clean, so Bobby fell in line behind his black Chevrolet, drafting with it to the lip of the top five. Then Irvan took a monstrous hit against the second-turn wall, opening pit road. As Petty watched his crewmen whir around their Pontiac, emptying two eleven-gallon gas cans into the parched tank and flinging four new tires on its wheels, he couldn't help but get caught up in the moment. Overriding Robbie on the radio, he shouted, "It's up to you, buddy. Go for it."

On new tires, Earnhardt went into the first turn hard behind second-place Jeff Burton, flinging himself down, then up, then, when Burton drifted high in the third turn, pushing past and powering up to Gordon. Stealing a bit of the drama from their 1995 title battle, Earnhardt dove beneath Gordon to take first.

"He's real brave on new tires, but it won't last long," the confident Gordon radioed his pit. Just as he said this, Ken

Schrader in the groove above him blew a tire and went crashing into the wall.

Robbie faced the seminal call of the year. With Schrader behind the wall, Bobby Labonte was next in line to knock them out of the top ten. He'd already led once. If he made his way to the front again and held on to win, they'd need *106* points—a *nineteenth*-place finish—to keep Labonte from stealing tenth. By ordering a pit stop now, what was the chance he might sabotage that? A stuck lug nut, an air gun break, a bad set of tires? Any of that could happen. And it didn't take much for a car to drift back to the middle of the pack, where desperate drivers tended to do desperate things.

The thought gave him a chill as he scanned his tire wear sheets. They should wear well, he thought. Oh hell! For his last call of the season, he'd put the race in his driver's hands.

"Stay out," he radioed as Bobby became the leader for the second time in as many races. "It's your race now."

Off the restart, Bobby Labonte was doing everything he could to keep the STP team from New York. Speeding into the first turn, he dove three wide under Earnhardt and Gordon to grab third, then surged past Rudd to pull to Bobby's bumper.

In the pits tire changer John "Hollywood" Hayworth ran to publicist Chuck Spicer and started hugging him. Despite his nickname, Hayworth was born so country, the local doctor had to be called out to a cotton field to deliver him. Now, jumping up and down as Bobby passed, he shouted a line from his favorite Tom Hanks film: "Run, Forrest! Run!"

Bobby was sure as hell trying. He was wide open, holding nothing back. The only sound he wanted to hear on his radio were his lap times, repeated like a hypnotic mantra to keep him throttling in rhythm. He heard Robbie call out, "30.72." Then, a lap later, "30.75."

In his rearview mirror the sun was beating on two cars behind him—the Chevrolet driven by Bobby Labonte and the second-place Ford of Ricky Rudd—covering them in blinding light. Rudd had been patient, hoping Bobby's lap times would slack off more, but Labonte had the faster car. In a quick burst, the young Labonte swept past Rudd and maneuvered to the STP Pontiac's tail. Labonte dared Bobby high in turn four, but it was just a taunt. As the men carried each other through turn two, though, it became real. Hamilton tried holding Labonte off in the low lane, but his tires didn't have the bite. *Let . . . him . . . go,* Robbie thought, chewing his lower lip.

Bobby did—and went from the fat right into the fryer. No sooner had the young Labonte passed than Jeff Gordon was filling Bobby's mirror. Thirteen laps into the race, the kid was two laps down; less than a hundred laps later he was back on the lead lap. You couldn't kill him. Ain't no time to be a cowboy, Bobby thought as the negative g forces pulled at his skin and he drifted high into the banking of turn two. Seeing a blur sweep past beneath him, he said good-bye to Gordon.

What next? How about Earnhardt again? Spilling into the backstretch inches off Bobby's tail, Earnhardt twitched left, then right, then went for the clean pass on the outside. Rudd, in Earnhardt's draft, became the fourth car to glide beneath the red-and-blue Pontiac.

Bobby heard through his radio, "31.45." Okay, the freight train had done its damage.

As if taking a deep breath, Bobby powered up in the first turn and, using the length of the backstretch, took back fifth. Watching Bobby speed by, Hayworth had the rest screaming, "Run, Forrest! Run." Robbie cupped his hand over his radio's microphone and said, "Good job, you're keeping yourself in it, Buddy."

Unfortunately, all this skirmishing let the first three cars get two full seconds ahead, and Jarrett and Terry Labonte were closing on him fast. Feverishly racing to close out a storybook season, Jarrett forced Hamilton high in the first turn to nab fourth. But more impressive was the yellow hood that filled his rearview mirror next. Labonte was six days away from his fortieth birthday, driving with a broken hand that was killing him, and the man didn't need to finish better than eighteenth to win the Winston Cup. And yet, three and a half minutes after his younger brother dusted Bobby, Terry was doing the same, taking fifth. Hamilton had to hand it to the man. He was tough.

With the exception of a run that Jarrett put on Bobby Labonte to lift himself to second place, the six men stayed where they were for the next thirty-four laps. As the checkered flag fell on Bobby Labonte in first place, and he and Terry took what was said to be the richest victory lap in NASCAR history, pit road seemed to fold into a V with every grease monkey and scene maker trying to poke into their pits.

Gordon was gracious in ceding the Winston Cup title to his teammate, though he couldn't help but advertise his youth by pointing out that his recovery from two laps down "showed we're a championship-caliber team and we plan to be like that a long time."

Jarrett was ebullient as he was swarmed by reporters at the gas pumps. The tall, broad-shouldered son of Hall of Fame racer Ned Jarrett had gone from being Ernie Irvan's tortured understudy to NASCAR's newest marquee face. He would have the whole winter to count the millions he'd be making.

Earnhardt, who finished fourth in the race as well as the final point standings, began looking to the 1997 season from the moment he parked by the gas pumps. "That's the hardest I've ever driven here," he said, making no attempt to hide his disgust. "Definitely wasn't the kind of day I wanted to have."

In all the chaos, Bobby Hamilton slipped out of his car and easily made it past the reporters as he walked toward his hauler. At long last he had the kind of year he didn't have to explain away. And so Loomis ran up to him, and the two men clasped their hands tightly and chest-bumped.

"Damn, that wasn't too bad. What'd we end up with?"

"Sixth in the race. Ninth in the standings," Loomis said.

Bobby looked at the larger-than-life portrait of Petty on the side of the team's hauler. "Ninth, huh?" he said, rolling the word around on his tongue to see how it tasted. "About damn time."

At that, he disappeared inside, leaving Robbie staring at it too. Tomorrow the crew chief would tell his men that he'd been offered the Earnhardt job and turned it down to stay with them another year.

But for now, as the circus started shutting down and the sunset threw pink light over the garage, he turned to watch his crew hugging one another.

"You gotta love this sport," he said.

The Waldorf-Astoria Hotel in New York was decorated for Christmas. A green velvet sleigh in the lobby was buried beneath shiny wrapped boxes with red ribbons. The ladies who lunch were all coming back from Saks, trailed by bellhops and their bags. The prominent four-sided Waldorf Clock, the 1893 model with a Statue of Liberty on top, was its usual busy meeting place.

Bobby peeked out almost furtively from behind the clock. By the French chairs a boy with his family was looking for autographs. The kid was buzzing over a Kyle signature he'd just added to his book. Two men who looked as if they were from Merrill Lynch were stationed by the concierge desk, waiting for Rusty Wallace.

Bobby pointed to a small café in the lobby, but before he could make it inside, the kid blocked him and the brokers were on the move. Trapped, Bobby accepted a glossy photo of himself in Phoenix. He didn't so much as sign it as move it under his pen. Then he sent the kid off with something that wasn't quite a smile, and sent the brokers away with even less.

Later that night, when he heard his name called, he slowly walked up onto the stage of the Waldorf's Grand Ballroom. It had been five years since he'd been there for his installation as Rookie of the Year, but it seemed longer. The intervals between promise and fulfillment usually do.

He looked out at Earnhardt in the front row, at Petty to his side, at the television broadcaster whose face was burned into his mind like a computer chip, and said something simple and unremarkable.

Bobby Hamilton was no more ready for fame than he was before he won his first race, before he got hired by the King, before he made it to Winston Cup. He was not like John Andretti or Robby Gordon, who chose stock car racing after their agents and lawyers analyzed the career potential; like Earnhardt or Irvan, who used NASCAR to reinvent themselves as something more than small-town men with pasts to leave behind; or any of the brothers or sons who followed their famous relatives.

Hamilton is a rarer case, an ordinary guy made special by The Show. Once they were all like him. But that was a while ago.

Now NASCAR has opened an office in Manhattan, two blocks away from the Waldorf on Park Avenue. It was a deliberate move, done to leave behind any trace of its old image. NASCAR's neighbors aren't moonshiners or rednecks or even small-town businessmen. Not anymore. Its new neighbors are Major League Baseball, the NBA, and the NFL.

Bobby is too set in his ways to be a major star in this new world. He doesn't have an agent or handlers. Which is as he wants it. It wasn't that long ago that he'd been fired from Sabates's operation and was wandering the garage looking for work. And so he said, "I wanted to be the one to put Richard's car in the winner's circle so my family could shut up all the people who kept saying, 'He ain't gonna ever win nothin'.' I know it sounds silly, but I feel good that it's their turn. And they got all winter to do it."

Bobby watched a family walk by, and took a long sip of Sprite.

"If my dad hadn't been on a government check, he wouldn't have had a nickel," he continued. "As it was, all he had was four hundred dollars in a locked box. He thought that was just tons of money. It was all he wanted." The racer paused here, looking into his empty glass. "I know my age is getting to be a factor and there'll be a time where we can't do any better. But I hope that comes after a championship. For now, all I want is five more years in a race car."

EPILOGUE

February 1997

When the eighteen-wheelers pulled up to Daytona for the start of the 1997 season, NASCAR's long journey out of the small-town South and into the maw of the big-city sports machine was nearly complete.

Having established beachheads in Fort Worth and Los Angeles, Bill France Jr. was eyeing his 1998 schedule, looking for an opening to fit a sparkling new track in Las Vegas, and his 1999 one to add another track near Miami. Though the grand old oval in Darlington was among the old-time tracks that would still hold two races in 1997, the Winston Cup schedule couldn't afford them that luxury much longer—not when there were still major media markets to conquer. Bruton Smith was already eyeing land around Atlantic City—once a hotbed of racing—and there was talk of breaking ground near Chicago.

Moreover, France was looking forward to the fall, when he'd take the Winston Cup series to Suzuka, Japan, for the second time. The Japanese had been underwhelmed by his first effort to bring them American stock car racing; the exhibition race staged near Tokyo in November 1996 didn't even sell out. But Major League Baseball didn't catch on right away either. France saw Japan as an important new market for NASCAR, one that a self-respecting juggernaut with its own product lines could ill afford to ignore.

Big Bill Sr. never competed with the companies that

sponsored his sport's race cars. He saw them as partners, and told his children that you didn't take food off a partner's plate. But as Bill Jr.'s son, Brian, gained influence as vice president for marketing, that line in the sand began to blur, and then disappeared entirely. This France would be the first to stumble on a remarkable find: NASCAR had been the passion of three generations of southerners, and they held its name holy. When he started leveraging that trust by selling the NASCAR name for use on consumer products, it took off. Now the NASCAR name may be found on Jell-O molds and Band-Aid boxes, its own line of car care accessories and magazines, even mall directories with a national chain of NASCAR Thunder stores and cafés.

Behind the smoked-glass doors of NASCAR's corporate affiliate, International Speedway Corp., Big Bill's other son, James, was girding for war.

ISC went into 1996 with four wholly owned tracks (Daytona, Talladega, Darlington, Watkins Glen) and a 50 percent interest in Martinsville. But as soon as Smith began his acquisition spree, Jim France saw the urgent need to shore up his family's position. In the summer of 1996, he bought 11 percent of Penske Motorsports, giving ISC interests in the Michigan, California, and Rockingham speedways, among others. Then, in 1997, he added two more venues—the Phoenix raceway, which holds the season's penultimate race, and the art deco motorsports complex near Miami that his brother is likely to add to the schedule in 1999. If anyone was keeping score, ISC controlled—or had influence over—tracks where fifteen Winston Cup races were held; Smith's Speedway Motorsports had eight.

With James running ISC, Brian branding the NASCAR name, and nothing happening in the garage area without

Bill Jr.'s okay, the Frances had become one of the wealthiest families in sport, worth $750 million in ISC stock
alone.*

But in growing NASCAR so large, they lost the one
thing that always set it apart from the other sports: their
seeming ability to control every last detail in the world
they created. That became painfully evident in December
1996, on the eve of the Winston Cup banquet to honor
Terry Labonte's championship season and Hendrick
Motorsports' second straight title.

As the admirers of Labonte and car owner Rick Hendrick began filling the Waldorf-Astoria hotel, a disturbing
dispatch arrived from Charlotte. A probe into American
Honda that netted twenty bribery and corruption convic-
tions of former executives had expanded to include Hendrick, Honda's largest U.S. dealer. His competitors had
long wondered how he was able to corner the market on
hard-to-get imports and dealerships in the 1980s. Now the
U.S. Attorney was supplying an alleged answer: He made
huge cash payments to the company's top salesmen,
helping one even buy a pair of homes. Hendrick didn't
deny making the payoffs, though he insisted he expected
nothing in return. And he wasn't the only dealer named in
the probe. He was, however, one of the few not to be given
immunity, a sign prosecutors were underwhelmed by his
offers of cooperation. A federal grand jury indicted them
on fifteen counts of money laundering, and single counts
of conspiracy and mail fraud.

NASCAR rallied around its favorite son, blasting the
timing as a shameless publicity grab by an ambitious
prosecutor. (A friendly cover story in the *Winston Cup
Scene* would suggest the case reeked of vendetta, noting

*The figure is based on the family owning roughly 60 percent of 38 million
outstanding shares, with each share trading at $21.

the prosecutor had kept Hendrick's photo on his wall.) Ignored in all of this was the irony that the case never would have received national coverage if NASCAR wasn't feting itself in the media capital of the world. But after the banquet was over, and the business of getting ready for the 1997 season begun, more solemn news emerged. Though there was never an indication Hendrick was in less than good health, a routine physical had revealed the presence of a leukemia that kills half of its sufferers within four to six years of diagnosis. The news, contained in an affidavit by his lawyers to postpone the federal conspiracy trial, stunned the sport.

Hendrick stayed home from the Daytona 500, his immune system debilitated, his body racked by ulcers and drug cocktails. On Sunday, February 16, he became the first Winston Cup owner ever to have his cars take the checkered flag in first, second, and third place in the Daytona 500. Six months later, on August 18, his condition had deteriorated so much that prosecutors agreed to let him plead guilty to a single count of mail fraud.

There were other notable absences from that race. Bobby Allison, for one, would not be fielding a car for the first time since 1961. After his team fell apart at the end of the '96 season, friends began giving him odd jobs in public relations. It was enough for him to finally buy back his house in Hueytown and take down that For Sale sign. In time, the good days began to pull even with the bad ones, and when people asked him to tell his story, he obliged, accepting his new role as NASCAR's de facto Official Tragic Figure.

R.J. Reynolds was also preparing to become an absentee friend. In April 1997, Steven Goldstone, chairman of RJR Nabisco Holdings, sat down in a Washington, D.C. hotel with five other tobacco CEOs and the representatives of forty state attorneys general to settle suits over health claims. The result was a $368 billion settlement that included strict curbs on tobacco financing of sporting events. But the pact quickly ran into trouble in Congress. Winston Cup remained safe at least through 1999.

In its statements, NASCAR reacted with appropriate dismay at this intrusion in the affairs of a partner of twenty-five years. But the Frances couldn't have been as displeased with the prospect of losing the tobacco money as they let on. The climate for hawking cigarettes had become ugly, and with NASCAR selling its drivers as cartoon characters—particularly in *Racing for Kids*, the publication owned by Jeff Gordon and Dale Earnhardt, and the Hot Wheels toys that were a spin-off of Kyle Petty's sponsorship—the marriage of stock and cigarettes had grown more strained than ever. Money was no longer the issue it was in 1972, when Junior Johnson had to beg for $100,000. The line to replace RJR was long now.

The small-town South of tobacco fields and cotton mills nurtured NASCAR, but it was time to leave them behind. It was time to move on.

The winter of 1996–97 was a time of reconciliation for the Bodine brothers. It started on Christmas day, with the family around Eli, whose emphysema had worsened. Mindful that his father didn't get out much, Brett presented him with slippers and a bathrobe. Eli seemed delighted. "That's all I wear now," he said, trying to be sunny. Two days later, Brett got a phone call at 5:45 in the morning that paramedics were at his father's house. He rushed to the hospital, but by then Eli was dead. "My mom gave me the bathrobe back," Brett says. "Dad got to wear it once." In the days after, the Bodine men tried to relearn the language of being brothers. As Brett put it, "We forgot about everything else and became a family again. We didn't talk about the past, and I don't think Geoff or me ever will again. We've buried it deep."

Geoff's advice about owning a race team—"You should think before you buy, because your life changes more dramatically than you could ever imagine"— haunted him through 1997. In a move that first seemed bold and turned out to be suicidal, Geoff hired a well-regarded drag racer, Bob Glidden, to improve the horse-power in his motors. They performed well during the first spate of short-track races, then began blowing on the larger ovals. He lost seventeen $30,000 motors, and plummeted to thirty-first in the points standings, bringing home the dregs of the purses. His balance sheet shot and his bankers balking at any more loans, Geoff ended his odyssey as an independent by selling 90 percent of his operation. The new owners promised him that he'd be able to drive his own car for three more years, presumably at a hefty enough salary that he could begin crawling out of debt, and maybe retire at the age of fifty.

"It's the oldest story in NASCAR," one reporter quipped. "You have to lose a huge fortune before you make a small one."

As opposite as Geoff and Brett are, their lives were running in eerie parallel. Not only had the men bought race teams within two years of each other, lost sponsors, and then struggled to find new ones, but Brett, like Geoff, was nearing financial ruin.

Carl Smith's "Close Call" phone card had been an unmitigated disaster as a new product launch. The cards were delayed by months, and Smith quickly fell $1.5 million in arrears to the Bodines. Then, on July 10, the *Winston-Salem Journal* reported that Junior Johnson was suing Brett over the hundred grand that Lowe's refused to pay after the missed Martinsville race in September 1996. Instead of chasing Brett, Lowe's took the easier course, deducting it from the money owed Junior. Brett found $50,000 to reimburse the old man, and went to New Hampshire hoping to win the rest. On the race's very first lap, he got caught up in a wreck and ended the day *245 laps* down.

The people who smell blood in situations like this are never shy, and they kept the phone ringing off the hook with offers to bail him out in exchange for majority control. By late July, he was still defiant, though the smile had long since drained from his face. "There are no partners out there," he said. "If I wanted a partner, I'd just drive for someone else again." The thought seemed to disgust him, and he twisted his face. "No, I'm gonna see this through, however it turns out." But with their cash reserves so low that they could afford to buy motors through August 10, the breaking point came during qualifying for the Brickyard on July 31.

The Bodines desperately needed a big-money weekend, but Brett qualified fourth worst on Thursday and by the time second-round qualifying came on Friday, August 1, he climbed into his Ford believing this was where it would end. He was nearly four-tenths of a second off the pace and low enough in points that if he qualified past thirty-ninth place he'd be ineligible for a provisional. Watching her husband disappear into the first turn, Diane Bodine thought, He shouldn't be out there. He's not thinking clearly.

And then she started crying. She'd never cried during a qualifying lap. Is this what it had all come down to? Being so afraid, so strung out, that she was crying over qualifying? Before that lap was done, she gathered herself up and thought, I'm not going to lose my husband like this. It's not worth it. We're getting a partner.

Brett narrowly snuck into the Brickyard with the last available provisional, rallying Saturday to finish eighteenth and bank $80,000. The following Wednesday, he announced that Andrew Evans, a Seattle investment banker with close ties to Microsoft founder Bill Gates, was becoming 50 percent owner of a new team being called Scandia/Bodine Racing.

Gary Claudio was wearing out his living room carpet watching his Pontiac players. The Joe Gibbs team that he'd lured from Chevrolet was seventh in the standings. Everyone else, including the Richard Petty outfit, was struggling to stay out of the back twenty.

"Mutts," he groused. "I got mutts."

Petty was on the road nearly all the time now—promoting his racing schools, tending his truck team, making appearances for the companies he endorsed, nurturing Kyle's PE2 team. The inhuman pace he kept as a racer—"I was fortunate startin' young and not having any habits as far as eating or sleepin, 'cause my body don't care what time it is," he once said—was the pace he now used in business. But in his absences, the STP team was drifting.

"There were five races we could have won," Bobby Hamilton complained in July. "Instead we're in twenty-first place. *I don't like that shit one bit.*"

The Pocono 500 hurt most. After starting the year strongly, the STP team fell to sixteenth, but Pocono was a track Bobby ran well on and Robbie Loomis marked the weekend as a turning point. Bobby stoked his crew chief's expectations by winning the pole on Friday, then leading the first twenty laps Sunday. He cut a tire shortly thereafter but maintained his composure, battling back from a lap down to get into the top ten by lap 129. Scanning his tire wear sheets, Loomis radioed that he wanted Bobby to pull into pit road on the next pass. Hamilton never got there.

Speeding out of the second turn, he felt his right front explode and girded for getting thrown into the wall at 180 mph. The impact was savage, and in the dim afterglow of a concussion, he felt for his eyes. They were open, but he couldn't see a thing. One minute passed. Then five. Then ten. Nothing. He'd been blinded before, but never for this long. He was scared, scared to damn death. After fifteen minutes, he finally began to see light, shadows, and then blurred shapes.

Laid up with double vision for two days, Bobby had plenty of time to think about the changes that had come over Petty Enterprises—changes dictated by Kyle's presence. The year before, the shop had churned out six cars. Now it was producing twenty. "It's like havin' a baby," Robbie said, trying to assure him. "We gotta put up with certain things to get the rewards of seeing him walk." But when Bobby turned down more lucrative offers for the 1997 season, he did it to be happy. Not patient.

When Kyle passed him in the standings on July 13, friends began encouraging him to call Robert Yates, who was not extending Ernie Irvan's contract into 1998. Yates had stood by Irvan for three years after his near-fatal crash, but Ernie squandered his ministerial patience with jealous fits and falling-outs. The capstone was an incident outside the Cornelius nightclub in Charlotte, when Ernie's wife, Kim, traded punches with another woman and her boyfriend. Irvan tried to get out quick, but the story leaked, mortifying Texaco's image-conscious executives. Yates looked pained when he announced he'd be searching for a new driver. "You wouldn't understand unless you lived through it," he said.

Bobby couldn't see the logic of trading one two-car team for another, and cast an eye toward the high-profile number 4 car, whose owner, Larry McClure, and driver, Sterling Marlin, had lost the magic (not to mention the crew chief) that let them finish 1995 in third place and 1996 in eighth. McClure had a great speedway program but was frustrated by his inability to notch top tens on short tracks. Bobby, among the best short-track drivers in NASCAR, was frustrated about his speedway driving skills routinely getting overlooked.

"You come with me and I'll guarantee you a Daytona 500," McClure told him.

After a long talk with Petty in a Holiday Inn room at Watkins Glen, Bobby decided that things had simply run their course. "I've been down that road," he said. "I know what it feels like when things get stale."

Petty nodded. They'd done a world of good for each other, the legend and the driver whose career he helped re-build. But they'd always had an uneasy alliance, and Hamilton couldn't get McClure's words to stop ringing in his ears. As he walked back to his room, Bobby made up his mind that he'd be running the 1998 Daytona 500 in the yellow Kodak car.

Going to sleep that night, he wondered what it would feel like when he won the Super Bowl of stock car racing.

Over the winter, Dwayne Leik called everyone he could think of on behalf of Dave Marcis, trying to replace Prodigy.

He called Duracell, figuring Dave was perfect for their slogan, "Stronger Longer"; Master Locks because he knew they didn't run their usual million-dollar Super Bowl ad and might want to spend that money on Dave; Alka-Seltzer because . . . well, duh. In all, he'd reached out to five hundred sponsors, dividing index cards with their names into three piles labeled "No way," "Didn't say no way," and "Maybe."

The "Maybe" stack was mighty thin.

Then, in mid-January, Richard Childress called to ask, "What you got going for the beach?" When Dave replied, "Nothing much," Childress sent him Bill Jordan, owner of the Realtree camouflage clothing company. Jordan agreed to a one-race deal—just the Daytona 500. Unfortunately, it didn't look as if Dave would even get that far. The qualifying lap he ran earned him only forty-sixth place, and as a result he was penciled into the twenty-second starting spot for his Gatorade 125 qualifying race. It was far enough back that his slow Chevrolet seemed to have no chance to climb to fourteenth—the cutoff to win a transfer into Sunday's "Super Bowl." But during his practice on Wednesday, Dave accidentally drifted high on the track. "Hey, I'm lighting up here," he realized. At the end of the day he gathered his crew around and said, "Dammit, we got a chance. Dammit, I feel good now." On Thursday the old man of the Winston Cup tour flew out of the gate and right up to a checkered-flag finish of eleventh place, keeping his string of consecutive Daytona 500 appearances alive at thirty. As usual, reports of his demise had been greatly exaggerated.

Jordan extended his sponsorship after that, but he had only a million dollars to give—33 percent less than Marcis Auto Racing had received from Prodigy. Dave tried, but you couldn't stretch a million bucks the way you used to. By July he'd missed three races and fallen to thirty-seventh place in the standings, barely hanging on. (Teams that fall out of the top forty are no longer eligible for provisionals.) A man from *Sports Illustrated* called, wanting to do a story on athletes who were the last of their breeds. "That's us," Dave's daughter, Shawn Marie, said with a sigh. "A dying breed."

On Friday, July 18, Dave took to the Pocono raceway to practice for the Pennsylvania 500. As his glass-smooth tires passed over a few drops of oil left on the third turn, the Monte Carlo launched into a hapless spin, flinging itself against the concrete wall, smacking on the driver's side. The impact smashed the steering wheel into his ribs, snapping two of them. Most men of fifty-six would take a day off. Not Dave Marcis. Things were too desperate for that, falling apart around him. He had to keep going, get that backup car ready, get to second-round qualifying. But when things are falling apart, nothing works. His motor blew and he used a provisional to get into Sunday's race, only to go out after forty laps with a blown backup motor in a backup car.

"This has been the worst weekend of my life," he groaned.

But the weekends would get worse, and worse, and worse. Dave missed ten of his next fourteen races, a streak that spent him to near-total exhaustion. By the end of the 1997 season, the last of the independents was still hanging on.

But barely.

Just barely.

As NASCAR raced away from its old world, it also said good-bye to some of its most colorful figures—gentle country layabouts like Elmo Langley, who competed from 1958 to 1981, then went on to fifteen years of mini-celebrity as NASCAR's pace car driver.

Langley traveled abroad only twice: in the late 1980s, when NASCAR went to Australia for an exhibition, and again in November 1996, when it made its maiden voyage to Suzuka, Japan.

On November 21, 1996, Langley climbed into his pace car to give the racer-turned-broadcaster Buddy Baker a quick tour of Suzuka's road course. Coming out of the first turn, Langley saw Rusty Wallace and went throttle down, sweeping past his glossy black Miller Ford. Giggling with delight, Langley turned to Baker and said, "We dusted his ass, didn't we?"

Suddenly the car slowed, and Baker told his old friend, "Elmo, if you don't put your foot on the gas Rusty's gonna dust us." But instead of speeding up, Langley brought the car to a stop. Then he heaved his last breath and died from a massive coronary.

"God took him the way he would have wanted," his ex-wife, Nancy, said. "Until his last breath, he was going wide open."

AFTERWORD

At the end of the 1990s, NASCAR had all but finished the journey it started at the dawn of the decade. Bill France seemed dizzy as he gave a speech to a national group of sports editors, reporting that his television ratings were second only to the NFL, and that NASCAR had nine out of the ten most highly attended events of 1997. Coca-Cola took its big dollars away from football and put them into NASCAR's pockets, while Pepsi signed Jeff Gordon to a contract that helped make him America's most sought-after sports spokesman next to Michael Jordan, Tiger Woods, and Arnold Palmer.

The press continued to be breathlessly impressed, as if it never expected things to get this far, and the sheer weight of the inspection started to lend NASCAR the trappings of a genuine cultural phenomenon. This had to do partly with America's resurgent love affair with all things southern, and partly to do with the fact that the world of sports marketing was exploding. Corporate America was expected to spend $4.5 billion promoting its products through sports in 1998, with fully ten percent of that aimed at NASCAR—more than the entire sum spent on baseball, basketball, football, and hockey.

But while NASCAR was being hailed as one of the great business successes of the decade, the veterans who'd been around through good times and bad couldn't help but worry about where all this was leading. In the summer of 1998, Deb Williams of the Winston Cup Scene gave this view from the garage:

"When a technical person says he can't talk to a driver any more because the driver is more interested in how his souvenirs are selling, the sport has problems.

"When a corporate person, who has never invented a safety device or piece of equipment for a race car, feels he should receive the same respect as a person who has toiled in the sport for twenty or fifty years, the sport has problems.

"When a sanctioning body won't take disciplinary actions that might be needed, such as suspension, because it's concerned about offending corporate sponsors, the sport has problems. As one person said to me in Dover, 'It looks like those of us who want to race may have to go find another series because this is becoming strictly an entertainment show.' "

The season's start certainly provided its share of entertainment, as Dale Earnhardt lifted the burden of nineteen years—and ended a losing streak that began in March 1996—by winning the Daytona 500. Bounding into Victory Lane, he trained his glare at more reporters, then attended a White House press briefing and shouted, "I'm here, and I've got that goddamn monkey off my back." Six weeks later, his son, Dale Jr., won his first NASCAR race in Texas, this one in the Busch series. On the last lap, the twenty-three-year-old, who was making just his seventeenth start, tore a page from the old man's playbook by bumping veteran Joe Nemechek from behind, and going throttle-down for the win. (Twelve races and four wins later, after the young Earnhardt had climbed to first place in the standings, he was penalized for rough driving in South Boston. The next day, his father nearly bumped Jeff Gordon out of a race a few hundred miles away in Pocono, PA.)

Dale Jr. learned at the feet of his father, just the way his father learned from his daddy, Ralph, and the way count-less crewmen and racers learned from theirs. It's what has made NASCAR such an insular, closed, familial world, and a foreboding one, too. But every so often, an outsider on a shoestring budget manages to pierce it, someone like Alan Kulwicki, who showed up one day with a briefcase, a degree in mechanical engineering, and an inventor's wile. The old timers snickered at the improbable Polish American who kept a decal of Underdog on his Thunder-bird and rarely had more than a couple of scruffy mechan-ics around him. The snickering stopped when he won his first race in 1988; by 1992, the year he won his title, he'd become feared. The emergence of an iconoclast like Kul-wicki can make the garage electric and filled with inven-tion. Williams's fear—which is shared by everyone who's watched NASCAR become increasingly interventionist about its competition—is that a $2 billion a year enterprise can't afford, and won't allow, surprises.

It's a compelling point. But early in the 1998 season, something happened to remind everyone that there is still room—maybe just a crack, but still room—for an under-dog to bubble up. It happened when a racer named Kevin Lepage, who spent fourteen years on Vermont's short tracks, got hired by a Cinderella operation so broke it didn't have enough men to practice pit stops, and stunned the sport by making fourteen of fifteen races with just one motor. (For perspective, Hendrick Motorsports has 140 engines in its inventory.) Of course, as soon as Lepage got hot, he signed with the five-car Roush Racing empire. Nevertheless, his success gave hope to every underdog in the garage.

There's a euphemism that people use in NASCAR when they don't believe something is right, but are disin-clined to speak out. They curl their lips and excuse it by saying, "Well, it's for the good of the sport." The sport is doing very "good" indeed. But as the same half-dozen or

so drivers keep making their way into Victory Lane, NAS-
CAR needs to remember the underdogs, too. For the good
of the sport.

Bobby and Debbie Hamilton spent the start of the 1998 season looking around the Kodak racing team like new home-
owners still unsure about whether the old tenant had been
entirely truthful. The Hamiltons never looked back at their
decision to leave Petty Enterprises, though it continued to
be bittersweet. In October of 1997, with just three races remaining to his contract with The King, Bobby dominated
the AC Delco 400 in Rockingham, leading three times for
thirty-seven laps and shocking everyone who assumed he,
like any racer about to leave a team, had given up. Later
that night, he flew to Level Cross, where he ordered pizza
for his crew, autographed their mementos, and collected a
$100,000 check from Petty, who'd bet him over dinner one
evening that he wouldn't win another race all year. "I don't
know why Richard couldn't have just said, 'Here's a hundred thousand dollars to stay,' " Debbie Hamilton remarked
later.

The Kodak team lured Bobby because of its knack for
winning at speedways. But the 1998 season was getting off to
a slow start. After seven races they were in eighteenth place.
Then the tour wound its way to the tiny oval in Martinsville. Taking the still young season on his shoulders, Bobby
dominated the race, letting his Chevrolet roll so freely
through the corners that it led 378 of 500 laps. "Sometimes
you just have them days," he said gleefully to reporters.

Two weeks later, in the wine country north of San Fran-
cisco, on a road course he once said "is a garbage dump we
ain't got no business coming to," Bobby was on the verge
of winning again. He led sixteen laps, and was pulling
ahead with ten to go when Jeff Gordon charged through
the field to pass him on a wild, skidding trip through the

eleventh turn. After Gordon slid into his right quarter panel to knock him out of the groove, Bobby bumped back several times, causing a NASCAR official to run up to Ray Evernham and order the combatants to calm down. "But they're racing for the lead!" the crew chief shouted. When Bobby took a run at what Gordon later described as "a million miles an hour," Gordon calmly let him pass widely in the outside of the eleventh turn, then nailed him with a surgical arc to his inside. Bobby was far from unhappy, though. "That was a hoot!" he said after he'd sped under the checkered flag in second place, his place as one of Winston Cup's best brawlers secure.

The Hamiltons still don't have much money, not millionaire money anyway. What they take in they devote almost entirely to their son, who came home from a failed marriage to see if he had his father's gift as a racer. But at forty-one, Bobby Hamilton is at peace with his talent and his family. What started out as a dream in a town truck has turned into one respectable ride.

In March of 1998, Brett Bodine found a letter on his fax machine that showed how frayed his relationship with his new partner, Andrew Evans, had become. The fax contained the news that Evans was filing suit to fire Brett as president of his own racing team.

Brett knew that things weren't progressing as fast as they should. In fact, he'd shaken up his operation in just the season's second race by removing his crew chief/brother-in law, Donnie Richeson. Months later, Richeson was found in the Busch Series garage, where he'd taken a job supervising six people instead of twenty-five. "I had to leave before it started coming in the house," he said. "We just couldn't have four people from one family in the eye of the hurricane."

The Bodines had lawyers everywhere. Besides being

entangled with Evans, they were suing Carl Smith and his Catalyst Communications. Smith's failure to deliver $2 million of promised sponsorship money in 1997 left them so broke that they had to put their team's salaries on personal credit cards, and beg Jack Roush to let them spread the payments out on their leased engines. When Evans appeared in Indianapolis with an offer to spend $1 million on half their race team, the Bodines reluctantly leapt at it. "Carl Smith cost me half of my team," said an embittered Diane.

In his speech to the national sports editors, France remarked, "Our athletes are paid for performance and performance alone. If drivers want a raise, they just go out and race for it." Few people have raced harder to stay in the game than Brett and Diane. Their perseverance has surprised a good many people, though it shouldn't have. A couple who've run through their savings, and have nothing left to lose, are bigger gamblers than the billionaire they're in bed with. At the halfway point of the 1998 season, Brett was holding steady in twentieth place. More importantly, he still was holding it all together.

"We're still an operating race team," Brett said when asked to give a grade to the past two years. "Just look around the garage. It's not easy to say that anymore. There are a lot of bodies dropping."

"I don't want no one feelin' sorry for me," Dave Marcis said. "I'm gonna turn this thing around, right from here, even if I have to go slap-ass broke doing it!"

It was nearing August, and Dave had missed eight of thirteen races. These weren't wide misses, or accidents of age, not at least as Dave was concerned. "I feel like I'm thirty-five," said the fifty-seven-year-old. "I'm fightin' because I still want to make these darn races."

Unfortunately, NASCAR was making it harder, not easier, for the oldest active racer.

A rules change that had been initiated in the off-season gave drivers in the top twenty-five of the Winston Cup points standings unlimited chances to take provisional starting spots if they were about to miss a race because of a poor qualifying time. In years past, teams got four provisionals at the start of the year, regardless of where they were in the standings. (They didn't get another one until every eighth race.) Now, the "top-twenty-five" rule was being used by a middling driver like Steve Grissom to enter races just about every week. In New Hampshire, Dave gritted his teeth as Grissom squeezed him out of the starting line-up, even though Dave had the faster speed! "The way they got the rules written," he said, his voice cracking, "I wake up Saturday halfway down the son-of-a-bitchin' road home. It's killin' me bad."

Dave had always preached that good would come of helping him fight against time, but the pews were starting to get thin. His chassis man of a dozen years left to become a mechanic with the state's Department of Agriculture, and he lost his truck driver to shot nerves and dyspepsia. He talked about the usual things—how "there ain't no loyalty anymore," and how "I'm doing too much, for chrissake." But the truth was that Dave was going to keep showing up to the track until he was too wretched to move, and maybe too blind to see.

He was in fiftieth place, with just $204,926 in winnings, when he said, "I don't want no hand-outs. I just want a fair shake." That was the weekend the *Boston Herald* called him "the best-loved totally doomed also-ran in motorsports, and maybe all sports."

Dave just shrugged at the title, and went back to his Chevrolet, where he crouched over its engine and asked it the very thing he'd been asking it every weekend for years.

"Where are you hiding that other tenth, you son-of-a-bitch? Where?"

ACKNOWLEDGMENTS

What convinced me to write this book was the line I kept hearing on the November 1995 weekend that I attended my first NASCAR race: "Anything you need, you just call, hear?"

Was it possible that people could really be this friendly?

Well, yes and no. As my reporting began in earnest, I discovered that the politics of NASCAR isn't for the faint of heart. That friendliness is a veneer, polished and fraught with intrigue. People have lost millions mistaking who their friends are and aren't. But as the months wore on, dozens of people took me into their confidence, and extended enough help for me to find my way through a world that is equal parts political swamp, con game, circus, and soap opera.

One of the first was Bob Zeller of the *Greensboro News & Record*. Bob gambled by introducing me around the garage, opening up all sorts of doors that otherwise would have remained closed. Much of the material on Junior Johnson's moonshining days comes from his wonderful work, but his reasoned voice and advice run through all its pages.

The second, Stan Creekmore, is a natural reporter—someone who can casually look at an engine and see that a crew chief has tried something crafty, or that something is amiss. His encyclopedic knowledge kept me from shooting myself in the foot on countless occasions. I also can't say enough about Marty Snyder, a broadcaster with Motor Racing Network, and Rick Houston of the *Winston Cup Scene*. Both were unselfish with their notes and their friendship.

As far as books, *American Zoom* by Peter Golenbock is a must for anyone interested in oral history; equally indispensable is Greg Fielden's authoritative *Forty Years of Stock Car Racing*. I also turned quite often to William Burt's *RaceFans Reference* guide, and Allan Girdler's *Stock Car Racer*.

Publicists occupy a unique role in NASCAR. While they keep the pressroom supplied with official grist, they also serve as a mix of spy, seducer and special envoy. Chuck Spicer and Dwayne Leik are the best of their breed. Both men wanted to be racers, but their heads for business made them too valuable behind the scenes for that. Chuck, who functions as Richard Petty's aide-de-camp, was one of the architects of his 1992 farewell tour. Dwayne saved Dave Marcis from extinction the day he walked into Marcis Auto Racing. The pair were responsible for giving me the access to write half of this book.

I'd also like to warmly thank Richard Petty for letting me ride the campaign trail; Homer Wood of the Railroad Cafe in Eden, North Carolina, for his strawberry moonshine; Ken of Tuscaloosa for guarding me with his gun the night I spent in the Talladega infield—even though I was never even remotely threatened; and everyone who ever invited me onto their RV or school bus to watch a race and drink a beer.

Other people who were indispensable to my education include Bill Armor, Karen Byrnes, Gary Claudio, Steve Crisp, Wayne Estes, Jerry Gappens, Charlie Harville, Brian Hoagland, Dean Kessel, Jeff Kettman, Cal Lawson, Clyde McCloud, Phil Parsons, Joy Pinto, Jon Sands, Brian

Simons, and Deb Williams. Special thanks go to Kymberly O'Brien, who rides shotgun with Jeff Gordon, and Tracey Eberts, who keeps NASCAR's press office afloat. It's not easy to book accommodations to thirty-two races in a year. Ruth Topol and Amy Griffith made sure I only had to sleep in my car once. Amy Scheibe at Random House made sure everything else went like clockwork.

When I returned from my first race in November 1995, this wasn't even an idea yet. Shelly Youngblut, with her uncanny sense for what will be hot, encouraged me to pursue NASCAR. But Glen Waggoner was the one who helped turn it into a book with his curiosity and encouragement. Then he went further by introducing me to his agent, Dominick Abel, and his editor at Random House, Peter Gethers. He is, and always will be, the definition of Man at His Best.

Both Dominick and Peter saw past a poorly written proposal, and took a chance on an untested book writer. If not for Dominick's British calm, it would have been a more nerve-racking journey. If not for Peter's considerable editing gifts, this manuscript would be much more confusing to read.

Mark Warren, the features editor of *Esquire*, shepherded my profile of Richard Petty into that magazine in March 1996. In doing so, he helped me find the voice that I used through much of this project. As the editor of *ESPN's Total Sports* magazine, Gary Hoenig gave me the time to do this book. But more importantly, he gave me the self-confidence. I'll always be grateful for that.

Being a writer's wife isn't easy, especially when your husband goes traveling around the country, leaving you alone to run a store and raise a three-year-old. Ellen spent a year hiding her stresses so I could write this book. It is as much hers as mine. It is also Jake's, since the site of him running around our Manhattan apartment, pretending to be Bill Elliott behind the wheel of the McDonald's car, gave me more joy than can be imagined.

Most of all, let me thank Dave Marcis, Bobby Hamilton, and Brett Bodine for inviting me into their worlds. All three are gamblers who've dared to live their lives large. Don't judge them until you've driven a mile—or five hundred miles—in their driver's seat.

1996 NASCAR Season Standings

Pos.	Driver	Points	Starts	Wins	Top 5	Top 10	Money Won
1	Terry Labonte	4,657	31	2	21	24	$4,030,648
2	Jeff Gordon	4,620	31	10	21	24	3,428,485
3	Dale Jarrett	4,568	31	4	17	21	2,985,418
4	Dale Earnhardt	4,327	31	2	13	17	2,285,926
5	Mark Martin	4,278	31	0	14	23	1,887,396
6	Ricky Rudd	3,845	31	1	5	16	1,503,025
7	Rusty Wallace	3,717	31	5	8	18	1,665,315
8	Sterling Martin	3,682	31	2	5	10	1,588,425
9	Bobby Hamilton	3,639	31	1	3	11	1,151,235
10	Ernie Irvan	3,632	31	2	12	16	1,683,313
11	Bobby Labonte	3,590	31	1	5	14	1,475,196
12	Ken Schrader	3,540	31	0	3	10	1,089,603
13	Jeff Burton	3,538	30	0	6	12	884,303
14	Michael Waltrip	3,535	31	0	1	11	1,182,811
15	Jimmy Spencer	3,476	31	0	2	9	1,090,876
16	Ted Musgrave	3,466	31	0	2	7	961,512
17	Geoff Bodine	3,218	31	1	2	6	1,031,762
18	Rick Mast	3,190	31	0	1	5	924,559
19	Morgan Shepherd	3,133	31	0	1	5	719,059
20	Ricky Craven	3,078	31	0	3	5	941,959
21	Johnny Benson	3,004	30	0	1	6	947,080
22	Hut Stricklin	2,854	31	0	1	1	631,055
23	Lake Speed	2,834	31	0	0	2	817,175
24	Brett Bodine	2,814	30	0	0	1	767,716
25	Wally Dallenbach	2,786	30	0	1	3	837,001
26	Jeremy Mayfield	2,721	30	0	2	2	592,853
27	Kyle Petty	2,696	28	0	0	2	689,041
28	Kenny Wallace	2,694	30	0	0	2	457,665
29	Darrell Waltrip	2,657	31	0	0	2	740,185
30	Bill Elliott	2,627	24	0	0	6	716,506
31	John Andretti	2,621	30	0	2	3	688,511
32	Robert Pressley	2,485	30	0	2	3	690,465
33	Ward Burton	2,411	27	0	0	4	873,619
34	Joe Nemechek	2,391	29	0	0	2	666,247
35	Derrike Cope	2,374	29	0	0	3	675,781
36	Dick Trickle	2,131	26	0	0	1	404,927
37	Bobby Hillin	2,128	26	0	0	0	395,224
38	Dave Marcis	2,047	27	0	0	0	435,177
39	Steve Grissom	1,188	13	0	1	2	314,983
40	Todd Bodine	991	10	0	0	1	198,525

Pos.	Driver	Points	Starts	Wins	Top 5	Top 10	Money Won
41	Mike Wallace	799	11	0	0	0	169,082
42	Greg Sacks	710	9	0	0	0	207,755
43	Elton Sawyer	705	9	0	0	0	129,618
44	Chad Little	627	9	0	0	0	164,752
45	Loy Allen	603	9	0	0	0	130,667
46	Gary Bradberry	591	9	0	0	0	155,785
47	Mike Skinner	529	5	0	0	0	65,850
48	Jeff Purvis	328	4	0	0	0	91,127
49	Jeff Green	247	4	0	0	0	46,875
50	Randy MacDonald	228	3	0	0	0	33,910
51	Billy Stanridge	198	3	0	0	0	27,780
52	Jim Sauter	170	2	0	0	0	51,172
53	Chuck Bown	168	3	0	0	0	38,867
54	Jack Sprague	136	2	0	0	0	22,720
55	Dorsey Schroeder	129	1	0	0	0	22,745
56	Stacy Compton	128	2	0	0	0	18,115
57	Robby Gordon	123	3	0	0	0	33,915
58	Butch Leitzinger	103	1	0	0	0	22,705
59	Jeffrey Krogh	98	2	0	0	0	19,680
60	Tom Kendall	84	1	0	0	0	20,730
61	Lance Hooper	64	1	0	0	0	9,645
62	Larry Gunselman	55	1	0	0	0	10,200
63	Richard Woodland	52	1	0	0	0	10,095
64	Hermie Sadler	52	1	0	0	0	13,055
65	Scott Gaylord	49	1	0	0	0	10,005
66	Ed Berrier	46	1	0	0	0	11,395
67	Randy Baker	40	1	0	0	0	12,550

1997 NASCAR Season Standings

POS.	DRIVER	POINTS	STARTS	WINS	TOP 5	TOP 10	MONEY WON
1	Jeff Gordon	4,710	32	10	22	23	$4,201,227
2	Dale Jarrett	4,696	32	7	20	23	2,512,382
3	Mark Martin	4,681	32	4	16	24	1,877,139
4	Jeff Burton	4,285	32	3	13	18	1,858,234
5	Dale Earnhardt	4,216	32	0	7	16	1,663,019
6	Terry Labonte	4,177	32	1	8	20	1,951,844
7	Bobby Labonte	4,101	32	1	9	18	1,943,239
8	Bill Elliott	3,836	32	0	5	14	1,377,607
9	Rusty Wallace	3,598	32	1	8	12	1,505,260
10	Ken Schrader	3,576	32	0	2	8	1,109,782
11	Johnny Benson	3,575	32	0	0	8	1,120,814
12	Ted Musgrave	3,556	32	0	5	8	1,128,404
13	Jeremy Mayfield	3,547	32	0	3	8	943,794
14	Ernie Irvan	3,534	32	1	5	13	1,492,739
15	Kyle Petty	3,455	32	0	2	9	834,639
16	Bobby Hamilton	3,450	32	1	6	8	1,350,335
17	Ricky Rudd	3,330	32	2	6	11	1,863,040
18	Michael Waltrip	3,173	32	0	0	6	1,015,384
19	Ricky Craven	3,108	30	0	4	7	1,139,860
20	Jimmy Spencer	3,079	32	0	1	4	1,016,109
21	Steve Grissom	3,061	31	0	3	6	1,045,374
22	Geoff Bodine	3,046	29	0	3	10	1,021,114
23	John Andretti	3,019	32	1	3	3	1,115,725
24	Ward Burton	2,987	31	0	0	7	977,044
25	Sterling Marlin	2,954	32	0	2	6	1,287,570
26	Darrell Waltrip	2,942	31	0	1	4	946,179
27	Derrike Cope	2,901	31	0	1	2	707,404
28	Joe Nemechek	2,754	30	0	0	3	732,194
29	Brett Bodine	2,716	31	0	0	2	936,694
30	Mike Skinner	2,669	31	0	0	3	791,819
31	Dick Trickle	2,629	28	0	2	2	656,189
32	Rick Mast	2,569	29	0	0	2	829,339
33	Kenny Wallace	2,462	31	0	0	2	926,501
34	Hut Stricklin	2,423	29	0	0	1	802,904
35	Lake Speed	2,301	25	0	0	0	715,074
36	Chad Little	2,081	27	0	0	1	555,914
37	David Green	2,038	26	0	0	0	483,833
38	Morgan Shepherd	2,033	23	0	1	3	662,999
39	Jeff Green	1,624	20	0	1	2	434,685
40	Robby Gordon	1,495	20	0	1	1	622,439

POS.	DRIVER	POINTS	STARTS	WINS	TOP 5	TOP 10	MONEY WON
41	Wally Dallenbach, Jr.	1,475	22	0	0	1	461,279
42	Dave Marcis	1,405	19	0	0	0	427,364
43	Robert Pressley	984	14	0	0	0	252,478
44	Gary Bradberry	868	16	0	0	0	251,930
45	Greg Sacks	778	12	0	0	0	320,714
46	Mike Wallace	541	7	0	0	0	159,303
47	Bobby Hillin, Jr.	511	10	0	0	0	211,978
48	Lance Hooper	402	6	0	0	0	134,150
49	Kenny Irwin	390	4	0	0	1	61,230
50	Billy Standridge	366	6	0	0	0	149,824
51	Steve Park	326	5	0	0	0	74,480
52	Todd Bodine	310	5	0	0	0	125,845
53	Rick Wilson	306	3	0	0	0	101,685
54	Jerry Nadeau	287	5	0	0	0	118,545
55	Ed Berrier	255	3	0	0	0	90,195
56	Kevin Lepage	231	3	0	0	0	57,720
57	Jeff Purvis	152	3	0	0	0	80,526
58	Loy Allen	119	2	0	0	0	75,239
59	Ron Barfield	97	1	0	0	0	64,935
60	Butch Gilliland	91	1	0	0	0	21,410
61	Tommy Hubert	79	1	0	0	0	21,350
62	Phil Parsons	70	1	0	0	0	12,845
63	Dorsey Schroeder	70	1	0	0	0	11,630
64	Sean Woodside	64	1	0	0	0	20,905
65	Rich Bickle	61	1	0	0	0	56,410
66	Jeff Davis	52	1	0	0	0	30,745
67	Larry Gunselman	49	1	0	0	0	20,720
68	Jack Sprague	43	1	0	0	0	18,650
69	Randy MacDonald	40	1	0	0	0	20,600
70	Buckshot Jones	34	1	0	0	0	2,087

*NASCAR's hottest star
comes roaring to life in . . .*

NATURAL BORN WINNER
The Jeff Gordon Story

by George Mair

Who says you can't have it all? Racing star Jeff Gordon is twenty-six years old, married to a former beauty queen, worshipped by his fans, respected by his rivals, and the youngest Winston Cup Rookie of the Year and Winston Cup champion. Gordon always knew he wanted to drive fast—and he meets that challenge every time he hits the tarmac with the help of the Rainbow Warriors.

A must for every racing fan, NATURAL BORN WINNER tracks Jeff Gordon from his childhood in California and Indiana right up to the 1997 NASCAR season, providing valuable insight into this phenomenal young champion.